Digital Modernism

MODERNIST LITERATURE & CULTURE

Kevin J. H. Dettmar & Mark Wollaeger, Series Editors

Digital Modernism

Making It New in New Media

Jessica Pressman

OXFORD
UNIVERSITY PRESS

OXFORD
UNIVERSITY PRESS

Oxford University Press is a department of the University of Oxford.
It furthers the University's objective of excellence in research, scholarship,
and education by publishing worldwide.

Oxford   New York
Auckland   Cape Town   Dar es Salaam   Hong Kong   Karachi
Kuala Lumpur   Madrid   Melbourne   Mexico City   Nairobi
New Delhi   Shanghai   Taipei   Toronto

With offices in
Argentina   Austria   Brazil   Chile   Czech Republic   France   Greece
Guatemala   Hungary   Italy   Japan   Poland   Portugal   Singapore
South Korea   Switzerland   Thailand   Turkey   Ukraine   Vietnam

Oxford is a registered trade mark of Oxford University Press in the UK and certain other
countries.

Published in the United States of America by
Oxford University Press
198 Madison Avenue, New York, NY 10016

Library of Congress Cataloging-in-Publication Data
Pressman, Jessica.
  Digital modernism : making it new in new media / Jessica Pressman.
    p.   cm. — (Modernist Literature & Culture ; 21)
  Includes index.
  ISBN 978-0-19-993708-0 (hardcover : acid-free paper)—ISBN 978-0-19-993710-3
(pbk. : acid-free paper) 1. Hypertext literature. 2. Modernism (Literature) 3. Electronic
publications. 4. Literature and technology. I. Title.
  PN56.I64P74 2013
  802'.85—dc23

                                                                    2013020714

9780199937080
9780199937103 (pbk.)

Images from *The Mechanical Bride: Folklore of Industrial Man* by Marshall McLuhan
copyright 1951 used with permission

For Brad

Contents

Series Editors' Foreword

What is digital modernism?

"Digital modernism" is deployed here by Jessica Pressman, the first critic to elaborate the term, to describe second-generation works of electronic literature that are text based, aesthetically difficult, and ambivalent in their relationship to mass media and popular culture. Such works offer immanent critiques of a contemporary society that privileges images, navigation, and interactivity over complex narrative and close readings.

Second generation?

Yes. The first generation, to use the term advanced by Katherine Hayles, designates a body of digitally born texts (as opposed to digitized print texts) composed mainly of hypertexts, a genre of text-based narrative that promotes multilinear reading paths. Print antecedents include Nabokov's *Pale Fire* and Cortazar's *Hopscotch*. Second-generation works explore and exploit the features of new authoring software packages, especially Flash, which enabled the production of multimedia, multimodal, and interactive aesthetics. Representative examples can be found at http://www.poemsthatgo.com/poems.htm, an archive for the defunct online literary journal *Poems That Go* that includes "The Last Day of Betty Nkomo," a Flash poem by Young-hae Chang Heavy Industries (YHCHI), whose work is the subject of *Digital Modernism*'s Chapter 3, "Speed Reading: Super-Position and Simultaneity in Young-hae Chang Heavy Industries's *Dakota* and Ezra Pound's *Cantos*."

Hold on. Despite the reference to Pound, shouldn't this book be called *Digital Postmodernism*? After all, YHCHI's *Dakota* appears to be a twenty-first century digital text, and haven't we learned from Fredric Jameson that modernism, echoing the cultural logic of capitalism, has been superseded by postmodernism, echoing the cultural logic of late capitalism, and that the kind of digital works and digital world addressed by Pressman are quintessentially pomo productions, inscribed as they are within a flattened ahistorical space epitomized by the computer screen, a space that explodes history into ever expanding zettabytes of digital information (occasionally congealing, like particles into planets, into memes) that stretch the historical imagination and the very possibility of narrative beyond their breaking points, leaving us afloat, drifting among simulacra and cat videos and longing for the pull of history to reground us, like Sandra Bullock in *Gravity*, in the marshy margins of the real?

No.

So you're saying that this book isn't called *Digital Modernism* simply to be included in this series, which is, after all, called Modernist Literature & Culture?

The suggestion is as wrongheaded as it is rude.
Adduce two reasons to support your claim.
First, this isn't the 1980s anymore, the cultural epoch described by Lyotard, Jameson, and Linda Hutcheon, whose accounts, focused on the now of the postmodern as it appeared to them then, are so often taken as descriptions of now's now, as if they were written in Gertrude Stein's prolonged present and are not then's now. If the lobby of L.A.'s Hotel Bonaventure, built in the mid-1970s, expresses the impossibility of locating oneself in the space of postmodernism's evacuation of history, in the early twenty-first century we live in what media scholar Henry Jenkins calls convergence culture, the primary affect and aspect of which is interactivity, with content flowing across media platforms and cultural communities, as epitomized in our moment's central cultural artifact, the game. Second, if older criticism, under the influence of Andreas Huyssen, often distinguished between modernism and postmodernism by means of a "great divide" between high art and mass culture, that grand narrative of postmodernism has long since lost its purchase insofar as modernism, like the second-generation electronic texts studied here, has always been permeated by lowbrow and mass media. And like early twentieth-century modernism, digital modernism, according to Pressman, rebels against its media moment—if yesterday's targets were closed poetic forms and narrative closure, today's is interactivity—by returning to an aesthetic of difficulty and the avant-garde stance it invokes.

So digital modernism, rather than a celebration of cool new technologies, is back-ward looking?

Half right. What's true of modernism more generally is true of digital modernism as well: it is "a strategy of innovation that intentionally employs the media of its time to reform and refashion older literary practices in ways that produce new art." Just as Joyce returned to Homer, and Pound borrowed "make it new" from an an-ecdote about an eighteenth-century B.C.E. Chinese washbasin, YHCHI returns to Pound's *Cantos*, and a host of digital works return to *Ulysses*, from a Twitter-based performance of "Wandering Rocks" to an online narrative inspired by "Ithaca," Judd Morrissey and Lori Talley's *The Jew's Daughter*.

By any chance, does Pressman herself, reflecting on her own protocols of reading, return to early twentieth-century modernism to think about how to read second-generation digital works and about the status of computer code as text?

That's very acute: yes, she does. Given that close reading no longer can be taken for granted as a standard skill, *Digital Modernism* seizes the opportunity to reassess and refashion the practice to suit digital works. After all, "close reading is a histori-cal and media-specific technique that, like older literary practices, demands reno-vation as we embrace our modern age and its born-digital artworks." To that end, in her first chapter she returns to Marshall McLuhan (who studied at Cambridge with I. A. Richards and F. R. Leavis, and who in turn trained Hugh Kenner) as a figure whose work illuminates central convergences between literary and media studies while laying the ground for the new multimodal techniques of close reading appro-priate to today's digital texts. Chapter 5 traces a prehistory of discourse about the readability of computer code back to modernist fantasies of universal communica-tion as well as to Leibniz's binary logic, Norbert Weiner's computer-based machine translation, and debates about Global English and the World Wide Web.
Name a specific question that *Digital Modernism* attempts to answer.

How do we close read works that are not only multimedia and multimodal but also comprised of what Katherine Hayles calls flickering signifiers and of multiple layers of semiotic processes, including hidden programming text and computer code?
And a provocative observation about *Ulysses*?

"Ithaca" exemplifies a database aesthetic. Stream of consciousness has always been about media.
That was two. Name two of the broader questions addressed.

Why does close reading still matter? Why does modernism still matter? What does modernism tell us about our current moment, its reading practices, and the role of literature within it?

That was three. Use ten words to sum up the primary point of *Digital Modernism*. As texts evolve, so too must practices of critical analysis.

Should I not only read this book but also assign it in classes and give it to all my friends and family?

Absolutely.

Mark Wollaeger and Kevin J. H. Dettmar

Acknowledgments

This book has been a long time in the making, and it has evolved along with me. It began as a dissertation at UCLA; it was revised during my years as a faculty member at Yale; and found its final shape in San Diego, my hometown, where I have since settled.

An appropriate acknowledgments section would require a separate book altogether. But there are a few notables whose influence deserves proper mention and far more gratitude than I could ever express.

Kate Hayles has been my advisor, mentor, and advocate since my first year of graduate school. This book simply would not have been possible without her nor, frankly, would my field of study. Michael North, Mark McGurl, and Alan Liu all served as astute dissertation advisers, and they continue to serve as role models. Rita Raley was never an official reader or adviser, but she deeply inspired this project and my overall sense of what digital scholarship can do.

Various writing groups supplied a balanced blend of writerly advice and personal therapy: Julia H. Lee, Melissa Sodeman, Bonnie Foote, and Holly Crawford Pickett at UCLA; Mark Marino and Jeremy Douglass beyond it; Caleb Smith, Justin Neuman, R. John Williams, Paul Grimstad, and Susan Chambers at Yale.

In the English department at Yale University, I found intellectual inspiration in every beautiful corner of LC. I am grateful to my former colleagues and especially to Amy Hungerford, Michael Warner, and Lanny Hammer for helping me refine my scholarly skills and sense of purpose.

In San Diego, I found intellectual support and heart-warming smiles in the persons of Michael Davidson, Liz Losh, and Erin Graff Zivin. I am grateful.

My greatest debts are to my family. They taught me my priorities, and they remain mine. My parents encouraged me to dream and to work hard to make those dreams a reality. They have supported and nurtured me all of my life and in all that I do. I will have to write many more books with far more articulate acknowledgement sections in order to appropriately express my gratitude to them.

I used to call this book "my baby" until my babies arrived. Jonah and Sydney continually teach me to see my world anew and to delight in these discoveries.

Finally, Brad. He made this possible and desirable. I dedicate this book to him.

An earlier version of Chapter 3 was originally published in *MFS, Modern Fiction Studies* (Summer 2008, 54.2), and an earlier version of Chapter 2 was originally published in *American Literary History* (Winter 2011, 23.4). I am grateful to both journals for their permission to reproduce that material here.

Digital Modernism

Introduction

Tching prayed on the mountain and
     wrote MAKE IT NEW
on his bath tub
     Day by day make it new
cut the underbrush,
pile the logs
keep it growing.

—Ezra Pound, excerpt from "Canto LIII" (264–5)

Making it new may be the oldest trick in the book, but it has newfound urgency in contemporary digital literature. Ours is an age increasingly defined by engagement with new media and obsessed with newness. This is particularly true in regard to creative and technological innovation. But this book argues that digital literature—literature made and accessed in and through digital computing—offers a surprising counterstance to this privileging of newness.[1] A recent trend in electronic literature makes it new in ways that make visible the tradition of making it new and thus, I claim, illuminates and refreshes our sense of literary history. As Ezra Pound suggests in the excerpt I selected as an epigraph, making it new means razing the underbrush of the recent past in order to seek out the older, taller trees that can serve as a foundation for new poetic structures. This strategy implies an ability and willingness to shift between seeing the trees and the forest, between focusing on individual literary works and on the larger network, field, or dataset they comprise.

Electronic literature is born-digital. It is computational and processural, dependent upon the operations of the machine for its aesthetic effects. Electronic literature emerges through a series of translations across machine codes, platforms, and networks; its resulting onscreen content depends upon algorithmic procedures, software, hardware, and (often) Internet compatibility. I use the terms "electronic literature" and "digital literature" interchangeably, for they both describe a diverse array of creative works that employ computational processing to produce text-based art. Electronic literature has been celebrated as a postmodern literary form that grows out of technologies, subjectivities, and poetics from the middle of the twentieth century, but this book provides an alternative genealogy. Across diverse genres and programming platforms, I examine a subset of contemporary online electronic literature that remixes literary modernism. These works adapt seminal texts from the modernist canon (e.g., Pound's *Cantos*, Joyce's *Ulysses*), remediate specific formal techniques (e.g., stream of consciousness, super-position), and engage with cornerstone cultural issues (e.g., the relationship between poetics, translation, and global politics). They employ a strategy of renovation that purchases cultural capital from the literary canon in order to validate their newness and demand critical attention in the form of close reading.

All of the works of electronic literature examined in this study are web-based and published on or after 2000, but what binds them is what makes them distinct from the majority of born-digital art—a commitment to literariness and a literary past. These works challenge assumptions about electronic literature that have become commonplace, such as expectations for reader-controlled interactivity or the assumption that electronic literature forfeits substantive content to formal experimentation. The works that sustain my attention are text based, aesthetically difficult, and ambivalent in their relationship to mass media and popular culture. They support immanent critiques of a society that privileges images, navigation, and interactivity over complex narrative and close reading. Instead of celebrating all that's new in new media, these works challenge contemporary culture and its reigning aesthetic values.

They do so by adopting a modernist practice of seeking inspiration and validation in a literary past. I call this strategy of renovating modernist aesthetic practices, principles, and texts into new media "digital modernism." Writers involved in digital modernism assess the state of electronic literature, and of literature in general in our digital age, and they decide to raze and rebuild. To do so, they cut the recently grown underbrush of digital literature and seek out the older, taller trees—modernist strategies of conceptualizing, crafting, and presenting literary art. They reframe literary tradition in ways that complicate simple designations of "new" even as they faithfully uphold and reconsider Pound's mantra.

Exemplary of this strategy is Young-hae Chang Heavy Industries (YHCHI), the collaborative duo that anchors Chapter 3 and inspired the inception of this book. YHCHI creates web-based animations that flash lengthy narratives onscreen one word or phrase at a time at heightened speeds. The text is rendered nearly illegible by the speed at which it flashes, and the result is an aesthetic of difficulty exacerbated by the fact that readers cannot stop or slow the animation. YHCHI revel in the challenge their work poses. "We can't and won't help readers to 'locate' us," they coyly state; "Distance, homelessness, anonymity, and insignificance are all part of the Internet literary voice, and we welcome them."[2] And yet, as I explore in detail in Chapter 3, YHCHI *do* locate their most acclaimed work in a particular cultural context. In interviews and artist statements, they repeatedly claim that *Dakota* (2002) "is based on a close reading of Ezra Pound's *Cantos* part I and part II." What is at stake for YHCHI, and other contemporary writers like them, in claiming association with the experimental-made-canonical movement of modernism? What does this *use* of modernism tell us about our current moment, its reading practices and the role of literature within it? These questions motivate the chapters that follow. For, rather than an instance of idiosyncratic cultural remixing, I see YHCHI's use of Pound and of modernism more generally as exemplary of a larger contemporary movement—digital modernism—in which twenty-first century writers purchase cultural capital from the literary canon in order to validate new aesthetics, promote traditional reading practices, and demand that their work be taken seriously.

My study of digital modernism makes the case for considering these digital creations as "literature" and argues for the value of reading them carefully, closely, and within the tradition of literary history. Analyzing these digital adaptations also provides a fresh perspective on modernism, specifically an opportunity to assess how modernist literature engaged with the new media of its own moment. This book thus pursues a dual purpose: it situates contemporary digital literature in a genealogy that rewrites literary history, and it reflects back on literature's past, and on modernism in particular, to illuminate the crucial role that media played in shaping the ambitions and poetics of that period. *Digital Modernism* thus conjoins literary studies and media studies to illuminate their shared past and necessarily entwined future.

Part I. Defining My Terms

Modernism

By "modernism" and its inclusion in the term "digital modernism" I mean a creative strategy rather than a temporal period or movement organized around certain key figures. I understand modernism to be a strategy of innovation that employs the media of its time to reform and refashion older literary practices in ways that produce new art. In other words, I will argue, using works of digital modernism to guide me, that modernism is centrally about media.

"A Return to Origins Invigorates,"[3] Ezra Pound claims, and the digital writers I examine in this study concur. They employ a deliberate anachronism that marks the form and content of their works in ways that express a larger, shared ambition. Pound is a central figure in this book. His poetry and criticism, but also his influence on other writers to explore the relationship between literature and media, permeates the pages that follow. Pound describes making it new as an act of recovery and renovation, not an assertion of novelty. That is why he defines literature as "news that STAYS news," and he begins *The Cantos* by renovating the news of ancient Greece: "Canto I" begins with Odysseus diving into the underworld in an adaptation of Book XI of Homer's *The Odyssey*. James Joyce's *Ulysses* is an example of this approach, as T.S. Eliot claims. In the essay "*Ulysses*, Order, and Myth" (1923), Eliot validates *Ulysses* by describing how it updates much older "news." "In using the myth," Eliot writes, "in manipulating a continuous parallel between contemporaneity and antiquity, Mr. Joyce is pursuing a method which others must pursue after him."[4] Eliot sees Joyce's renovation of a classical past as forever altering the foundation upon which future writers will build. But making it new is not just about reinventing the past. It is also about using new media to do so. In "Canto LIII," from which my epigraph is taken, Pound locates efforts to make it new in specific sites of medial inscription—on the interface of the bathtub's walls and the sliced logs piled high to make new structures. Making is building, building requires material, and this material matters. Thus, making it new, I insist, is about renovating the past *through* media.

Whatever ambiguous qualifications are used to define "modernism," the late decades of the nineteenth century and the early decades of the twentieth century is certainly the classical period of our contemporary technological age. Our modern mediatized consciousness emerged during this first electric age. In his seminal *The Culture of Time and Space 1880–1918*, Stephen Kern shows that new conceptions of time and space accompanied new technologies of communication and, in turn, so too did new artistic methods of representing this experience also emerge. More recently, Enda Duffy's *The Speed Handbook: Velocity, Pleasure, Modernism* presents an "epistemology of speed in the specific historical period . . . [that] corresponded to the culture termed 'modernist'" by exploring the causal connection between new technologies and modern(ist) aesthetics.[5] Literary scholars have studiously detailed the relationships between modern technologized life and experimental art movements such as Futurism, which particularly informed modernism. The narrative of this period's technoliterary history is well rehearsed indeed.[6] Media scholars, too, have recognized this period as transformative for laying the foundation for modern media culture. Friedrich Kittler's *Discourse Networks 1800/1900* identifies a decisive epistemic shift in the period that gave birth to modernism; this rupture is represented as a forward-slash in the book's title. Kittler claims that Western culture at the end of the nineteenth century experienced a monumental change in "the network of technologies and institutions that allow a given culture to select, store, and produce relevant data."[7] The governing cultural "discourse network" of the previous epoch, he argues, was based in oral and analog modes of communication that supported a sense of embodied connection between human beings through such media as handwriting, whose flow of letters directly inscribes the enacted movements of one person for another. But the "continuous connection of writing" that exemplified the earlier discourse network of analog communication media was then disrupted by the emergence of new media.[8] "The historical synchronicity of cinema, phonography, and typewriting," Kittler writes, "separated optical, acoustic, and written data flows, thereby rendering them autonomous."[9] This new media epoch initiated the transition to discourse network 1900.

New media critic Lev Manovich also identifies the modernist period as a decisive moment of medial shift that paves the way for the digital. In *The Language of New Media* he argues that innovations in cinema, and in montage in particular, foregrounded modularity and interchangeability in ways that produced a new cultural perspective. "A hundred years after cinema's birth," Manovich writes, "cinematic ways of seeing the world, of structuring time, of narrating a story, of linking one experience to the next, have become the basic means by which computer users access and interact with all cultural data."[10] But before Kittler, Kern, and Manovich, Marshall McLuhan, the father of media studies, identified modernism as the foundation for modern electric age. As I show in Chapter 1, McLuhan established media studies by reading the contemporary period through the lens of modernism and by adapting New Critical reading practices to approach and analyze electronic media.

If modernism is, as McLuhan and more recent media critics claim, the first electronic age, and if making it new is the cornerstone of literary modernism, and if this mantra implies, as I argue, a focus on media, then literary modernism invites media studies. The implications of this fact are evident in works of digital literature that remix modernism and refocus attention on the role of media within earlier modernist works. Digital modernism thus allows us to reconsider how and why media is (and always has been) a central aspect of experimental literature and the strategy of making it new.

Electronic Literature

Electronic literature is still in its nascent stages, but in just over two decades of existence it has already witnessed the passage of at least two generations, the development of a small but certain canon, and the rarefaction of expectations about what electronic literature is and does. Electronic literature emerged and gained critical interest in the late 1980s and early '90s. This "first generation of electronic literature," as Katherine Hayles calls it, was comprised primarily of hypertexts, a genre of text-based narrative that promotes nonlinear, or more accurately multilinear, reading paths.[11] Electronic hypertexts have print predecessors in experimental novels like Vladimir Nabokov's *Pale Fire*, David Foster Wallace's *Infinite Jest*, Julio Cortazar's *Hopsotch*, and the *Choose Your Own Adventure* young adult book series, all of which use footnotes or other textual devices to connect chunks of text and enable navigation of the narrative as a network rather than a linear path. Most electronic hypertexts were either uploaded to the Internet by individual authors or published by Eastgate Systems (founded by Mark Bernstein in 1986), a small publisher dedicated to electronic literature, on discs or CD-Roms.[12] Eastgate's tagline, "serious hypertext," described not only individual works but also an ambition shared by the publisher, writers, and readers alike—to gain serious attention for the emerging field of electronic literature. Eastgate's tagline also had the effect of aligning all electronic literature that took itself seriously with hypertext. Academic advocates supported this endeavor by taking hypertexts very seriously and strenuously vocalizing this claim. Victorian scholar George P. Landow hailed hypertext as the culmination of poststructuralism's decentered and writerly text.[13] Postmodern fiction writer Robert Coover's infamous article "The End of Books" (*New York Times Book Review*, 1992) brought hypertext to the public eye with death threats to a favorite reading technology. A few of the first generation hypertexts so vociferously lauded comprise the emerging canon of electronic literature, including Shelley Jackson's *Patchwork Girl* (Eastgate, Storyspace version, 1995), Michael Joyce's *afternoon: a story* (Eastgate, Storyspace 1990 [1987]), and J. Yellowlees Douglas's "I Have Said Nothing" (Eastgate, 1994); excerpts from the latter two were included in the Norton print literary anthology *Postmodern American Fiction* (1997) and thereby ensconced in the literary canon where they are assured to be taken seriously.

In the mid-1990s innovations in graphical interfaces transformed the text-based Internet into the image-laden web, exponentially expanding its users and possibilities. The nature of electronic literature changed dramatically. First generation electronic literature, the lengthy text-based hypertexts built in Storyspace or HTML (like Adrienne Eisen's web-based "Six Sex Scenes" [1996]) gave way to a second generation of dynamic, visual, and animated works. Second generation works explore and exploit the features of new authoring software packages. Most dominant among them was Flash (formerly Macromedia Flash), which enables the production of multimedia, multimodal, and interactive aesthetics. First generation text-based narratives quickly looked outdated in comparison to the flashy facades of new, Flash-based works. For example, the online literary journal *Poems That Go* (www.poemsthatgo.com) exhibits exemplary works of second-generation, Flash-based electronic literature.[14] Although it has ceased publishing new issues, *Poems That Go* (thankfully) still maintains an archive of its past issues. The works I study here and designate as "digital modernist" were created after the emergence of the second generation of electronic literature, but they resist the characteristics of that classification in decisive ways.

Instead of exploiting the possibilities of Flash to pursue ever-new aesthetics through combinations of complex animations, detailed graphics, and immersive interactivity, digital modernism is characterized by an aesthetic of restraint. YHCHI remains the exemplary case, for they proudly claim to employ "a simple technique that *shuns* interactivity, graphics, photos, illustrations, banners, colors, and all but the Monaco font" (emphasis added).[15] The fact that these writers, and others like them, pursue minimalism as a conscious act of rebellion is, I contend, significant. The intentional rejection of fashionable trends and expectations serves as a strategy uniting contemporary digital writers. It also connects this movement to a longer tradition of similar rebellion, specifically, the modernist avant-garde.

To quote the oft-quoted modernist art critic, Clement Greenberg, "What singles Modernism out and gives it its place and identity more than anything else is its response to a heightened sense of threats to aesthetic value."[16] This statement expresses the standard story of modernism: that the popular, lowbrow culture spurred serious writers toward reactionary and decidedly highbrow aesthetics. According to this narrative, modernist literature is intentionally antipopular.[17] Digital modernism responds to a similar sense of threat in similar ways, but the fact that these artistic works are built in corporate software and displayed online alongside all forms of popular, lowbrow, consumer entertainment complicates any simple designations of high/low, modernism/postmodernism, counterculture/status quo, and so forth. Exploring the relationship between modernism and digital modernism exposes the central role of media and of mass culture in both periods' artistic endeavors. Approaching modernism via digital modernism thus shows how literary history is, at least in part, media history.

Digital modernist works share a revolutionary sensibility and a desire for confrontation with their modernist predecessors. This spirit is, in part, due to the shifting status of electronic literature in the early years of the twenty-first century. This shift is evidenced in the tale told by the publishing history of the literary journals dedicated to showcasing and distributing electronic literature in the 1990s. Like modernism in the early decades of the twentieth century, electronic literature emerged in and through a subculture of small literary journals. The late 1990s saw the proliferation of online magazines dedicated to publishing electronic literature and the critical discourse about this new field, including interviews with authors, book reviews, and scholarly articles. Some of the journals that came online in the last years of the twentieth century include *Beehive* (Talan Memmott, ed.) in 1998, *The Iowa Review Web* (Thom Swiss, ed.) in 1999, *Riding the Meridian* (Jennifer Ley, ed.) in 1999, *Cauldron.net* (Claire Dinsmore, ed.) in 1999, *Drunken Boat* (Michael Mills and Ravi Shankar, eds.) in 2000, and *poemsthatgo.com* (Megan Sapnar and Ingrid Ankerson, eds.) also in 2000. Such webzines flourished and brought attention to the second generation of electronic literature, but they did not last long. Creative and critical energy shifted, on the whole, from a focus on literary studies to media studies more broadly construed. Websites and blogs about emergent digital formats proliferated, particularly those focused on games and their scholarly study, then known as "Ludology."[18] Literary journals ceased operations and faded into the static of cyberspace. In the first few years of the twenty-first century, many of the mainstays of the electronic literature community stalled production: *Drunken Boat* in 2001, *Cauldron.net* in 2002, *Beehive* with its 2002–3 issue, and *Riding the Meridian* in 2003. *The Iowa Review Web* continued publication longer (stalling out in 2007), but whereas its first issues (1999–2001) were devoted to showcasing electronic literature, its later issues shifted to interviews with authors and critical essays about new media. Similarly, as of October 2012, Eastgate.com's home page showcases tools rather than just literary texts, and the majority of the literature it offers is over a decade old. There are, of course, exceptions to the broad-stoke narrative I present here, but the context serves as a relevant backdrop for understanding digital modernism.

Despite the situation implied by this quick survey of the early digital literary journals, electronic literature is neither dead nor static. It is alive and well, and it has a score to settle. There is a countermovement underway, this book argues, a serious effort to encourage digital literature to be taken seriously. This response is not limited to digital literature. The impact of digital literature and the reach of digital modernism also affect print, and my coda explores the influence of digital modernism on an exemplary bookbound novel. But the majority of this book focuses on Internet-based literature in order to show how and why one of the most maligned of literary spaces, the web—one accused of fostering reading habits that destroy deep attention and devalue hermeneutic analysis—is actually the place where serious literature stages its rebellion and renaissance.

"Digital Modernism"

The title of this project invokes decades of debate distinguishing modernism and postmodernism, the details of which have been thoroughly rehashed and do not need repeating here. However, a brief explanation of my chosen terminology might prove helpful. By titling this project "Digital Modernism" I conjoin electronic literature to the modernist period rather than its immediate predecessor, postmodernism, because I see points of connection between modernism, postmodernism, and digital modernism that would be lost by focusing only on the latter period.[19] There are two central reasons why the title of this book is not "Digital Postmodernism." First, the grand narratives distinguishing modernism from postmodernism based on "the great divide," as Andreas Huyssen famously described the relationship between high art and mass culture, now seem outdated.[20] Scholars have shown that instead of being opposed to popular culture, modernism was in fact deeply permeated by the lowbrow and mass media. Second, ours is no longer the same cultural epoch as that described by Jean-François Lyotard, Fredric Jameson, Linda Hutcheon, and others theorists of postmodernism writing in the 1980s. Personal computing, the Internet, and the technologies of global capitalism have altered cultural composition, capitalist economies, and systems of signification, let alone theories about them. Works of digital modernism are accessed online, within the infrastructure of e-commerce and popular technoculture, and this embeddedness is essential to their practice and immanent critique. These works represent and respond to the networked age and what Henry Jenkins calls "convergence culture," wherein content flows across media platforms and cultural communities.[21] If interactivity ("participatory culture" as Jenkins calls it) is the primary affect and aspect of convergence culture, games might be considered its central cultural artifact. As we will see, digital modernism rebels against this cultural situation and the affective mode exemplary of it—interactivity—by returning to an older aesthetic of difficulty and the avant-garde stance it invokes.[22]

It makes sense, then, that the only previous use of the term "digital modernism" I have been able to locate is as a substitute for "avant-gardism." Lev Manovich uses the term just once in an early nettime.com correspondence (from 1998) with fellow media theorist Geert Lovink in a thread titled "Digital Constructivism."[23]

It is not coincidental that the term should come from Manovich, for his work deeply influences my own. We both analyze digital media and its aesthetic effects by exploring connections to modernist art. However, our goals lead to different arguments, methodologies, and outcomes. As I mentioned earlier, Manovich's *The Language of New Media* charts a genealogy that connects digital media to cinema, and his text serves as bedrock for the field of new media studies. However, his argument about the absorption of modernism into new media technology is one that I seek to complicate. "One general effect of the digital revolution," Manovich writes, "is that avant-garde aesthetic strategies came to be embedded in the commands and interface metaphors of computer software. In short, the avant-garde became materialized in a computer."[24] Specifically, he means that the "avant-garde strategy of collage reemerged as the 'cut-and-paste' command, the most basic operation one can perform on digital data."[25] Such a claim is intriguing but problematic because it reduces a cultural movement with a message into a medium. The title and argument of his essay "Avant-Garde as Software" (1999) unabashedly identifies the avant-garde by the formal techniques it uses rather than the manner or goals to which they are employed.[26] Manovich sees modernism as "materialized" in a computer and thus as an involuntary, media-determined effect of digital art-making. The effect of this argument assigns avant-garde strategies to the machine rather than the human artist. This collapse of the avant-garde into the computer can be read as the ultimate fulfillment of Fredric Jameson's claim about postmodernism, wherein the capitalist system consumes all possibilities of critiquing it.[27] This is a conclusion that digital modernism resists, and, following the works, I do too. Instead of reading the computer as an avant-garde technology, I examine the conscious adaptation of modernist techniques as a formal practice and strategic alignment in specific digital works. I read literary objects produced through computing technologies whose techniques express an avant-garde strategy that is revised from the modernist period and repurposed for contemporary culture.

Digital modernism is aligned with strategies of the avant-garde: it challenges traditional expectations about what art is and does. It illuminates and interrogates the cultural infrastructures, technological networks, and critical practices that support and enable these judgments. Digital modernism thus remakes the category of the avant-garde in new media. My goal in making such statements is not to resuscitate tired cultural categories or to simply identify a new avant-garde movement. Instead, I seek to remind us of the transformative effects literature can have when we dedicate our attention to it and, specifically, to close reading it. This book pursues close reading as both subject and method. It models how close reading can be adapted to serve as media-specific analysis of digital literature and argues that such critical, formal, and analytical endeavors are vital to the current, digital moment.

Close Reading

"Close reading" describes a variety of methods for approaching a literary text in order to understand *how* it means, but the term focuses on the formal techniques used to produce a particular effect and affect. In other words, close reading explores the artistry and craft of literature. As the term implies, "close reading" asserts a relationship of closeness to the text. More than anything, it describes the careful application of focused attention to the formal operations in a literary text. Close reading thus entails slow, careful, and repeated reading.

Close reading became a central activity of literary criticism in a very hyper-moment, a period—modernism—that is, I suggest, similar to our own. It emerged as an affront to the speeding up of modern life due to new technologies of speed and automation such as the automobile, the telegraph, cinema, and ticker tape.[28] John Guillory reminds us that when I. A. Richards was laying the foundation for literary criticism in the early 1920s, he "notoriously offered no positive methodology of reading, only a set of tactics for removing the sources of misreading."[29] These "sources" were deeply related to the mediatized moment of the modernist period. "Richards was already confronting a media generation," Guillory writes; Richards saw "his generation as already overwhelmed by a saturated media environment, buffeted by stimuli that produce conditioned responses."[30] Richards sought a means of combating these stimuli by focusing attention on the details of an individual literary text. The speeding up of life in the early decades of the twentieth century had the ironic and significant effect of introducing new efforts to slow things down. Close reading was one such effort. Jeffrey Schnapp describes the modernist moment as one in which speed and "a sense of urgency" produced a "tempo and complexity [that] give rise to distinctive forms of slowness: distractions, bureaucratic delays, traffic jams. . . ."[31] I would add close reading to this list. Close reading tunes out the distractions of the speeding, technological world in order to focus, concentrate, and read slowly.[32] "The crucial thing is to slow down," Jonathan Culler writes in his description of close reading.[33] Close reading is slow and disciplined reading. As we will see, the New Critics codified close reading into a disciplined practice that became the primary professional and pedagogical practice of literary studies for much of the twentieth-century. But before we get to the New Critics, let me

pause for a moment to consider the central tenet upon which the reading practice of close reading is founded.

Close reading depends upon the belief that a text is worthy of sustained attention. The idea that a text could and should be studied for its content, aesthetics,
and formal attributes (rather than, say, because of who wrote it or what moral
lesson it imparts) was a radical one. It is hard for us—particularly those of us
who learned to close read as part of learning to study literature—to consider
disassociating literature from close reading or to recognize just how revolutionary the ambitions undergirding close reading really were. But it's worth recall-
ing this historical context in order to understand why I ground my argument
about digital literature in the history of modernism, the New Criticism, and
close reading.

The New Criticism

Like "close reading," "The New Criticism" is also an uncertain term. It shares with
"new media" and "modernism" an identification of presentness and suggests confrontation with (or rejection of) the recent past. "The New Criticism" describes
a critical movement that emerged in the 1930s and remained a staple of literary
studies until the 1970s, when New Historicism and other critical movements of the
postwar, postmodernist, and poststructuralist period arose to challenge the ideologies upon which the New Criticism was based (and which I will soon discuss).
John Crowe Ransom's book *The New Criticism* (1941) gave a title to the movement, but the definition and boundaries of that movement remained diverse and
ambiguous, even among its members. In an interview near the end of his life,
Cleanth Brooks, who, by all accounts was a central member of the New Criticism,
said, "What is it exactly that a New Critic does? Ransom never says."[34] But Brooks
does posit a suggestion. "As far as some sort of common pursuit is concerned,
I think it is safe to say that these people [the New Critics] generally took the text
very seriously."[35] Frank Lentricchia agrees. "The common ground," he writes, "is a
commitment to close attention to literary texture and what is embodied there."[36]
Focusing on what *is* there—that is, the words on the page—may seem like a simple
and obvious pursuit to us now, but in the 1920s and '30s it was radical. It might
prove challenging—in the wake of New Historicism, multiculturalism, and other
critical movements invested in deconstructing the ideological stakes of the New
Criticism as formalism—to appreciate just how diverse and avant-garde the New
Criticism really was.[37] But, before literary criticism became central to English departments and before the term "literary criticism" became interchangeable with

"literary scholarship," literary studies meant philology, literary history, and the passing down of *belle-lettrist* sensibilities.

The sea change in the Anglo-American academy began across the pond, at Cambridge University, with I. A. Richards. Richards was a pioneer in literary criticism and a great influence on the New Criticism. (In Chapter 1, I discuss his influence on Marshall McLuhan.) Richards's *The Principles of Literary Criticism* (1924) laid the foundation for literary criticism to emerge as a discipline. In the preface to this book, Richards writes, "This book might be compared to a loom on which it is supposed to re-weave some raveled parts of our civilization."[38] The specific part of our civilization Richards seeks to unravel and reweave is the way of practicing literary studies; and since the word "text" has its etymological root in the Latin word for "to weave," he urges a focus on analyzing a text's formal arrangement rather than just its linguistic content. Untangling the mess that constituted literary studies meant redefining the practice of critical reading and the type of writing it produced. Richards writes, "the reader, as opposed to the biographer, is not concerned with what as historical fact was going on in the author's mind when he penned the sentence, but with what the words—given the rest of the language—may return."[39] Reading for what the words "may return" demands that a reader "go deeper."[40] Deep reading implies a sustained focus on the words themselves and how they operate to produce a particular effect. Such a critical practice asks the reader to approach the text with the purpose of excavating it and bringing to light its internal functions.

For Richards, deep reading also implied attention to how a text affects the reader. More than the students he inspired, either directly (like F. R. Leavis and William Empson) or indirectly (like the American New Critics), Richards was interested in the psychological and neurological process of reading.[41] He was far more interested in the reader's mind than in the author's, and his advice to the reader to pursue slow, close reading is based in an understanding of how the brain operates. Richards writes, "a *very slow* private reading gives a better chance for the necessary interaction of form and meaning to develop than any number of rapid perusals" (emphasis in original).[42] "This simple neurological fact," he continues, "if it could be generally recognized and respected, would probably more than anything else help to make poetry understood."[43] Richards's insistence on reading with slow, focused attention and rigorous consideration of the "interaction of form and meaning" demands that critics study the work itself rather than just research around it. This shift in critical focus inspired a new generation of critics.

The New Criticism was, Andrew DuBois explains, "a *radical* response to arcane Indo-European philology on the one hand, and on the other to a body of historical scholarship that seemed more deeply interest in sociology and biography than in literature" (emphasis added).[44] The New Critics were "academic radicals," Gerald Graff states, for they "challeng[ed] the supremacy of the philologists, the literary and intellectual historians, and the literary biographers."[45] They did so, Miranda Hickman explains, by "treat[ing] literary texts as art, rather than texts documenting history, social developments, ethics, or philosophy."[46] The New Critics sought to legitimate literary criticism and defend humanistic inquiry. As Graff writes, "The New Criticism stands squarely in the romantic tradition of the defense of the humanities as an antidote to science and positivism."[47] Close reading was the critical method they developed to serve this pursuit. "The methodology of 'close reading,'" Graff explains, "was an attempt not to imitate science but to refute its devaluation of literature: by demonstrating the rich complexity of meaning within even the simplest poem."[48] Rather than seeking to explain what a text means, to provide one "true" meaning or utilitarian purpose for a work, close reading reveals complexity and multiplicity. "The tendency of science is necessarily to stabilize terms," Cleanth Brooks writes in the Well-Wrought Urn, "to freeze them into strict denotations; the poet's tendency is by contrast disruptive."[49] This is why the New Critics favor poetry and difficult texts, works that traffic in disruption and disorientation. This is also why their criticism and pedagogy focus on terms like "ambiguity" (William Empson's Seven Types of Ambiguity [1930]), "paradox" (Brooks's essay "The Language of Paradox" [1947]), "tension," and "irony." These formal techniques and patterns reward explication.[50] The New Critical close readings often rise to the level of creative acts themselves. For anyone who has read a good close reading, one that takes you through a journey in a text you've read before and teaches you to see it anew, you know how transformative that experience can be. A good close reading can change your mind. It can make you reread and reconsider. Close reading can be not only about art but can become art, and for the New Critics, this was part of the point.

The New Critics were great close readers, and many of them were poets themselves, including William Empson, John Crowe Ransom, Robert Penn Warren, and Allen Tate. They took inspiration from modernists like Eliot and Pound, who fused the roles of poet and critic. They understood poetry to be a discipline and craft; consider Eliot's dedication to Pound, il miglior fabbro or "the better craftsman." They understood this craft as requiring dedicated study; consider Pound's The Guide to Kulchur (1938). Following Pound and Eliot, the New Critics thought poetry and criticism should strive for the precise and objective rather than emotive, experiential, or sentimental. As T.S. Eliot famously states, poetry "is not a turning loose of emotion, but an escape from emotion; it is not the expression of personality."[51] Similarly, in language that echoes Eliot's, Richards calls for criticism that approaches the aesthetic experience "in terms of distinterestedness, detachment, distance, impersonality, subjective universality, and so forth."[52] The New Criticism that emerged thereafter valued an objective stance toward the aesthetic and a focus on form.[53]

This disinterestedness is often interpreted as disinterest with anything other than form, and the New Critics are routinely criticized as formalists who cared nothing for history, culture, and so forth. "No idea of the New Critics inspired more protests," writes Graff, "than their assumption of the 'objective' nature of the literary text, their view that a poem is an object whose meaning can be analyzed by a detached, ideally disinterested critic."[54] But as Robert Archambeau argues, such protest often "involves a fundamental misunderstanding of what is meant by disinterest."[55] Pursuing the philosophical threads that influence Richards (and, through him, the New Criticism more broadly), Archambeau argues that disinterestedness implied a balanced and open perspective, rather than the opposite: "The distinterested mind, as Richards defines it, *is* the dialogic mind" (emphasis in original).[56] The larger point here is that the primary critique leveled against the New Critics—that they isolated their object of study from its historical context—is in fact true of their critics. But I am getting ahead of myself.

The New Criticism emerged in the years immediately following the period of high modernism. Many of the theorists know as New Critics built their reputations reading and teaching these difficult works. Close reading provided a method of appreciating the experiments of literary modernism, and the New Criticism, in turn, served to canonize modernism. "New Criticism grew up partly to justify modernist literature," William Logan writes.[57] Indeed, the codification of close reading was essential to establishing literary criticism as a field with a modern literary canon, and modernist literature was central to that canon. "The most significant achievement of the New Criticism," Graff argues, "was not its dissemination of a new technique of reading (though this was certainly significant), but its popularization of the modernist idea of literature and along with it modernist assumptions about language, knowledge, and experience."[58] Close reading was a central part of this endeavor.

Close reading was never just a means of understanding literary works but also of discerning and assigning value to them. Evaluation and judgment was inscribed into the practice from its inception. As Richards writes, the critical "endeavor [is] to discriminate between experiences and to evaluate them."[59] Codifying a practice of critical reading instituted a value-system for literature and established a class of professional readers capable of assigning and describing these values. The

professional literary critic emerged as a manager of readerly taste as literary criticism became an academic discipline. Such was the goal, as John Crowe Ransom
stated it in "Criticism, Inc." (1938): "Criticism must become more scientific, or
precise and systematic, and this means that it must be developed by the collective
and sustained effort of learned persons—which means that its proper seat is in the
universities."[60] Close reading became a skill-set taught in English departments,
and particular types of texts best served this reading practice. As a result, certain
texts were deemed worthy of close reading while others were not. For example, the
New Critics privileged poetry over prose, imagistic, cerebral, and difficult works
over those with a direct, colloquial, or sentimental tone.[61] One result of this hierarchy was a relegation of the majority of female and minority writers to the margins. Guillory reminds us, "Canonicity is not a property of the work itself but of
its transmission."[62] The transmission of the New Criticism through pedagogy (in
classrooms and textbooks) and critical publications helped to codify a canon that
included modernist literature.[63] It also established literary criticism as a profession, extended the prestige of English departments within the American academy,
and confirmed close reading as the central skill taught within.

From a media studies perspective, one might claim that one of the reasons
close reading remained a staple of American English departments and literary
pedagogy more broadly is that it required little technological support. The New
Critical practice of close reading presupposes that literature is print based. It approaches a text with the assumption that the text is read in a printed form—a page,
a book, a handout, and so forth—and this assumption encodes certain ideologies.
Namely, the object of study is thought to lack dependency upon its material characteristics; its words, and not the material properties of the textual medium (ink,
paper, binding, edition, etc.), are considered relevant.[64] Many criticize the New
Criticism for not expressing interest in media, materiality, or other more tangible
aspects of a work's context (history, politics, publishing history, etc.). Indeed, the
New Criticism, and the critical methodology for close reading that it promoted,
has been simplified, caricatured, and even rejected outright. Formal analysis has
been deemed outdated or, even, associated with a different cognitive epoch.[65]
I challenge these conclusions and the assumptions about New Criticism upon
which they are built by excavating their history. Contemporary digital poetics
demands such efforts, for such literature requires the skills associated with close
reading. As I will repeatedly argue throughout this book, this new literature promotes renovation of older critical practices, and invites reconsideration of how
close reading is a technique that itself has a history deserving of excavation and
analysis.

I am not alone in desiring to reassess the New Criticism. A recent wave has scholars excavating the New Criticism, its influence, and the way its history has been written. One finding is that misconceptions about the New Criticism proliferate because the same essays by the same people get anthologized over and over again. The larger, more diverse spectrum of New Critical work remains largely unread, at least until recently. In *Praising It New: The Best of the New Criticism* (2008) Garrick Davis collects and republishes essays by modernist and New Critical writers in "the first anthology of New Criticism to be printed in fifty years," as the blurb on the book's back cover proclaims. Frank Lentricchia and Andrew DuBois's *Close Reading: The Reader* (2003) focuses not only on known New Critics but also on more contemporary efforts at close reading. This valuable volume includes essays by Helen Vendler, Franco Moretti, and Eve Kosofsky Sedgwick, which collectively show how close reading extends beyond the expected dates and political perspectives of those who first honed the craft. Lentricchia describes the collection as "intended to represent and undercut what we take to be the major clash in the practice of literary criticism in the past century: that between so-called formalist and so-called nonformalist (especially 'political') modes of reading" by exploring their "common ground": "a commitment to close attention to literary texture and what is embodied there."[66]

In addition to the republication of New Critical texts, scholarly volumes that reconsider the New Criticism are also emerging. Miranda Hickman and John McIntyre's recent collection *Rereading the New Criticism* (2012) is exemplary in its effort to "reevaluat[e] the significance and legacy of the New Criticism" by collecting contemporary scholarly essays that closely analyze the texts and contexts of the New Criticism in ways that rebuke misconceptions about that founding movement in literary criticism.[67] In this respect, this collection follows other important critical acts of reconsideration, including William J. Spurlin and Michael Fischer's collection *The New Criticism and Contemporary Literary Theory: Connections and Continuities* (1995) and Mark Jancovich's *The Cultural Politics of the New Criticism* (1993). These efforts begin with the recognition, in Miranda Hickman words, that "New Critical work is still widely misrepresented as ahistorical, apolitical, and acontextual."[68] The recent surge of interest in reconsidering the New Criticism provides welcome company and context for my own ambitions.

Mine is not a book about the New Criticism. Close reading is my arrow not my target. But my purpose and practice have certain key points of intersection with the New Critics. Most significantly, I make the case for the continued importance of literature and literary criticism in an increasingly digital, visual, and networked culture. Moreover, I do so by close reading specific works of literature. This book is structured around acts of close reading that endeavor to expose the aesthetic value of digital literature and the literary more broadly.

Part II. The Stakes of My Argument

Renovating Close Reading

"These days," Jane Gallop writes, "I worry about the fate of close reading."[69] For Gallop, close reading is "the most valuable thing English ever had to offer" and, moreover, "the very thing that made us a discipline."[70] Lamenting the current state of literary studies, wherein archival research has upended textual explication and literary history seems more important than analysis, Gallop states, "If practiced here and there, it [close reading] is seldom theorized, much less defended."[71] Jonathan Culler echoes Gallop's sentiments. In a recent article for the *ADE Bulletin* titled "The Closeness of Close Reading" (2010), he claims, "we cannot just take close reading for granted, especially as we welcome into the university a generation of students raised in instant messaging" and "in an age where new electronic resources make it possible to do literary research without reading at all."[72] The fact that reading (and close reading) cannot to be taken for granted as standard skills no more is an opportunity to deliberately reassess and refashion these practices to suit our modern age and its born-digital artworks. We need to recognize how close reading is a historical and media-specific technique that, like other critical practices, demands renovation as we embrace our modern age and its digital literature.[73]

This book is part of a recent movement in literary criticism that seeks to recall the benefits of close reading in order to facilitate its adaptation. A handful of new media critics have recently asserted the value of close reading digital art and literature. Roberto Simanowski's *Digital Art and Meaning: Reading Kinetic Poetry, Text Machines, Mapping Art, and Interactive Installations* (2011) shows how digital art promotes interpretation; Jan Van Looy and Jan Baetens's *Close Reading New Media* (2003) collects essays that close read individual digital art objects; Alice Bell and Astrid Ensslin's special issue of the online journal *Dichtung-Digital*, titled "New Perspectives on Digital Literature: Criticism and Analysis" (2007), highlighted "second-wave theory" of digital literature that "focuses on close readings and semiotic textuality."[74] In a recent essay in *Digital Humanities Quarterly* titled "The Materialities of Close Reading: 1942, 1959, 2009," David Ciccoricco critiques this "second-wave theory" or what he calls "second generation digital-literary criticism" (of which the aforementioned texts would be part) for their "celebration of

both the practice and the very possibility of close reading works of digital literature, while at the same time failing to adequately articulate what 'close reading'
means, or must come to mean, in digital environments."[75] I hope that my book
participates in the effort to advocate for close reading approaches to digital literature, and thus also for the value of digital literature, even as it sympathizes with
Ciccoricco's critique. What distinguishes the chapters that follow from other, earlier attempts at approaching digital literature through close reading (of the likes
that earn Circcoricco's scorn) is an effort to demonstrate the relevance of this approach while also theorizing and historicizing it.

After the boom and bust cycle of contentious claims about either the newness
or sameness of digital media and either the rupture or continuation that digital
literature poses to literary studies, we are left with the need to analyze the specific
effects of the symbiosis between literature and media as it bears itself out in particular works. I contend that literary scholars need to pay more attention to the
media aspects of literature and that media critics need to pay more attention to
the literariness of electronic literature. I close read digital literature because the
works deserve it. Indeed, you might not know it from reading most criticism about
electronic literature, but these works are of interest not only because of their technological properties and programmatical innovations but also because of their
narrative content and formal aesthetics. The medium is not the only message,
but it is a popular one among critics. The works that sustain my study invite and
reward close reading. They are rich and complex, filled with intertextual allusions
and complicated poetics that reward careful reading and rereading.

But how do we close read works that are multimedia and multimodal, comprised of "flickering signifiers" (rather than static and stable ones) and of multiple
layers of semiotic processes, including hidden programming text and computer
code?[76] Different answers to these questions have led to a crisis of sorts in the field
of electronic literary criticism or, at least, to proliferation of critical subspecializa-
tions. Because digital literature challenges our ability to locate "the text," it invites
diverse critical methods and sparks debates about what counts as literature and
as literary criticism. In the field of electronic literature, scholarly attention has recently shifted from the content displayed onscreen to the technological platforms
and programming code producing it, and this has stimulated a debate over what
and how to read.

Early in the study of digital poetics, Loss Pequeño Glazier (2002) identified
source code as a vital component of the digital text that deserved critical analysis,
and today more critics are pursuing such examination. Mark C. Marino proposes a
method of analysis that he calls Critical Code Studies which reads programmable

code *as* text to "analyze and explicate code as a text, as a sign system with its own rhetoric, as verbal communication that possesses significance in excess of its functional utility."[77] Other critics, like Florian Cramer and John Cayley, warn against reading code as text. Arguing that because code is an executable process, programmable text becomes code only when it runs. They conclude, code is not code when it is extracted for study.[78] Or as Cayley pithily titles his essay, "The Code Is not the Text (unless It Is the Text)."[79] Even with such precautions, however, a shift is underway in contemporary digital criticism—a turn away from reading onscreen aesthetics toward analysis of the technical mechanics of digitality. This trend is exemplified by MIT Press's two new book series: Platform Studies (edited by Ian Bogost and Nick Montfort), which "investigates the relationships between the hardware and software design of computing systems and the creative works produced on those systems," and Software Studies (edited by Matthew Fuller, Lev Manovich, and Noah Wardrip-Fruin) which "uses and develops cultural, theoretical, and practice-oriented approaches to make critical, historical, and experimental accounts of (and interventions via) the objects and processes of software."[80] These critical strategies are valid and valuable, particularly when they serve to promote a fuller understanding of digital textuality and the reading practices it promotes; but they should not replace rigorous analysis of the aesthetic ambitions and results of technopoetic pursuits.

I approach electronic literature by close reading its onscreen aesthetics, both its textual and nontextual elements. For this reason, *Digital Modernism* might be considered a kind of apologia for "screen essentialism" in digital literature.[81] Through this apologia, I argue that close reading digital literature is valuable training for twenty-first century media literacy. As I will suggest throughout, this book is not just about electronic literature or even about literature more generally; it is also about the value our culture places on critical thinking and analysis. I hope to show how studying the formal poetics of born-digital literature promotes reflective consideration of the practices we use to read, analyze, and judge.

Literary Analysis as Media Literacy for a Digital World

Digital Modernism positions literary analysis at the center of our technological culture. It shares this ambition with the New Critics. As I mentioned earlier, those critics sought to recuperate literary analysis from an increasingly devalued position in relation to the sciences in the early part of the twentieth-century, and they used close reading to do so. In the early part of the twenty-first century, we find ourselves in a similar situation. In a culture that seems to favor facts over critique, data over interpretation, positivism over poetics, we might draw some points of parallel to that period which inspired the New Critics to turn to the text and close read. An economic crisis has made a liberal arts education increasingly untenable for the majority of Americans, and the study of literature and the humanities seems particularly out-of reach. But we should remember that New Critics saw close reading as a pedagogical means of training students to read not only specific literary texts but also to learn to evaluate and judge culture more broadly. The pedagogical goal of the New Critics, Tara Lockhart writes, was for students to "become more capable of pursuing their own inquiries and more competent at generating critical responses to complex textual questions."[82] The goal remains the same today, although the complex textual questions are now just as likely to be written in lines of programming code as in poetic stanzas. In whatever form or medial format the text appears, however, close reading of it supports and enables critical thinking. This point, more than anything, is my polemic and purpose.

In our culture of technophilia, most people are users of ever-more complex media products containing ever-more sophisticated interfaces that hide the interworking of the technologies and the ideologies behind their design. Most users lack the skills to think critically about these objects and, moreover, about how these objects formally operate. How do we understand the interface of the Google home page? How does it formally produce meaning? When I ask my students this question, I am usually met with silence and confusion. The response is not because they don't know what the Google home page looks like but because they have never been asked to think critically about it. When I follow up with more specific questions about the formal properties of the interface, things begin to change. Students begin to notice the typography used to depict the company's name and recognize it as a deliberate choice employed for particular purposes: to present a playful poetic that imagistically enables a single word to become a corporation's name (a pronoun), a space and thing (a noun), and a mode of action for using the search engine (a verb). They start to explicate how the stark white background of the Google home page produces its central poetic effect—ambiguity (that poetic property that so fascinated the New Critics). Students begin to see this web page, which they have encountered hundreds of times before, as a *text* with complicated poetics—one which deserves to be analyzed.

If we want to train critical thinkers for a digital era, we need to teach them to close read new media objects and artworks. We can do so by teaching them to read and close read digital literature. The question of how to read digital literature is thus not only of interest to a sub-set of academics but part of a much wider cultural discussion about literacy in a digital age. In an earlier age, the New Critics turned to close reading individual works of literary art as a means of bridging the emergent divide between science and the humanities. We can learn from their example because now, more than ever before, close reading can serve to bridge this divide. When it comes to digital literature, there is no separation between science and literary art. Digital literature is algorithmically driven and technologically enabled; its content cannot be separated from its form or format.[83] Web-based digital literature exacerbates this point because it exists as part of a network (the Internet) and thus challenges the ability to identify the piece's perimeters or proclaim its autonomy. What we learn by close reading digital literature is that one cannot simply focus on textual formal devices but must consider how they are formatted and in which contextual networks they are produced, distributed, and accessed. This means a merger of formalism and textual studies, aesthetics and media studies. We *can* retain the productive and illuminative pleasures of formalist close reading while simultaneously recognizing and examining the material and historical contexts in which a literary work operates. We can also complicate simplistic distinctions between science and art, poetics and technology.

Electronic literature demands that we do so.

Part IV. Critical Influences

Digital Modernism seeks to builds bridges between modernism and digital literature, print textuality and computational technologies, literary criticism and media studies. This attempt to illuminate the recursive relationship between modernism and new media is inspired by revaluations of modernism by such scholars as Michael North, Garrett Stewart, Johanna Drucker, and Marjorie Perloff as well as the textual criticism of Jerome McGann, George Bornstein, Lawrence Rainey, and others who remind us that literature is always created, distributed, accessed, and archived in material contexts and media-specific conditions. Whether we realize it or not, these conditions inform the ways in which we read and study literature. In the field of new media studies, *Digital Modernism* stakes a claim for the importance of literature and literary analysis. Here I build upon the work of Katherine Hayles, Alan Liu, and Rita Raley, all of whom pursue media-specific analysis with scholarly vigor and historical breadth while remaining acutely attuned to literary poetics. Hayles, in particular, is a central and powerful node in the network of influences that inform my approach for, in many recent publications, she has drawn critical attention to the "intermediation" (her term) of natural language and computing code and to the need to reassess the implications of this situation, particularly as it informs literary studies.[84]

My decidedly literary approach participates in and benefits from cross-disciplinary conversations in media studies and media archaeology lead by the likes of Wendy Chun, Lisa Gitelman, Matthew Kirschenbaum, Lev Manovich, Terry Harpold, and others who work to reconceive the ways in which we theorize the relationships between old and new media. My commitment to caring about emergent literary aesthetics is informed by another strain of recent scholarly work—efforts by theorists such as Sianne Ngai and Rita Felski—who forcefully and gracefully assert the need to rethink aesthetics. In her treatise *On Beauty*, Elaine Scarry pens an apologia for aesthetics in a postmodern world that seems to reject it as a serious field of study. Wouldn't it be ironic if the post-postmodern period heralds the return of aesthetic theory *through* digital literature? In my effort to read aesthetics by renovating close reading, I am inspired by critics like Franco Moretti who strive to find creative methods of reassessing and reinvigorating the practices we lump together under the title "literary criticism." If I achieve my goals, this project will contribute to ongoing efforts by a diverse group of scholars who all seek to adapt traditional humanities criticism to illuminate, historicize, and contextualize the contemporary and the new. My particular intervention is to provide a framework for locating diverse points of connection across a century of literary history and across more recent but distributed conversations about the relationship between media and literary studies. In what follows, I read the literary aspects of individual digital works in ways that extend traditional literary criticism to digital objects and digital culture more broadly.

Part V. Chapter Summaries

Each chapter of this book examines a different aspect of digital modernism's relationship to modernism and shows how reading carefully between these literary acts provides an opportunity to reconsider literature and literary history through perspectives made possible by new media. Chapter 1, "Close Reading: Marshall McLuhan, from Modernism to Media Studies," introduces the father of media studies, Marshall McLuhan, as a modernist New Critic and argues for the importance of understanding how close reading serves his foundational writing. McLuhan studied at Cambridge under such eminent New Critics as I. A. Richards and F. R. Leavis, and this training provided the scaffolding for his later theories about media evolution. I examine how McLuhan adapted the New Critical practice of close reading and applied it to objects that the New Critics did not consider literary. In so doing, he built media studies from literary studies. Recognition of this fact places the literary at the heart of our medial moment. Taking seriously McLuhan's training in literature as well as his writerly prose is, I claim, crucial to understanding his theories of media but also the larger field of media studies that grew out of them. Although many people cite or refer to McLuhan, few close read his writings. Yet close reading his prose illuminates the ways in which he adapted modernist literature to serve his contemporary medial context. Sustained attention to how he refashioned the New Criticism illuminates central convergences between literary and media studies and reminds us how creative and versatile the critical activity of close reading can be.

My second chapter turns McLuhan's famous insight that the medium is the message into a strategy for close reading. "Reading Machines: Machine Poetry and Excavatory Reading" performs close reading as media archaeology and argues that the machines involved in producing a reading experience are crucial aspects of a literary work's aesthetics. I read William Poundstone's digital work *Project for the Tachistoscope: {Bottomless Pit}* (2005) as it flashes a stream of speeding text and icons onscreen in an act of poetically remediating a now-obsolete technology, the tachistoscope. In his digital work, Poundstone presents a tachistoscopic reading experience that archives the older technology and promotes excavation of it. This chapter pairs Poundstone's digital work with an earlier experiment in machine poetics that dates from the modernist period: Bob Brown's Readies machine (circa 1930). American avant-garde poet Bob Brown introduced his plan to build a reading machine that would speed up the way we read and thereby fundamentally change the kind of literature we write. He called his machine "The Readies." "The word 'readies' suggests to me a moving type spectacle," Brown writes, "reading at the speed rate of the day with the aid of a machine, a method of enjoying literature in a manner as up-to-date as the lively talkies."[85] The Readies was never built, but Brown's writing about the machine and his anthology of poetry for it (which includes out-of-print poems by Gertrude Stein, F. T. Marinetti, and Ezra Pound) serves as a crucial link between experimental writers of modernist and contemporary periods imagining literary revolution *through* innovations in the speed-reading machines of their own times.

Having established that digital modernism exposes media to be part of the poetic practice and thus deserving of critical analysis, the next two chapters consider specific literary techniques enabled by digital technologies and employed by digital modernism. Chapter 3, "Speed Reading: Simultaneity and Super-position," examines Young-hae Chang Heavy Industries's claim that their "*Dakota* is based on a close reading of Ezra Pound's *Cantos* part I and part II." I close read the digital work in relation to its proclaimed source material despite the fact that the speed at which *Dakota* flashes challenges efforts to do so. I show how YHCHI brilliantly adapt Pound's poetry at the level of content and form. For, not only do YHCHI remix the language of the first cantos but they also use Flash to renovate Pound's poetic technique of "super-position" or textual montage. This chapter examines the transformation of Pound's formal technique into Flash to show how the poetic result illuminates connections between the modernist and digital modernist texts as well as the literary periods they represent.

Chapter 4, "Reading the Database: Narrative, Database, and Stream of Consciousness," traces a constellation of digital modernist works that adapt stream of consciousness in ways that illuminate literature's effort to represent cognition with and through media. James Joyce's *Ulysses* is the central node in this network, the inspiration for a variety of digital modernist works: a Twitter-based performance of "Wandering Rocks" (by Ian Bogost and Ian McCarthy), a generative, database-driven work of performance art (Talan Memmott's *Twittering: a novel*), and a deeply complex narrative inspired by a section of Joyce's "Ithaca" chapter (Judd Morrissey and Lori Talley's *The Jew's Daughter*). Considering these diverse works together and in relation to their source of inspiration, *Ulysses* shows how stream of consciousness—that central literary technique for representing consciousness in twentieth-century literature, which came to the fore through modernism—is, at its heart, decidedly about media. This chapter shows how contemporary literature updates modernist techniques for depicting human consciousness to reflect changes as its subject becomes posthuman and its medium becomes digital.

I also explore a conceptual and technological parallel between stream of consciousness and electronic hypertext, the latter of which is often identified as a technological format that models the mental processes of associative cognition. *The Jew's Daughter* pursues an allusion to hypertext as it adapts "The Jew's Daughter" section of *Ulysses*, a decidedly nonhypertextual and non–stream of consciousness narrative section. I compare how these literary works represent cognition as a mediated process, and I focus on two points of connection. First, the juxtaposition between digital and modernist works shows how *Ulysses* employs a database aesthetic to depict cognition. Examining this point complicates contemporary critical debates about the difference between database and narrative. Second, and subsequently, literary fiction is seen to be a vital space for testing out theories about how media informs and affects cognition.

The fifth chapter, "Reading Code: The Hallucination of Universal Language from Modernism to Cyberspace," intervenes in a different topic of contemporary debate in media studies: discourse about the readability of computer code. I trace a prehistory of this discussion about code-as-text back to, yes, modernism. I draw a parallel between the idea that computer code enables universal communication and the idea that the Chinese ideogram is a universal medium for poetics, an idea most famously propagated by Ezra Pound via Ernest Fenollosa. Chinese has been a central part of Western discourse about universal language for centuries, from Leibniz's binary logic through to Norbert Wiener's computer-based machine translation and debates about Global English via the World Wide Web. This chapter traces this thread across the intertwined histories of poetics and computing. I read a work of electronic literature that incorporates ideograms into its interface design (Young-hae Chang Heavy Industries's *Nippon*) and a digital novel that confronts and rejects the idea that cyberspace enables universal translation (Erik Loyer's *Chroma*). These works, I claim, resist the ideological underpinnings that turn code into a universal language—either through the conceit that code is capable of universal machine translation or that code is an autonomous, unreadable entity on par with a natural language. These works, I argue, critique computational ideologies *through* literature. In so doing, they remind us that literature and its study are essential to understanding and critiquing digital culture and discourse.

Digital Modernism concludes with a coda, "Rereading: Digital Modernism in Print, Mark Z. Danielewski's *Only Revolutions*," that demonstrates how the strategy of digital modernism informs contemporary print literature. Danielewski's experimental print novel *Only Revolutions* (2006) employs the central modernist and digital modernist practice of adapting the past to pursue literary innovation and, even, revolution. The novel contains 360 pages with 360 words per page, and its design demands that readers turn the book around, literally *revolve* it (to use the language of the novel's title), in order to read the narratives of its two protagonists, which are printed at opposite ends of each page. *Only Revolutions* illuminates and exploits the possibilities of the codex as a medium for experimental literature even as it depicts this traditional reading machine referencing and relying upon the Internet for its bookishness. This novel displays print literature as part of, not separate from, the digital network. In so doing, it proclaims the vitality of print textuality in the digital age. Moreover, *Only Revolutions* enacts a digital modernist strategy by showing how the older medium (the book) and the literature it contains (whose poetic is, I will show, decisively modernist) are renovated through interaction with digitality. With this conclusion, I show how digital modernism extends beyond the screen and, thus, I hope, extends the relevance of my efforts to analyze it.

Collectively, the chapters in this book illustrate how literature adapts to a new age and its new media. And, as the texts we study evolve, so too must our practices of critical analysis continue to change. The challenges posed to traditional modes of analysis offer opportunities to update our critical practices and to see afresh the recursive relationship between technologies and textual expression. The chapters that follow strive situate electronic literature within literary history and push literary studies to evolve with our new media age. What is at stake is nothing short of a better understanding of the significance of literary art, critical reading practices, and humanistic culture in our networked age.

1. Close Reading

Marshall McLuhan, from Modernism to Media Studies

"it is the framework itself that changes with new technology, and not just the picture within the frame."

Marshall McLuhan, *Understanding Media*[1]

Marshall McLuhan, a.k.a. the "Oracle of the Electronic Age" and the "Patron Saint" of *Wired* magazine, coined the term "global village," taught us that "the medium is the message," prophesied the impact of the electronic technologies, and established the field that we now call media studies. McLuhan published his groundbreaking books in the early 1960s, in a period of social revolution, and achieved immediate fame and notoriety as a cultural guru and technocultural prophet.[2] He was an English professor who became a household name, and his face graced the covers of national magazines and international television shows; he even did a cameo in a Woody Allen's *Annie Hall* (1977).[3] His name became an adjective. "McLuhanist" or "McLuhanism" became a synonym for technodeterminism and rhetorical obliqueness. His work bridged academic and popular audiences; loved and hated by public intellectuals, it has been critiqued and admired for challenging conventional scholarly practices (in particular, the practice of eschewing citations and footnotes, let alone a clearly articulated, thesis-driven argument). Much has been written about McLuhan over the years (especially recently, since 2011 was the centennial of McLuhan's birth), and these writings usually take an extreme position in judging their subject.[4] His reputation has seesawed through extreme highs and lows, though it seems to be on the upswing these days.[5] Many people know McLuhan's name and cite his famous mantra—"the medium is the message"—but few actually read his works and still fewer close read them. But, as I hope to show, close reading McLuhan's seminal works from a literary perspective—in particular, *The Mechanical Bride: Folklore of Industrial Man* (1951), *The Gutenberg Galaxy: The Making of Typographic Man* (1962), and *Understanding Media: The Extensions of Man* (1964)[6]—provides invaluable insights into his interpretative methodology and opens up new avenues for addressing the intersection between media and literary studies.

McLuhan is a Janus figure between past and present, a modernist New Critic who transformed "practical criticism" into close reading media forms; and, I will show, in so doing, he pioneered a field of study. Media studies only came into its own in the last few decades, but as is often the case with "new" fields of study (particularly ones focused on "new" media), it lacks a sense of its own history. This chapter argues that contemporary media studies can be traced back to McLuhan and, through him, to modernist writers and critics. Recognizing this fact illuminates the continued influence of modernism on digital culture.

Amidst the hype and criticism surrounding McLuhan as digital prophet, it is often forgotten that he was, first and foremost, an English professor. McLuhan was trained in the New Criticism at Cambridge under I. A. Richards and F. R. Leavis, and he was deeply influenced by this experience. He relied on this education—in particular, the appreciation of modernist literature and the practice of close reading—as the foundation for his critical approach to media. As I will argue, he adapted the New Critical method of focusing on form into a means for thinking critically about forms of media. Sustained attention to how he did so exposes close reading to be a mode of media-specific analysis; conversely, media-specific analysis can be understood as a mode of close reading.[7] This claim may sound counterintuitive because, as I explained in this book's introduction, the New Criticism is commonly understood as rejecting all aspects of materiality in the practice of interpreting a literary text. But close reading McLuhan's texts challenges this view of the New Critics by showing how the version of practical criticism he learned at Cambridge was always about approaching the broader category of the literary *within* complex media ecologies.[8] Close reading McLuhan's writings reminds us that media-specific analysis is as much a literary endeavor as a technological one.

Understanding McLuhan

The "medium is the message" is a memorable, alliterative aphorism that rolls off the tongue, but what does it mean? That is not so easy to explain because McLuhan refuses to do so. His deceptively concise mantra in no way represents a larger body of writing consisting of clear, rational argumentation. His cameo appearance in *Annie Hall* pokes fun at the fact that McLuhan is famously incomprehensible. While standing in line at the cinema, Woody Allen's character grows increasingly aggravated by the man behind him explicating loudly and pompously about McLuhan's theory of hot and cool media. Allen turns around and confronts the man, who then introduces himself as a professor of television and culture at Columbia. Allen critiques the professor's summary of McLuhan and then steps aside to pull into the frame none other than Marshall McLuhan himself. As if to literally "back up" Allen's interpretation, McLuhan walks up to the professor and quips, "You know nothing of my work!" McLuhan's exclamation is more than an intellectual's fantasty, on the part of Allen's character; it is actually a self-deprecating comment whose comic punch line comes at McLuhan's expense. For, even an Ivy League professor of media studies can completely misunderstand McLuhan's work. His prose is just that oblique.

Let me pass along one more humorous story about McLuhan's famous incomprehensibility, which media scholar Lance Strate shares on his blog. Strate claims that Jerome Agel (the producer of *The Medium Is the Massage* and many of McLuhan's other, later visual books, too) once told him the following joke:

> Q: Did you know that McLuhan's *Understanding Media* has been translated into twenty-two languages?
>
> A: Really? Has it been translated into English yet?[9]

McLuhan's writing is hard to understand because it is fragmented and hypertextual but also dense and compact. Like much of the prose by the experimental modernist writers McLuhan admired, it disrupts formal expectations. One might even call his style "poetic"; he certainly would. His texts do not follow a clear, linear trajectory or build toward a single argument. His arguments do not even fit within the confines of a single codex but instead sprawl hypertextually across numerous genres and media forms—books, essays, interviews, and lectures captured in print and live and recorded performances. This point is important because McLuhan's provocations unfurl into arguments only for the reader who follows their recursive recombination across diverse media formats. In McLuhan's oeuvre, form and content are inseparable to the point that "reading" McLuhan is a difficult endeavor demanding a poetic, indeed a modernist, sensibility.

To understand his writing, one must read the textual content by paying attention to how it operates. Reading McLuhan's texts thus requires close reading. McLuhan writes about print culture with awareness of the book as medium, and, as I will show, the pages of his books express this fact in the arrangement and structure of their argument and page layout. "Our conventional response to all media," he writes, is to focus on "how they are used," but this "is the numb stance of the technological idiot. For the 'content' of a medium is like the juicy piece of meat carried by the burglar to distract the watchdog of the mind."[10] Form, not just content, should be the subject of media criticism; and media is, after all, form. "All the new media, including the press, are art forms which have the power of imposing, like poetry, their own assumptions."[11] McLuhan turns media into an object of study, one akin to art or poetry. As Umberto Eco describes McLuhan's main insight, "The *form* of the message is the real content of the message (which is the thesis of avant-garde literature and criticism)" (emphasis in original).[12] McLuhan learned about avant-garde literature and criticism during his time at Cambridge University.

Part I. McLuhan as New Critic

After graduating from the University of Manitoba in 1933, McLuhan studied at Cambridge under I. A. Richards and F. R. Leavis.[13] Richards and Leavis were pioneers in the New Criticism, and Cambridge was a hub of such innovative thinking. McLuhan was deeply influenced by this experience and relied on this education as he developed his own critical method and path. In a foreword to a collection of his essays of literary criticism, edited by Eugene McNamara, *Interior Landscapes: The Literary Criticism of Marshall McLuhan* (1969), McLuhan retrospectively acknowledges the impact of his Cambridge education. He writes, "My study of media began and remains rooted in the work of these men," meaning Richards and Leavis as well as his favorite modernist writers (Pound, Joyce, and Eliot) to whom he was introduced at Cambridge.[14] In a letter dated December 12, 1935, McLuhan writes, "Until I came to the Cambridge English School, my principle qualification was a boundless enthusiasm for great books, great events, and great men. Dr Richards and Dr Leavis have proved to be a useful supplement and corrective to that attitude."[15] McLuhan returned to North America in 1936, taking his first teaching position at the University of Wisconsin. In the words of biographer Glenn Willmott, McLuhan "saw himself, and sold himself, as a representative of the New Critical avant-garde."[16] McLuhan inherited from the New Critics a particular view of the role of literature, the literary imagination, and literary analysis. This view saw the distinction between poetry and criticism, poet and critic, as unnecessary. The goal of poet and critic is to challenge conventions and teach the rest of the world to see from a new perspective.

McLuhan saw himself as a critic-seer witnessing a great technocultural transformation. The emergence of electric technologies, he thought, was comparable to the revolution produced in the fifteenth and sixteenth centuries by the invention of the printing press. The electric age of radio and television would, he was convinced, similarly transform the ways in which we read, write, and think. Within this period of massive medial shift, McLuhan saw himself poised, in the language Ezra Pound uses to describe the role of the artist, as "the antennae of the race."[17] McLuhan writes, in words that echo Pound's, "It's always been the artist who perceives the alternations in man caused by a new media, who recognizes that the future is the present, and uses his work to prepare the ground for it."[18] McLuhan inherited from his teachers, the modernists and New Critics, a sense of urgency and responsibility as a critic. He saw his purpose in pedagogical terms, as a Romantic bard translating the poet's recognition to a broader audience. He describes his education at Cambridge as "a shock" because "Richards, Leavis, Eliot and Pound and Joyce in a few weeks opened the doors of perception on the poetic process, and its role in adjusting the reader to the contemporary world."[19] The impact of this education should not be underestimated; for it was at Cambridge that McLuhan learned to see how literary study could have real-world relevance. This understanding supported McLuhan as he refashioned literary criticism into media studies.

McLuhan's Media Theory

McLuhan presented a media-based theory of history, and it goes something like this: the printing press introduced repetition and uniformity into the production of texts and, in so doing, made repetition and uniformity the cornerstones of human experience. "Homogeneity, uniformity, repeatability" are, according to McLuhan, the result of a print-based society.[20] The technology of printing press builds words from individual letter blocks in an assembly-line manner, and the results of this technological process are ever-present. McLuhan argues that they are felt deeply and psychically at the individual level and also in the culture at large. He writes, "from the invention of the alphabet there has been a continuous drive in the Western world toward the separation of the senses, of functions, of operations, of states of emotions and politics, as well as of tasks."[21] The resulting "typographic Man" privileges vision over his other senses and reads in silent isolation the static, discrete, and linear, alphabetic text of print. Typographic man forgoes the real-time embodiment of interpersonal interaction ascribed to oral cultures and is cut off from the holistic sensibilities of multisensory communication. In McLuhan's view, print fosters a fixed point-of-view rather than a sense of simultaneity; it thus supports ideologies of individualism over tribal connection.[22] The mechanical principle of Gutenberg technology becomes a state of being and a way of seeing: "the most obvious character of print is repetition, just as the obvious effect of repetition is hypnosis or obsession."[23] Or, as he more clearly explains the causal connections, "The invention of typography confirmed and extended the new visual stress of applied knowledge, providing the first uniformly repeatable commodity, the first assembly-line, and the first mass-production."[24] The repercussions of print technology are only becoming visible to us now, McLuhan argues, because we are in the midst of transitioning away from a print-based culture and into an electric age.

Whereas "previous technologies were partial and fragmentary," McLuhan writes, "the electric is total and inclusive."[25] Electronic technologies thus, McLuhan argues, usher in the dawn of a new era. McLuhan's thesis is summarized in the following statement, taken from *The Medium Is the Massage: An Inventory of Effects* (1967): "The alphabet and print technology fostered and encouraged a fragmenting process, a process of specialism and of detachment. Electronic technology fosters and encourages unification and involvement."[26] These new media, in some sense, promote a return to an earlier era, one inclined toward the tribal or "the global village." McLuhan writes, "our age translates itself back into the oral and auditory modes because of the electronic pressure of simultaneity."[27] The emergence of electric technologies promise to unify man and reconnect mankind. For this reason, he writes, "the greatest of all reversals occurred with electricity, that ended sequence by making things instant."[28]

For the purposes of my argument, it is important to recognize that McLuhan identified the decisive historical moment of this reversal in the media-based history he writes as taking place in the modernist period. Not only did the late decades of the nineteenth century and early decades of the twentieth century experience an emerging electronic mediatization, as I suggested in my introduction, but this technological fact was imprinted and expressed in that period's art. McLuhan claimed that modernist literature and art hold the keys to understanding the medial shift to the electronic age. "Cubism," he declares, "by seizing on instant total awareness, suddenly announced that *the medium is the message*" (emphasis in original).[29] Modernist literature and art translated the instantaneous and simultaneous affect of technological innovations (such as radio, the telegraph, and airplanes) into artistic expressions, including Cubist art, Gertrude Stein's "continuous present," and cinematic montage.[30] "The printed book encouraged artists to reduce all forms of expression as much as possible to the single descriptive and narrative plane of the printed world," McLuhan writes; "The advent of electric media released art from this straitjacket at once, creating the world of Paul Klee, Picasso, Braque, Eisenstein, the Marx Brothers, and James Joyce."[31] McLuhan posits modernism as a period of media revolution, the origin of our modern media age. He built his theory of media upon this understanding of modernism, an understanding cultivated at Cambridge under Richards and Leavis.

Adapting the New Criticism

The particular type of New Criticism that McLuhan learned and adapted was Practical Criticism. In 1929 Richards published *Practical Criticism: A Study in Literary Judgment* and pioneered a new approach to the critical reading of poetry. Richards attempted to provide for literary studies a kind of scientific methodology, and he introduced his goals for his book in decidedly scientific rhetoric: to "introduce a new kind of *documentation*," "a new *technique*," and "to prepare the way for education methods *more efficient* than those we use now" (emphasis added).[32] The book contains documentation from a series of studies Richards conducted in his classroom, efforts to reconsider the method of teaching literary criticism. In these now-famous pedagogical experiments, Richards gave his students poems stripped of common indicators used to identify, locate, and ascertain the value of a text, ways of assigning value passed down from the *belle-lettrisic* education of old: author's name and poem's title. Canonical and noncanonical poems were mixed together, and students were asked to analyze and judge the texts before them. Richards then compiled his students' responses into a "record of a piece of field-work in comparative ideology."[33] The result: "On the whole it is fairly safe to assert that the poems received much more thorough study than, shall we say, most anthology pieces get in the ordinary course."[34] By stripping away the historical context, Richards turned his students' focus to the poem itself. Richards describes the experiment as promoting awareness that a poem's success lies in its ability to communicate how it works, not just what it communicates. He writes, "poetry itself is a mode of communication. What it communicates and how it does so and the worth of what is communicated form the subject-matter of criticism."[35] *Practical Criticism* supports Richards's larger ambition, "to provide a new technique for those who wish to discover for themselves what they think and feel about poetry (and cognate matters) and why they should like or dislike it."[36]

McLuhan took part in these pedagogical exercises. He wrote home to his mother (from Cambridge in 1935) with an air of skepticism about "the 'great' discovery" Richards supposedly made through them.[37] "I have some doubts about the method of giving *one* poem of any person as a test," he writes; "A really cultivated taste might hit the nail most of the time, but uncultivated people can enjoy many things in a *volume* by one writer, where the merits of his craft and ideas and feelings are permitted to permeate the consciousness from 1000 different angles" (emphasis in original).[38] Although he had his reservations about the conclusions one can draw from the experiment (which are, indeed, valid critiques), McLuhan expresses willingness to consider how different data sources and circuits of flow constitute a literary experience. He would later, we will soon see, experiment formally in pursuing different ways of "permeat[ing] the consciousness from 1000 different angles" to produce a sense of simultaneity in critical prose. Although, rather than examine poetry, McLuhan would apply his skills in practical criticism toward analyzing media.

Practical Criticism was "a companion volume," as Richards called it, to his first book, *Principles of Literary Criticism* (1924). The preface to the 1928 edition of *Principles of Literary Criticism* opens with an oft-quoted line, "A book is a machine to think with."[39] The sentence continues, although its second half is cited less often, and the quotation in its longer form affected young McLuhan. "A book is a machine to think with, but it need not, therefore, usurp the functions either of the bellows or of the locomotive."[40] In the opening lines to a text that would become the cornerstone work in the field later known as literary criticism, Richards suggests a need for comparative media studies, for considering the relationship between media forms as a means of pursuing criticism. *Principles of Literary Criticism* proceeds from the foundation that a comparative mode is central to analysis and that this comparative mode is often neglected. "The central question," Richards writes, "What is the value of the arts, and why are they worth the devotion of the keenest hours of the best minds, and what is their place in the system of human endeavors?"[41] That question, Richards laments, "is left almost untouched" in the annals of Western critical thought.[42] But with *Principles* and *Practical Criticism*, Richards sought to pave the way for others to approach poetry comparatively by considering it as a form of communication that employs language and specific media forms. Thinking comparatively about poetry, Richards suggests, will have the effect of making literary criticism relevant not only to poetics but also to other forms of cultural communication. "Criticism will justify itself as an applied science," he writes, "when it is able to indicate how an advertisement may be profitable without necessarily being crass."[43] Success in literary criticism depends upon an ability to explain *how* a text works, not only what it says. As we will soon see, McLuhan takes Richards at his word in this regard. In his first book, *The Mechanical Bride: Folklore of Industrial Man* (1951), McLuhan shows the value of literary criticism by close reading advertisements to show how they work.

But before we return to McLuhan, we must first attend to the other leading figure at Cambridge who also greatly influenced him: F.R. Leavis. Leavis also practiced a form of Practical Criticism, but in ways that distinguished him from other New Critics and established him as a particularly important mentor for the young McLuhan. In *How to Teach Reading: A Primer for Ezra Pound* (1932), Leavis pays attention and tribute to Pound as critic, which McLuhan would follow suit in doing. Leavis begins that book by stating that Pound's *How to Read* (1929) "has, one hopes, been widely read" for "its value" lies in the fact that "it is a thing to quarrel with."[44] Grappling with Pound's suggestions about how—and more so *why*—to read in a world that lacks a Common Reader or reading list is important, Leavis claims, for "Literary history pursued in this spirit will be very different from the usual accumulation of dead and deadening knowledge about authors and periods."[45] Leavis describes and disdains the current state of literary studies wherein "we have, passing for an educated interest in literature, the elegant cult . . . of *belles lettres*."[46] Instead of trying to read everything labeled as important by someone else, Leavis "recommend[s] close analytic study of a few poems of each of the authors in question."[47] Such efforts in focused, *close* reading will open up literary study, Leavis suggests, enabling literary study to go beyond reading only those texts. Indeed, such practice will even translate these critical, close reading skills to nontextual objects. Leavis claims as much in the conclusion to *How to Teach Reading*, stating that "a serious concern for education in reading cannot stop at reading"; and then, "Practical criticism of literature must be associated with training in awareness of the environment—advertising, the cinema, the press, architecture and so on, for, clearly, to the pervasive counter-influence of this environment the literary training of sensibility in school is an inadequate reply. Here is raised the whole question of the relation of reading to education and culture"[48] The "close analytic study of a few poems," that is, close reading, is a bridge to reading larger cultural environments. This is one of Leavis's main points and one that significantly impacts McLuhan's own development as a critic.

Zooming out from a few poems to the culture at large suggests the importance, exigency, and even moral certitude of the analytical act. This connection between whole and part, cultural and object of study, education and close reading, permeates and undergirds Leavis's approach to analysis. Consider the opening of *Culture and the Environment* (1933), in which Leavis and Denys Thompson survey the situation of literary studies in a modern, mediatized world:

> Many teachers of English who have become interested in the possibilities of training taste and sensibility must have been troubled by accompanying doubts. What effect can such training have against the multitudinous counterinfluences—films, newspapers, advertising—indeed the whole world outside the classroom? Yet the very conditions that make literary education look so desperate are those which make it more important than ever before; for in a world of this kind—and a world that changes so rapidly—it is on literary tradition that the office of maintaining continuity must rest.[49]

Leavis and Thompson acknowledge the changing medial landscape and the challenges this "whole world" of "film, newspapers, advertising" pose to literary study. In response to this new and mass media, they assert the continued relevance of literary training. McLuhan agrees, and he relies upon his literary training to explain, in Leavis and Thompson's words, "the very conditions that make literary education look so desperate." McLuhan's innovation is to show how a "literary education"—its critical reading practices (i.e., close reading) and objects of study (i.e., literary works)—can serve the new media, electronic moment.

McLuhan departs from Leavis in his method of pursuit. "Of course the trouble with Leavis," McLuhan writes in a letter dated from 1944, "is that his passion for the important work forbids him to look for the sun in the egg-tarnished spoons of the daily table."[50] In other words, Leavis was too highbrow in his focus of study. McLuhan learned from his New Critic teachers that the study of poetics could be something other than "romantic rebellion against mechanical industry and bureaucratic stupidity."[51] Whereas Leavis and Thompson position literary criticism as an antidote to the passive consumption of modern mass culture, a means of counteracting (serving "against") an increasingly mediatized cultural environment, McLuhan sees the relationship to be synergistic rather than antagonistic. Literary analysis and, specifically, the ability to close read is not positioned against the medial environment but situated squarely within it. It can serve to teach the reader to accept, adjust, and even appreciate the aesthetics of the modern technological age and offer a way of understanding this environment. In contrast to the Frankfurt School or other theorists inspired by modernist literature and literary theory who saw aesthetics as an outpost from capitalism and the commodification of consciousness,

McLuhan takes the New Critical practice of isolating a text for analytical explication in another direction—as a way of reading the mediatized moment.

McLuhan learned from Leavis to assert a larger purpose for literary criticism. In an essay published in 1944 in *The Sewanee Review*, a publishing pillar of the New Criticism, McLuhan (then signing his name H. M. rather than the full-fledged "Marshall") distinguishes between Richards (and his followers) and Leavis based on the moral purpose expressed in their individual approaches. McLuhan describes Richards as an astute rhetorician who analyzes the specific instance of a literary moment and thus reinvigorates the critical enterprise, while Leavis offers a larger, ethical purpose in and through his criticism.[52] As he puts it in a letter home to his mother (while still Richards' student at Cambridge in 1935), McLuhan writes, "Richards is a humanist who regards all experience as *relative* to certain conditions of life" (emphasis in original); this point-of-view, McLuhan concludes, is "such ghastly atheistic nonsense".[53] In contrast, McLuhan writes of Leavis, in his essay for *The Sewanee Review*, "his method is that of an artistic evaluation which is inseparable from the exercise of a delicately poised moral tact."[54] Specifically, McLuhan claims, "the method of Leavis has superior relevance to that of Richards and Empson because he has more clearly envisaged not only the way in which a poem functions, but the function of poetry as well."[55] Literary criticism and the method of close reading associated with it should not be employed solely to explicate an individual poem, McLuhan suggests, but should aspire to address the larger role of Poetry, with a capital P. McLuhan took from Leavis the sense of performing moral duty through literary criticism, of seeing critical analysis as an opportunity to help establish "the index to the moral quality in the age that 'produced' the poems" and thus enlighten that quality of the present age.[56]

McLuhan was a recent and dedicated convert to Catholicism; he was a believer, and his socially conservative beliefs inspired his learning at Cambridge and his criticism throughout his life. This connection might not be immediately visible in the content of his prose, presentations, and interviews, but the confidence of his religious beliefs infuses his work and working persona.[57] This certitude informs the way McLuhan refuses to adopt the traditionally staid tone of academic criticism. He strives not for objectivity and critical distance, nor does he deign to appropriate the cautious and careful tone of the scholar. He opts instead for declaration and prophecy, leaving readers and listeners to either accept or reject his claims, and many choose the latter. Yet, in our own moment, wherein the electric age is becoming digital, many of McLuhan's prophecies seem to be coming true. His influence on media theorists is irrefutable, and it seems high time to reconsider his work, its influence, and also its origins.[58]

The Mechanical Bride: McLuhan's Emerging Style

McLuhan's style of media studies is hardly recognizable to us now. Postmodernism claimed the death of grand narratives, and thus the style of sweeping narratives of media evolution presented by McLuhan, and later by Elizabeth Eisenstein and Friedrich Kittler, has been supplanted by a rigorous analysis of individual media forms. One need only think of the emergence of media archaeology as a recent, vital field of study.[59] McLuhan does not carefully analyze specific media formats; he is not attuned to examining any individual form of technology or its particular effects on literary aesthetics. He sets his sights wider—on the goal of analyzing and understanding media more generally (hence the title of his groundbreaking book, *Understanding Media*). This panoramic perspective is adapted from his New Critical origins; just recall the title of Leavis and Thompson's *Culture and the Environment*. But McLuhan's method of using literature to read culture works by adapting and practicing close reading in ways that also offer an implicit critique of the tendency in the New Criticism to use formalism to push toward intellectual isolationism.[60] McLuhan's indebtedness to and active adaptation of the New Criticism and literary modernism are most evident in his first book, *The Mechanical Bride: Folklore of Industrial Man*.

The *Mechanical Bride* shows how practical criticism can be adapted and applied to assess some of the most influential texts from popular culture: advertisements. The book's title is an allusion to a painting by Marcel Duchamp, *The Bride Stripped Bare by Her Bachelors, Even* (1915–23), and it suggests an alignment with Richards's goal to pursue criticism by comparing art across media forms. In his preface, McLuhan introduces his critical practice in distinctly artistic terms: the "objects and processes" that follow are, he writes, "unfolded by exhibit and commentary as a single landscape."[61] McLuhan thus begins his book of cultural criticism by claiming a creative pursuit. His book is an artistic "object" and a creative approach or "process." McLuhan then proceeds not by declaring a thesis and proving it using examples and explications of them; instead, he admits to seeking "not conclusions" but ideas that "are intended merely as points of departure."[62] He will later use the word "probes" to describe these points of departure and also the critical method and prose style they constitute.

McLuhan is often quoted as declaring, "I DON'T EXPLAIN—/ I EXPLORE."[63] His manner of presenting provocative ideas rather than proving a rational argument or a cohesive theory echoes Ezra Pound's view of what criticism should be. In "A Retrospect" (1913), Pound writes that criticism "provides fixed points of departure. It may startle a dull reader into alertness. That little of it which is good is mostly in stray phrases."[64] McLuhan uses his probes for precisely this purpose. As a result, his criticism strives toward the poetic. He clearly differentiates his practice from the norm. "This is an approach," he writes in *Understanding Media*, "which it is hard to make clear at a time when most books offer a single idea as a means of unifying a troupe of observations."[65] Contemporary criticism reflects the larger constraints of print culture, as McLuhan sees it, wherein typographic man expects a single idea per book and expects that idea to be presented in a clear, linear fashion presented chronologically from page one onwards. McLuhan challenges these conventions. He seeks to defamiliarize the formal expectations of literary criticism and to expose the larger constraints and ideological forces informing the practice. To put it another way, McLuhan pursues an avant-garde approach to writing literary criticism. The results are prose texts that require a readerly response derived from reading avant-garde modernist poetry—that is, close reading.

McLuhan's probes, exhibits, and processes are intended to promote slow and careful close reading. "A whirling phantasmagoria can be grasped only when arrested for contemplation," McLuhan writes, "And this very arrest is also a release from the usual participation."[66] The arrested state of contemplation, the slow and careful attention paid to a text, is not, McLuhan claims, the "usual participation" of readers, but it is necessary for understanding the world of the electric. McLuhan demonstrates this reading practice in the pages of *The Mechanical Bride*. From its first pages, *The Mechanical Bride* presents a pedagogical effort to train readers to see how advertisements work, how they operate formally to produce certain effects. "Why not use the new commercial education as a means of enlightening its intended prey?"[67] He close reads the cultural artifacts of mass culture, advertisements, in order to teach others to critically read the world around them.

The Mechanical Bride proceeds as a series of "exhibits." The pages present advertisements extracted from magazines, movie posters, and newspaper pages as textual objects for close reading. These images are introduced by provocative probes, questions or statements printed in larger font, alongside a large question mark. The suggestions of bullet-pointed questions frame the image and the explication of them that follows. The paragraphs of textual explication that surround the image show McLuhan addressing the probes, albeit obliquely, as he close reads the image (see Figure 1.1). The structure of presentation resonates with the pedagogical style of practical criticism that McLuhan learned from Richards's classroom experiments, wherein students were asked to analyze a text at-hand without supplementary explanatory materials. The page layout of *The Mechanical Bride* also registers the influence of *Culture and Environment*, which does not use images but is structured around what Leavis and Thompson call "examples" and which serve

Fig 1.1 Marshall McLuhan, *The Mechanical Bride: Folklore of Industrial Man*. (Gingko Press, 2002 [1951], 80–81.) Reprinted with permission of the publisher.

a similar function as McLuhan's "exhibits." *Culture and Environment* pursues its practical criticism through examples taken from popular culture, quotes from advertisements and books, which are then followed by analytical discussions of them. Leavis and Thompson explain, "the exposition is largely by way of 'examples'—i.e. suggested exercises, bringing home the point at issue."[68] McLuhan expands upon this methodology by applying it to non-textual objects of study taken from mass culture and incorporating these visual objects into the pages of his book.

McLuhan does not limit himself to the text contained in the ads but also addresses their visual design. In Leavis and Thompson's text, the visual aspect is only suggested, but in McLuhan's it is manifest and central. For example, on the verso side of the page presented above, McLuhan lists questions that subtly present an argument about the advertisement contained on the recto side (e.g., "Just another stallion and sweet kid?" and "The Greeks manage these matters in myths?"). The title of the exhibit is "Woman in a Mirror," and the first line of McLuhan's text explains his title by comparing the advertisement to an unexpected modernist source: "This ad employs the same technique as Picasso in *The Mirror*."[69] McLuhan goes on to describe Picasso's visual practice of operating though "juxtaposition and contrast" and then claims that ad men pursue a similar strategy. "The opposition of the cool elements, phallic and ambrosial, provides a chain reaction,"

McLuhan writes of the image.[70] The figure of the upscale woman, the "good girl" and "sweet kid," is presented next to the image of a horse representing classical sculpture (rather than a raging beast), suggested by the allusion to Greek myths in the opening questions and by McLuhan's claim that the horse's appearance suggests "the trailing clouds of culture as from some European castle."[71] The high-class woman and specially bred horse share a sense of stature; both are desirable objects to assess and possess. Within the context of the advertisement, they are paired as a couple and double each other. They both stand upright and look toward the right. The slanted text of "Palomino" ("*the* stocking color for Spring '47") bridges their bodies and aligns their value. "Palomino," the ad suggests, describes the color of both of their legs, since this is an advertisement for a new color of Berkshire stocking. But McLuhan argues that the pairing or juxtaposition of these two seemingly disparate figures suggests a deeper and more base level of communication, one that "could never pass the censor of consciousness," let alone the censor of published materials.[72]

The ad sells sex. The diagonal line of text that visually connects the two figures moves between their lower-halves. The reader's eye is drawn from the bottom-half of the upright horse (whose genitals are not visible but should be based upon the horse's positioning) to just below the woman's hips, where her gloved hands cross each other to form an X. X marks the spot, and it is there that her hands clutch a stark, white purse with the emblem of a horse on it. The appearance of the horse on the woman's purse suggests the penetration of the palomino into the lower-right-hand corner of the page, the spatial register occupied by the woman and female sexuality. Juxtaposition is used to invoke sexual desire in order to stimulate consumer desire, and McLuhan concludes, "The layout men of the present ad debased this technique," and this technique of juxtaposition exemplified Picasso.[73] We can hear McLuhan's conservative morals coming through, for certainly Picasso's paintings also express sexuality and sexual desire. But the point here is that McLuhan's text exposes the use of an artistic technique, the formal device of juxtaposition, as precisely that which makes the ad (and Cubist art) effective, artistic, and deserving of analysis. McLuhan writes, "Effective advertising gains its ends partly by distracting the attention of the reader from its presuppositions and by its quiet fusion with other levels of experience."[74] Precisely because ads seek to distract, one must pay particular attention to how they operate, to the techniques they employ. One must, in other words (and following McLuhan's lead), close read.

The description of McLuhan's argument in this particular exhibit from *The Mechanical Bride* might seem straightforward, but my close reading of his text actually obscures the radical poeticness of his prose. In the process of explicating the advertisement and the technique of juxtaposition it employs, McLuhan performs his own textual play. He moves from referencing Picasso to Madame Bovary and then quotes A. N. Whitehead as well as Fitzgerald's *The Great Gatsby*. This accumulation and juxtaposition of sources produces claims like the following: "This sort of thing in Fitzgerald pretty well does what the present ad does."[75] The exact meaning of "this" is not specified, but the effect lumps Fitzgerald and the ad men together through their shared use of an artistic technique and a tendency to trade in sexual subtexts. McLuhan's oblique explication of this advertisement, it bears repeating, is by no means straightforward. The six-paragraph exhibit accompanying the image employs the formal practice it describes; it uses juxtaposition, not elucidation, and produces poetic dissonance rather than a clear or rational argumentation.

The Gutenberg Galaxy

The pages of McLuhan's second book, *The Gutenberg Galaxy: The Making of Typographic Man* (1962), continue to exhibit Leavis's imprint even as they venture out into new forms of experimentation. In *Culture and Environment*, large block quotes stand out from the rest of the page, and this selected text identifies the "books that the reader is intended to examine for himself."[76] McLuhan takes the practice of using block quotes to incorporate a critical bibliography into the pages of one's text and turns it into a central organizational mode for presenting his argument in *The Gutenberg Galaxy*. Instead of using block quotes to craft a syllabus for future reading, as Leavis and Thompson do, McLuhan builds a bullet-point argument *across* the pages of his book (see Figure 1.2). A reader can flip through the pages to quickly read these pull-quotes, which themselves comprise an argument dispersed across the codex. The pull-quotes form a reading path that promotes a hypertextual reading practice, one more aligned with the habits of reading online in a skim-and-plunge mode (to use Steven Johnson's words) than with the sustained and focused attention exerted when close reading poetry.[77] McLuhan uses these bullet points and block quotes to promote a reading practice that is both hyper and deep that actually complicates the division between them.[78] Whatever approach one takes to reading the content presented on the pages of this book, the pages themselves demand attention as medial interfaces.

McLuhan's use of the pull-quotes expose the page to be a kind of canvas upon which text blocks lie like tiles in mosaic. These text tiles reflexively illuminate the interface of the page and the medium of the book, which is also part of the content of McLuhan's argument. McLuhan reflectively theorizes his formal practice before the book even begins. In a page of text that appears before the prologue, McLuhan writes, being, he ensnares himself in it; and each language draws a magic circle round the people to which it belongs, a circle from which there is no escape save by stepping out of it into another.[5]

Such awareness as this has generated in our time the technique of the suspended judgment by which we can transcend the limitations of our own assumptions by a critique of them. We can now live, not just amphibiously in divided and distinguished worlds, but pluralistically in many worlds and cultures simultaneously. We are no more committed to one culture—to a single ratio among the human senses—any more than to one book or to one language or to one technology. Our need today is, culturally, the same as the scientist's who seeks to become aware of the bias of the instruments of research in order to correct that bias. Compartmentalizing of human potential by single cultures will soon be as absurd as specialism in subject or discipline has become. It is not likely that our age is more obsessional than any other, but it has become sensitively aware of the conditions and fact of obsession beyond any other age. However, our fascination with all phases of the unconscious, personal and collective, as with all modes of primitive awareness, began in the eighteenth century with the first violent revulsion against print culture and mechanical industry. What began as a "Romantic reaction" towards organic wholeness may or may not have hastened the discovery of electromagnetic waves. But certainly the electro-magnetic discoveries have recreated the simultaneous "field" in all human affairs so that the human family now exists under conditions of a "global village." We live in a single constricted space resonant with tribal drums. So that concern with the "primitive" today is as banal as nineteenth-century concern with "progress," and as irrelevant to our problems.

The new electronic interdependence recreates the world in the image of a global village.

✻ It would be surprising, indeed, if Riesman's description of tradition-directed people did not correspond to Carothers' knowledge of African tribal societies. It would be equally startling were the ordinary reader about native societies not able to vibrate with a deep sense of affinity for the same,

[5]Quoted by Cassirer in *Language and Myth*, p. 9.

31

Fig 1.2 Marshall McLuhan, *The Gutenberg Galaxy: The Making of Typographic Man*. U Toronto Press and Signet Books, 1962. Reprinted with permission of the publisher.

"*The Gutenberg Galaxy* develops a *mosaic* or field approach to its problems. Such as mosaic image of numerous data and quotations in evidence offers the only practical means of revealing the causal operations in history.

The alternative procedure would be to offer a series of views of fixed relationships in pictorial space. Thus the *galaxy or constellation* of events upon which the present study concentrates is itself a mosaic of perpetually interacting forms that have undergone kaleidoscopic transformation—particularly in our time" (emphasis added).[79]

Explaining how he has carefully performed a "means of revealing" the historical narrative he is about to tell (in which technology provides the "causal operations" for cultural transformation), McLuhan suggests that this unconventional writing style is intentionally pursued. It suits the content it presents. McLuhan thus describes his formal approach with artistic intention and a media-specific intention. As Bonnie Mak argues in her illuminating new book, *How the Page Matters*, the page is a medium that matters: "To matter is not only to be of importance, to signify, to mean, but also to claim a certain physical space, to have a particular presence, to be uniquely embodied."[80] Also recently, Elena Lamberti focuses on the significance of the mosaic as formal structure in McLuhan's writing; she describes the mosaic as "a non-linear form of writing which reconfigures the linear alphabetic form in order to give the written page a tactile and multi-sensorial dimension."[81] Connecting Mak and Lamberti's points as a means of approaching McLuhan's prose, we can see how his text is not only about media but also about depicting and embodying its own printed materiality. And, he does this far before his more famous and obvious experimentations with page and book design, as in his collaboration with Quentin Fiore on *The Medium Is the Massage*. From his very first book, McLuhan presents a text in which form and content are inseparable.

Turning to the content of *The Gutenberg Galaxy* with recognition of McLuhan's literary training, we might not be surprised that he positions literature at its center. McLuhan selects, excerpts, and juxtaposes creative and critical texts from writers across the disciplinary spectrum, including selections from his own writings. He employs the formal structure of juxtaposition that, in *The Mechanical Bride*, he attributed to Picasso. *The Gutenberg Galaxy* opens with Shakespeare—"When King Lear proposes . . ."—and then proceeds by piecing together a literary mosaic with quotes from Donne, Chaucer, Milton, and Yeats, all within the first eight pages.[82] The next fifteen pages include quotations from Bertrand Russell's *History of Western Philosophy*, an article in the journal *Psychiatry*, Plato, David Riesman's *The Lonely Crowd*, and Heisenberg. McLuhan's patchwork produces a network of interconnections across the timeline of intellectual history and across the physical space of the page. He builds an argument by presenting a visual collage of text, and the formal practice reflexively illuminates the medium of print and its constraints. At the same time, he strives to capture on the page the simultaneity that he ascribes to electric media.

McLuhan bombards his reader with an array of quotations taken from sources sampled from across a historical timeline, and he creates a sense of information overload. The reader must constantly shift and redirect her attention in order to absorb his argument about the epistemic shift produced by electric media. Lamberti describes McLuhan's use of the mosaic strategy as a formal way "to question traditional ideas of knowledge and to move the reader from a linear (logical, ordered, exclusive) to an acoustic (non-logical, simultaneous, inclusive) perspective."[83] But his formal strategy also imitates the acoustic effect of electric media within the pages of a paperbound book. The effect produces a poetic tension (to use a New Critical term) that invokes the medial shift McLuhan describes while also displaying the inseparability of form and content in printed prose. Lewis H. Lapham describes McLuhan's prose as, "By turns brilliant and opaque, McLuhan's thought meets the specifications of the epistemology that he ascribes to the electronic media—non-lineal, repetitive, discontinuous, intuitive, proceeding by analogy instead of sequential argument."[84] Form follows function; the medium is the message. The result is provocative and perplexing, and both are intentional.[85]

Like the modernist writers he admired and the New Critics who canonized them, McLuhan rejected a distinction between creative and critical writing, and the results are evident in his writing on media. No other modernist writer/critic merged poetic and critical writing more—and inspired McLuhan more—than Ezra Pound, and it is to Pound's influence on McLuhan that I now turn.

Part II. McLuhan and Modernism

Before he had published the books that would establish him as the iconic prophet of the new mediatized age, McLuhan wrote to Ezra Pound, "Your portrait by Lewis adorns our mantle."[86] The portrait was a reproduction of a charcoal sketch by Wyndham Lewis, whom McLuhan also greatly respected and with whom he developed a close personal relationship.[87] McLuhan's act of framing Pound's portrait and placing it in the center of his home is more than a curious and colorful footnote in literary history. It is an early point of connection between literary history and media studies, a moment full of significance and symbolism for the trajectory of digital modernism that this book traces. I'd like to suggest that McLuhan's act of placing Pound's representation over his mantle is a gesture that parallels his more public acts of reframing the modernist poet for a new generation of readers.

McLuhan intended to write a book on Pound. In a letter to Pound's wife, Dorothy Shakespear Pound, dated September 1948, McLuhan writes, "Next job, a book on E. P. If I can summon the courage. Because the more I read him the less competent I feel to do a good job."[88] He never did find the courage to write that book, but he did inspire one of his students to do it instead. During the years that McLuhan corresponded with Pound while the poet was detained at St. Elizabeths Hospital (a government-run psychiatric facility), McLuhan introduced the aging poet to a young literary scholar named Hugh Kenner. The result is literary history.[89] Kenner's seminal *The Pound Era* (1971) nearly singlehandedly recuperated Pound, whom the literary academy had shunned as a political traitor after Pound's pro-Mussolini radio broadcasts during World War II.[90] Kenner not only helped to revive Pound's reputation but also identified him as the central figure of modernism, as the title of his book expresses, defining the entire modernist period as Pound's era. As the initial mediator between Pound and Kenner, McLuhan played an important role in the transmission of the modernist poet and critic to readers and writers in the second half of the twentieth century. In his own writings as well, McLuhan asserted Pound's significance for literary, cultural, and media studies. He viewed Ezra Pound not only as a great poet and critic but also a media theorist. McLuhan always asserted that the electric age and its study have their origins in the Pound Era.

I am suggesting, as others have done before me, that McLuhan established media studies upon his appreciation and understanding of modernism, in particular, the writings of Pound and also James Joyce.[91] These two writers are not only of central interest for McLuhan but, as I show in the following chapters, also for digital modernism. Joyce's influence on McLuhan's texts has been well documented, especially by Donald Theall, and it is not my intention to repeat that work here.[92] But understanding why Joyce and Pound appeal to the first modern media theorist helps elucidate the hold these writers continue to have over contemporary media culture and authors working within it.

Media Studies as Modernist Studies

In the pages of *The Mechanical Bride*, McLuhan confronts his reader with a challenge posed as a query: "You never thought of a page of news as a symbolist landscape?"[93] He continues, "the French symbolists, followed by James Joyce in *Ulysses*, saw that there was a new art form of universal scope present in the technical layout of the modern newspaper."[94] McLuhan uses Joyce, via Symbolism, to position his own practice of critically analyzing the formal artistry of lowbrow newspaper advertisements within a highbrow modernist literary framework. He makes this point more forcefully when he suggests a comparison between himself and Joyce through their shared study of popular culture and advertisments. "To write his epic of the modern Ulysses," McLuhan writes, Joyce "studied all his life the ads, the comics, the pulps, and popular speech."[95] McLuhan makes this comparison even more directly later in *The Mechanical Bride*, when he writes, "Joyce explored popular phraseology and heroes with a precision which this book cannot emulate."[96] Although he expresses humility before his modernist idol, McLuhan obviously seeks not only to emulate Joyce's technique but also to situate his own work in the company of the modernist writers he so deeply admired.

Eric McLuhan, Marshall McLuhan's son and a literary scholar and media critic in his own right, reflects on his father's relationship to Joyce:

> "my father used Joyce as a colleague. Whenever he made a discovery about technology and culture, he would open the Wake and read for a bit, and there, sure enough, he would find that Joyce had already been over the ground, decades earlier. . . . He did not merely use Joyce to confirm an insight, but also used Joyce as the stimulus for fresh awareness of the present moment."[97]

Marshall McLuhan's sense that he was Joyce's colleague is particularly evident in *The Gutenberg Galaxy*, wherein he claims that he pursues a formal approach similar to that in *Finnegans Wake*. He writes, "James Joyce devised an entirely new form of expression in *Finnegans Wake* in order to capture the complex interplay of factors in the very configuration that we are considering here."[98] McLuhan derives from Joyce an understanding of literary technique as a form of *techne* or medium. He explains that the second page of *Finnegans Wake* exposes how Joyce "is making a mosaic, an Achilles shield."[99] McLuhan then adapts this mosaic method for *The Gutenberg Galaxy*. Donald Theall and Joan Theall explain, "the working title for both *The Gutenberg Galaxy* and *Understanding Media* was *The Road to Finnegans Wake*."[100] "Whatever else McLuhan was up to in his sometimes exasperating and, often enigmatic writings," they write, "he developed a theory of communication which he considered to be 'applied Joyce.'"[101] Eric McLuhan recalls that his father "once remarked to me, as I know he did to many others, that his work on media and culture was, in the main, 'applied Joyce.'"[102] He then goes on to conclude,

"Conversely then, it might be fair to say that no one can claim a serious appreciation of Joyce's work without a complete familiarity with the full spectrum of McLuhan's work."[103]

The concept of "applied Joyce" is a poetic act that, I'd like to suggest, shares an impetus with the digital acts of adapting modernism that I will examine later in this book. McLuhan's formal engagement with Joyce and his more symbolic act of framing and hanging Pound's portrait are both gestures that connect McLuhan to modernism and to digital modernism, making him a midpoint in the literary genealogy this book traces. When we turn to the influence of Pound on McLuhan, which is somewhat less-examined than Joyce's imprint, we recognize how literary studies and modernism are central to digital culture. We also have a chance to see modernism from a new perspective; in this case, to see Ezra Pound as an early media theorist before media studies was a recognizable field of study.

McLuhan and Pound

During the years 1948–1957, McLuhan corresponded with Pound while the poet was restrained at St. Elizabeths, and his letters illustrate that McLuhan understood Pound to be not only an important poet but also an insightful analyst of media. At this time, Pound's poetry had been overshadowed by his politics. After his stint supporting Mussolini in radio broadcasts during World War II, Pound was detained by the US government for treason and found mentally unfit to stand trial. But the imprisoned and disgraced poet did not lack visitors, many of them luminous literati but also young upstarts like McLuhan who visited *il miglior fabbro* seeking him out as a guide for interpreting culture. This is a role that Pound cultivated throughout this life, as *Guide to Kulchur* expresses. In an undated letter, placed around 1948 (to Felix Giovelli), McLuhan describes his admiration for Pound's taste: "Everything he mentions has to be read."[104] McLuhan found Pound's pedagogy so compelling that, in a letter dated September 22, 1949, he wrote to Pound, "Have just this minute been bracing myself with the pages on prosody in your ABC of Reading. May my pate become a flue-pot if I dont [sic] try to get that book reprinted."[105] McLuhan's interest in Pound was neither tangential nor trivial but central to the theoretical enterprise he was undertaking. Indeed, it was during the period of his correspondence with Pound that McLuhan developed the central aspects of his criticism: methods of close reading media and examining the connections between language, culture, and media.[106] In a letter to Pound dated July 16, 1952, McLuhan lays out in detail the sections of the book on which he is working and which would establish his reputation, *The Gutenberg Galaxy:*

The Making of Typographic Man. He then asks Pound for advice, not with style or organization, but with content: "But are there some big facts I've missed?"[107] From his letters, it is obvious that McLuhan identified Pound as not only a father of modernism but also as a forefather of media theory.

Pound was deeply aware of the specificities of media and their impact on literature and reading. In *ABC of Reading* (1934) Pound writes, "In all cases one test will be, 'could this material have been made more efficient in some other medium?' "[108] In personal correspondence with Harriet Monroe (in a letter dated August 18, 1912), Pound queried, with evident frustration and lament, "Can you teach an American poet that poetry is an art, an art with a technique, with *media. . .?*" (emphasis added)[109] Or, consider the following media-specific statement in "A Retrospect": "When Shakespeare talks of 'Dawn in russet mantle clad' he presents something which the painter does not present."[110] In "How to Read" (1929) he boldly queries, "WHY BOOKS? This simple first question was never asked."[111] McLuhan follows suit by reminding us that the book is a technology (and by doing so in a bolded statement): **"Our obsession with the book as the archetype of culture has not even encouraged us to consider the book itself as a peculiar and arty way of packaging experience"** (emphasis in original).[112] He continues, "But until the book is seen as a very specialized form of art and technology we cannot today get our bearings among the new arts and the new media."[113] McLuhan shared with (and learned from) Pound the idea that new ideas, poetry, and media must arise from a knowledge of the older forms.

Pound experimented with technology and media, especially the technology of the codex, in his poetry, and I will explore how he did so in more detail in Chapter 3; but one well-known example taken from Hugh Kenner's analysis will suffice to make the point. Kenner argues that Pound's use of the typewriter is evident in his groundbreaking imagist poem "In a Station of the Metro" (1913). When Pound strikes the space bar twice, the action is not only meant to separate words but to serve as an aesthetic "gesture," Kenner writes, by which "something intrinsicate to his feeling of how the lines sound and of how meanings are built up."[114] In a letter to Pound dated January 22, 1957, McLuhan focuses on a similar aspect of Pound's writing: "you were the one man of our time who had seen the typewriter as a new art form and had used it imaginatively."[115] He continues his letter in this line of thinking, presenting an interpretation of media's role on the message it presents: "As a form of publication the typewriter has obviously had much to do with habits of verbal arrangement both written and oral."[116] McLuhan then requests a response from Pound, whom he identifies as his teacher: "Anything you have to say on this subject will have interest for the student of your work."[117] Pound straight out refused to answer the question, responding, "Yu go right on writin' me letters-but dont xpect me to answer questions-even if answers are known" (June 18, 1948).[118] McLuhan did not need answers because he found in Pound's *The Cantos* an inchoate media theory that provided inspiration for his own nascent ideas.[119]

In a letter to Pound dated June 16, 1948, McLuhan describes *The Cantos* as "the first and only serious use of the great technical possibilities of the cinematograph," because they provide "perceptions of simultaneities."[120] He compares *The Cantos* to film because the poetry expresses an aesthetic of simultaneity that he would later ascribe to electric media and strive to mimic in his own writing. Reading McLuhan reading Pound returns us to my earlier examination of the role of the New Criticism in the development of media studies. In a letter to Pound dated June 30, 1948, McLuhan writes with admiration, "Your poems—the Cantos—make heavier demands on the reader than anything else of your time."[121] The compliment is based in the fact that *The Cantos* demand hermeneutic interpretation and close reading. For McLuhan, this is a good thing. "Pound's prose is precise," McLuhan writes, "It has to be read *very* slowly" (emphasis in original).[122] First, there is the demand (italicized for emphasis) to slowly and closely read Pound's prose. Second, McLuhan identifies how Pound adapts a poetic formal method of condensing his ideas into poetic form even in his prose criticism. McLuhan draws upon Pound's own poetic symbol for representing language at its most precise and imagistic, the ideogram, to describe the aesthetic to which he himself aspires. "His method in prose and verse is the ideogram," McLuhan writes, "That is the sculp[t]ed item, whether historical, excerpted or invented."[123] In Chapter 5, I examine Pound's ideo-grammic method in relation to media history and theory, but for now the relevant point is that McLuhan follows Pound in turning to literature as a means of think-ing about media (both the media of cinema and electric simultaneity but also the printed book). McLuhan sees in Pound's use of the ideogram a condensation of content that demands unpacking by a careful reader. McLuhan appreciates this data density as artistic practice and critical rhetoric. The ideogram demands close reading, and the impact of this point is evident in McLuhan's own media theory, particularly in the distinction he makes between hot and cool media.

In *Understanding Media: The Extensions of Man*, McLuhan distinguishes be-tween hot and cool media based on the level of participation they require from the user. Hot media (radio, film, photographs, books, etc.) are high definition and leave little to be filled in from the audience while cool media (the telephone, car-toons, oral speech, and, perhaps counterintuitively, television) require high levels of participation from users. The distinction is less valuable for the often arbitrary and outdated divisions it makes between individual media forms than for the fact that the impulse toward distinction is based on the amount of user interaction they elicit.[124] In other words, data density informs readerly interaction and defines the type of media by its level of participation. McLuhan understands this emphasis on interactivity to be a facet of modernism and its vestige into the electronic age. "It is strange," he writes, "that modern readers have been so slow to recognize that the prose of Gertrude Stein with its lack of punctuation and other visual aids, is a carefully devised strategy to get the passive visual reader into participant, oral action. So with E. E. Cummings, or Pound, or Eliot."[125] The lack of traditional grammar and syntax in modernist literature makes reading and comprehension difficult and requires high levels of reader interaction. This is a good thing because it requires close reading and critical analysis from the reader. The intentional strategy on the part of modernist writers to elicit reader interactivity, McLuhan suggests, not only demands readers to close read but also prepares them to pursue similar reading techniques in the electric age. This is the main point and the foundation for understanding media through modernism via McLuhan. Understanding close reading to be the refinement of the readerly participation necessary to engage with modernist literature—and modernist literature as origin of our contemporary electric media age—McLuhan takes what he learned at Cambridge and adapts it toward approaching and understanding media.

Part III. McLuhan as Digital Modernist

The Rear-View Mirror

In *Understanding Media*, the book that made him famous, McLuhan argues that a new cultural epoch is upon us, and it is characterized by speed. In the mechanical age, actions could be distinguished from their consequences because they happened slowly, but, McLuhan writes, "Today the action and reaction occur almost at the same time."[126] This is in part because, "[i]n the electric age," McLuhan explains, "our central nervous system is technologically extended to involve us in the whole of mankind."[127] Hence, the book's subtitle: "The Extensions of Man." The Typographic Man of the Gutenberg Age, who, recall, McLuhan identified as isolated and individualistic, is transformed through technologies that extend his senses, his nervous system, and his community. As a result, McLuhan writes, "we approach the final phase in the extensions of man—the technological simulation of consciousness, when the creative process of knowing will be collectively and corporately extended to the whole of human society, much as we have already extended our senses and our nerves by the various media."[128] McLuhan published these words in 1964. Reading them now, they burn with insight about our contemporary digital moment.

Cybernetics, AI, and posthumanism pursued "the technological simulation of consciousness," and the extension of our senses by media is now visible everywhere in daily life. Bluetooth earphones and iPod devices strapped to arms extend our auditory sense and turn humans into cyborgs; Web 2.0 social networking sites extend our ability to communicate and participate in virtual spaces, conversations, and friendships; cellular and mobile devices track our location and broadcast our whereabouts, extending our sense of presence and physicality. Creative human consciousness as we know it is, without doubt, to some degree collective and physically incorporated. The extension of our senses in this manner transforms the way we see our world and ourselves. Moreover, as McLuhan argued, it changes the way we see. "The partial and specialized character of the viewpoint, however noble" that was associated with the earlier mechanical age "will not serve at all in the electric age."[129] To see things differently we need to adapt our traditional modes of seeing, reading, and thinking. We need to privilege new patterns and practices. McLuhan theorized this situation and modeled such new methods in his prose.

As I have been arguing, McLuhan adapts close reading to examine electric culture. Simultaneity is the name of the game in the modern, mediatized, electronic world, but this does not mean that slowness has no value. To the contrary. Close reading, slow and focused analysis, is central to our hyper-mediated world. We have seen how McLuhan identified simultaneity as a central facet of modernism, as exemplified by Cubism, cinema, and Pound's *Cantos*; and he adapted close reading, the practice of slowly and carefully analyzing these artworks, into a means of approaching this medial environment. His mode of close reading might not immediately resemble what we think of when we think about close reading and, perhaps, neither does my practice of close reading his writings, but such is the adaptation of the New Critical practice into the new media age. Following McLuhan, I focus not solely on text but also on images, design, and patterns of design as meaningful modes of communication. Indeed, the design and patterns of print become the subjects of close reading alongside the content they present. Such is the subject and form of one of McLuhan's later books, *COUNTERBLAST* (1969, designed by Harley Parker), a work that conveys McLuhan's modenist ambitions and aligns with the impulse of digital modernism.

After his meteoric rise as public prophet and cultural commentator, McLuhan released a manifesto-like book that further solidified his modernist ambitions through its formal design. *COUNTERBLAST* updates *Blast*, the publication

Wyndham Lewis and Ezra Pound released in 1914 that contained the vorticist manifesto and groundbreaking experimentation with typography and page design. The pages of *COUNTERBLAST* resemble modernist manifestos with their blaring typography and probing, combative statements. Its cover visibly imitates its modernist inspiration.[130] The cover art contains a spiraling vortex at its center and presents the text of the title in a pinkish color that invokes *Blast's* own bright pink cover. The recently published facsimile edition of *COUNTERBLAST 1954*, a "never-before published manuscript that McLuhan distributed as a hand-made 'zine," further testifies to McLuhan's insistence on his modernist heritage and his remix spirit.[131] Both books titled *COUNTERBLAST* situate themselves in a feedback loop between old and new literature and the medial ecologies that enable them. McLuhan intended *COUNTERBLAST* to adapt the message blasted from the pages of that earlier modernist publication, and through it, he declares himself part of a modernist lineage. "The term COUNTERBLAST does not imply any attempt to erode or explode BLAST," McLuhan writes, "Rather it indicates the need for a counter-environment as a means of perceiving the dominant one."[132] McLuhan presents the electric environment as a form of counterculture, and study of it serves to illuminate the constraints of the previous cultural and medial period.

"We look at the present through a rear-view mirror," McLuhan writes.[133] We only begin to recognize the constraints, affordances, and consequences of print because that previous epoch is passing. *COUNTERBLAST* expresses the idea that the emergent electronic world enables us to see more clearly the world of print and its psychological, social, and communicative effects. Like *The Medium Is the Massage* (designed by Quentin Fiore [1967]), *COUNTERBLAST* depends upon creative graphic design and experimental typography to present a message that is literally inseparable from its medium. These highly designed texts focus attention on the page as interface and the book as medium. They serve as evidence that the new media environment promotes understanding of—and possibly even appreciation and nostalgia for—the previous print epoch.[134] This impetus to return to and reconsider the past in light of the current, medial moment is the central motivating force of digital modernism.

Conclusion

McLuhan not only wrote at the midpoint of the twentieth century, but he is also himself a midpoint between modernism and digital modernism. Donald Theall writes, "since the mid-point of the century a single name, McLuhan, has brooded ghost-like, over social and cultural understanding of the intersection of communication, computers, persuasion, and the emergence of a technoculture."[135] Moreover, McLuhan is a bridge between literary and media studies because he adopted the role of the modernist poet/critic in the postmodern period using an understanding of literature that he gained from the New Critics to explain the age of television. I hope we can now see how retracing McLuhan's connections to the New Criticism shows how he adapted the practices of an earlier cultural moment to address his own. We can learn from McLuhan and do something similar. Indeed, understanding McLuhan in this way serves to remind us that we too can and, indeed, *must* renovate traditional critical practices to suit the needs of our emergent literary culture.

McLuhan saw the world in the midst of transformation due to medial shift, and he offered the following query. Posed in the language of modernism (and of vorticism in particular), it could easily serve as a thesis or a probe for the chapters that follow: "May not our job in the new electronic age be to study the action of the new vortex on the body of the older culture?"[136] Reading McLuhan as both a modernist and a theorist of new media, I answer "the Oracle of the Electric Age" in the affirmative. How exactly to go about studying the new vortex of the electric age and its impact on literature is my pursuit in the following chapters.

2. Reading Machines

MACHINE POETRY AND EXCAVATORY READING
in William Poundstone's electronic literature and Bob
Brown's Readies

"If you're searching for a godfather of the reading machine," a recent essay in the *New York Times Book Review* suggests, "you might look past Jeff Bezos and Steve Jobs to a nearly forgotten early-twentieth-century writer and impresario named Bob Brown."[1] Robert Carlton (Bob) Brown, an American experimental writer of the modernist period, shared a social network with the likes of Williams Carlos Williams and Gertrude Stein, and planned to build a reading machine that would speed up the pace of reading literature and thereby change the kind of literature we read. He called his machine "The Readies." "Revolutionize reading and a Revolution of the Word will be inkless achieved," he writes.[2] The Readies was never built and was, until recently, nearly forgotten. So too has Brown remained on the margins of literary history.[3] But recent events in the evolution of digital reading machines prompt excavation of the Readies and reconsideration of it as a vital part of the genealogy of contemporary technopoetics and literary practices.[4] This chapter pursues such excavation by reading the Readies in relation to recent machine-informed poetics in an individual work of electronic literature, William Poundstone's *Project for the Tachistoscope {Bottomless Pit}* (2005).[5] This digital work, I argue, explores and exposes how reading machines use speed toward poetic ends. Reading between Poundstone's electronic literature and Brown's Readies solidifies Brown's position as godfather of a contemporary generation of writers experimenting with the latest digital reading machines and thereby charts poetic connections between modernism and digital modernism.

I hope to show that technologies of reading, not just writing, are an integral part of American literary history, poetics, and close reading practices. To do so, I read across a triangulation of reading machines—computer, tachistoscope, Readies—in order to expose how digital literature demands that the study of literature also include the study of media and, more specifically, the study of reading machines.

By "reading machine" I mean a mechanized device that stores and presents literature, not just a readerly prosthesis for accessing text.[6] These reading machines participate in producing the literary experience. They often even read or process the text before the human reader can do so. Importantly, the literary texts I examine were written expressively for their reading machines. The poetics they pursue are thus dependent upon the reading machine and also inseparable from it. It is this situation, in which the reading machine is intentionally employed in the service of a medium-specific technopoetic, that I call "machine poetics." Machine poetics expose the reading machine to be part of the literary process and thus subject to literary analysis. Of course, in comparing the Readies and born-digital literature I am eliding the myriad differences between analog and digital reading machines. These differences are inarguably crucial, but explicating them is not my focus here. My goal is to show how reading machines and machine poetics have a foundation in literary history that precedes the digital computer and goes back, at least, to modernism.

By analyzing the specific poetics, aesthetic ambitions, and media-specific ways in which writers engage with their intended reading machines, we can start to see the various and diverse technologies that are subsumed under the broad descriptors "digital" and "analog"; and, we can start to reclaim the media studies part of literary studies. Brown and Poundstone are exemplary cases for pursuing this argument because they ground their poetic ambitions in the specificities of the reading machines used to display their works. I will begin with Poundstone's *Project*, a work of digital literature that remediates an earlier and now obsolete reading machine in ways that simultaneously illuminate and obfuscate the layers of technologies involved in delivering the digital literary text. I argue that this techno-reflexivity is not only central to this particular literary work but also to a more general understanding of how literary study is always already a media-informed practice.

Part I. Reading the Remediation

William Poundstone's web-based Flash animation *Project for the Tachistoscope {Bottomless Pit}* demands unpacking or, rather, excavation.[7] This is evident in the work's title, which uses curly brackets to bury the subject of the narrative, a story

about a bottomless pit, and make this content subsidiary to its larger formal project: the act of technological remediation at its center. *Project* resurrects an older
reading machine, the tachistoscope, through a newer one, the digital computer.
Jay David Bolter and Richard Grusin define "remediation" as "the representation
of one medium in another" and claim that remediation "ensures that the older
medium cannot be entirely effaced; the new medium remains dependent on the
older one."[8] Katherine Hayles refashions the idea of remediation into "intermediation" to express how relationships between media are not limited by a linear model
of evolution (between older and newer media) but include cyclical and recursive
interactions.[9] This latter concept more appropriately describes what is happening
within *Project* and in the relationship the work crafts between the tachistoscope
and the digital computer. Poundstone presents intermediation as an aesthetic
practice, one that illuminates the complex ecologies of technological and literary processes involved in reading. His formal remediation of the tachistoscope
through the computer purposely complicates our understanding of either technology and prompts reconsideration of that older technology by situating it within a
literary context.

The tachistoscope, whose etymology combines the Greek word for speed
(*tachistos*) with the act of viewing (*skopein*), is just that—a speed-viewing machine.
It was developed in the latter-half of the nineteenth century and used into the
twentieth for optical, psychological, and cognitive research. It projected a series
of fast, flashing images at a single location upon which a seated, staring viewer
focused intently.[10] The tachistoscope was used to measure attention and memory
as well as, later, to enhance recognition and reading speeds.[11] But the machine also
focused attention on how new technologies affect reading practices. Jonathan
Crary identifies the tachistoscope as pivotal to the emergence of modern visuality,
subjectivity, and the concept of attention. He describes the tachistoscope as "part
of a broad-ranging project to acquire knowledge that would allow a rationaliza-
tion of a perceiver and the management of attentiveness."[12] The tachistoscope thus
becomes a medium that shapes our idea of what it means to read—to manage
attention in order to maintain focus and, in the case of literary criticism, to close
read. Charles Acland identifies the tachistoscope as a largely forgotten but fundamental technology in enabling the medial shift from static print surfaces to flickering, electronic projection: "One of the tachistoscope's contributions was to reorient
reading from the page to the screen."[13] These interpretations of the tachistoscope
present it as a technology that reflexively disciplines the modern reading subject
to practice new reading modes and in new media formats. Poundstone's adaptation of the tachistoscope—produced through the computer, the Flash authorware,

and the Internet—thus begs the question: what does the latest incarnation of the tachistoscope tell us about what we take to be quintessential modern qualities of reading? In other words, how and why does Poundstone's tachistoscope shape its reader?

Project is a speed-viewing experience but one that, I argue, promotes close or deep reading. It complicates notions that speed reading and hyper-attention are opposed to close reading and deep attention. Katherine Hayles distinguishes between deep and hyper-attention, identifying them as epitomizing a larger cultural and cognitive shift. Deep attention, she writes, is "the cognitive style traditionally associated with the humanities, [and] is characterized by concentrating on a single object for long periods (say, a novel by Dickens), ignoring outside stimuli while so engaged, preferring a single information stream, and having a high tolerance for long focus times" while hyper-attention "is characterized by switching focus rapidly among different tasks, preferring multiple information streams, seeking a high level of stimulation, and having a low tolerance for boredom."[14] *Project* shows how literature can bridge the gap (or pit) by inviting *both* hyper- and deep attention in ways that promote reflexive attention to the media-specific act of reading. Moreover, the work exposes both types of cognitive modes, reading practices, and attentive experiences to be dependent upon media.[15] *Project* does this, I will show, by remediating the tachistoscope, a technology that stimulates hyper-attention in order to test and train deep attention. But first let me explain how *Project* practices remediation as poetic method.

The works presents a "project" intended for viewing on a particular reading machine, the tachistoscope, but it presents this project online where it is accessed via a computer, not an analog version of a tachistoscopic machine. This conceit, I argue, foregrounds remediation as poetic or aesthetic practice. This poetic practice serves to promote an excavatory reading practice in which close reading and media archaeology converge. I have already discussed close reading in detail in the introduction and first chapter of this book, so let me now introduce media archaeology.

Media archaeology is the examination of specific media technologies within their cultural and historical contexts. Media archaeology proceeds by excavating forgotten technologies, unknown uses of them, or unseen connections between media forms and practices in the past and the present. As a result, media archaeology seeks to continually rewrite media history and ruffle any smooth tales of evolution. Media critic Erkki Huhtamo describes media archaeology as having two main goals: "to study the cyclically recurring elements and motives underlying and guiding the development of media culture," and to promote "the 'excavation' of the ways in which these discursive traditions and formulations have been 'imprinted' on specific media machines and systems in different historical contexts."[16] Following Michel Foucault and Marshall McLuhan, media archaeology focuses on what Friedrich Kittler calls "discourse networks": "the network of technologies and institutions that allow a given culture to select, store, and produce relevant data."[17] For my purposes here, media archaeology reminds us how specific cultural conditions make possible the emergence of new technologies and reading practices.

What seems normal, deep, or hyper about our reading practices is always shaped by historical contexts and media formats. Reading practices, literary poetics, and reading machines emerge from and adapt to specific cultural ecologies. (McLuhan argued as much, as I showed in the previous chapter). The intertwined relationship between literature, reading, and media renders media archaeology a vital practice for literary criticism. It is also necessary for analyzing *Project*, for Poundstone's digital work presents the tachistoscope as a medial layer to be excavated and examined for its aesthetic effects. Doing so can tell us much about the tachistoscope but also about contemporary digital reading machines and reading practices.

Project not only promotes media archaeology but also uses excavation as its central operational metaphor. We will soon see that the work's narrative is about excavatory efforts to explain a bottomless pit, but excavation also describes the activity *Project* asks of its reader.

Terry Harpold uses the term "ex-foliation" to describe the kind of critical activity that approaches reading via the media involved in producing "a text." "*Reading is, before it can be anything else,*" Harpold writes, "*surface-work*" (emphasis in original).[18] Thus, reading beneath the surface requires excavation or ex-foliation. "I propose the term ex-foliation," Harpold writes, "for a loosely grouped set of procedures for provisionally separating the layers of the text's surfaces without resolving them into distinct strata or hierarchies, with the aim of understanding their expressive concurrencies."[19] *Project* remediates the experience of "reading" through a tachistoscope in ways that draw attention to how this remediation happens. I place the word "reading" in scare quotes because the question of whether one reads or sees, comprehends or consumes, is uncertain; indeed, this uncertainty was precisely why the tachistoscope was employed to test and measure cognitive reception and recognition.[20]

Project employs Flash software to produce an onscreen experience similar to that of sitting in front of a tachistoscope, and it does so in ways that complicate the distinctions (and thus the hierarchies) between attention and distraction, passive and active reading, deep and hyper-attention. It makes these deconstructive moves in and through a focus on media, directing attention to the technological means through which text is presented, that is, to the reading machines that are a neglected but vital part of literary history. *Project* thus promotes media archaeology by initiating the excavation of an older technology in ways that demonstrate the literary work theorizing its own medial layers and encouraging the reader to do the same. The reader approaches the work by digging deep into its layers of media and remediation, thereby renovating the traditional practice of close reading to produce a critical method that enables rediscovery of the intertwined relationship between media and the literary. To see how this happens, let's now turn to the work.

Project narrates the story of a natural and unexplainable bottomless pit that appears in the middle of what appears to be the American Midwest, and the work's Flash-based, flashing aesthetic works to create a pit of readerly attention onscreen. The animation proceeds by flashing single words and images at the center of the computer screen. These "imagetexts" (to use W. J. T. Mitchell's neologism) consist of three layers: narrative text, simple white icons, and colored clip-art photographs that periodically overlay the words to produce a palimpsest collage.[21] The work's primary design feature is a vortex comprised of concentric circles that shift in color through variations of blue. The vortex pulses in an ongoing movement of contraction and expansion, emanating depth and drawing the reader's eye into its bottomless pit. (See Figures 2.1 and 2.2.) The circles remain ever-present onscreen, and it is atop these circles that the imagetexts flash. The result is a layered sense

Figs 2.1 and 2.2 Nonconsecutive screenshots from William Poundstone's *Project for the Tachistoscope {Bottomless Pit}* (2005) showing various configurations of layered image and text. (Used with permission from the author.)

of depth created on the flat computer screen. A heavily synthesized electronic soundtrack accompanies the visuals and sets a rhythmic background beat. The music oscillates between a calm, meditative tone that supports a steady reading pace and a heightened state of anxiety. When the music rises in pitch and seems to speed up, so too does the reader's pace. Though the work creates a sense of depth onscreen and though the music informs the reading pace, through it all, *Project* remains extremely noninteractive: it proceeds as an animation that requires no input from the reader other than clicking "Start." *Project* operates through a central paradox: it overwhelms the reader with multimodal stimuli in ways that force the reader to sit still, stare at the center of the screen, and passively consume the onslaught of flashing information. But it also, I will show, promotes close reading of the layers of narrative design and media it employs.[22]

Project's narrative describes a scene of excavatory reading that elicits a similar type of reading practice, both from the characters within the story and also from the reader at her computer screen. The narrative begins by detailing how construction efforts to build a highway near the pit proceed without problem or delay until, on the fifty-ninth day, workers "felt the ground rocking beneath their feet. Those who could run to safety did. Behind them a great chasm opened in the earth. 73 workers and nearly four million dollars worth of government equipment disappeared into a cavity of unknown depth." In response, "The state brought in geologist Nelson Playfair who had experience with deep wells." This specialist's task was to read and explain the Pit, but "Playfair's attempts to measure the depth of the Pit by triangulation failed owing to poor visibility at the lower levels." He could not see, so he could not read. The next line of the narrative implies that this failure to read the Pit is not simply due to inappropriate reading technologies (i.e., illuminating machines) but to a larger, more systemic problem: "The Pit is not an isolated phenomenon. It is only an extreme case of what has been happening all along in this region where integration of geologic layers has become compromised." The earthly foundation that once appeared stable and seamless suddenly shifts to expose the fact that things aren't what they seem to be. As a result, readers of all sorts, from geologists to neighbors and tourists alike, journey to the Pit to explore and try to explain the situation. The sinkhole becomes a symbolic entity, a thing to read.

Project presents a parable about reading in the midst of medial shift. The literary work produces a parallel between the diegetic world and the reader's own. The last line of the narrative secures this analogy. The text ends with a statement that implies that the Pit and readings of it will continue to expand: "In recent years the Pit has both widened and gotten alarmingly deeper." This is reinforced formally, for the work does not stop, pause, or loop back to the "Start" screen. It plays continuously, repeating its text without a discernible break. The story about a bottomless pit becomes a bottomless pit for a reading experience that performs its message: the foundational layers upon which we as readers have built our methodologies for accessing and interpreting texts are in a state of seismic shift due to digital technologies.

Poundstone's allegory of our medial moment begs the question, how do we practice close reading when the foundations on which we see, read, and know have shifted so immeasurably that we know not even where to focus our gaze? Digital textuality involves so many layers of semiotic and operational codes and processes that it challenges our ability to locate "the text." As I noted in this book's Introduction, scholarly attention in digital studies has recently shifted away from focusing on the content displayed onscreen to analyzing the programming codes, machines, and platforms on which that content is distributed.[23] *Project* is an exemplary instance of a work of digital literature that promotes awareness of the technological layers involved in its production *through* its onscreen aesthetics. In other words, this work promotes media studies via poetics.

Part II. A Specific Literary Context

"The starting point of this piece is the historical coincidence that 'subliminal advertising' and 'concrete poetry' were introduced as concepts at nearly the same time," Poundstone writes.[24] That time is the 1950s, when corporate advertising became an art form and an object of study. In 1951 Marshall McLuhan published his first book, *The Mechanical Bride*, which, as we saw in the previous chapter, is an effort to apply close reading to advertising. McLuhan opens his preface by claiming, "Ours is the first age in which many thousands of the best-trained individual minds have made it a full-time business to get inside the collective public mind. . . . Why not assist the public to observe consciously the drama which is intended to operate upon it unconsciously?"[25] As I argued in the previous chapter, McLuhan adapts the literary practice of close reading to the advertising texts of consumer culture and thereby gives birth to media studies. Poundstone never mentions McLuhan in his opening paratexts, but he does highlight the role of Vince Packard's bestselling and hugely influential book, *The Hidden Persuaders* (1957), which shared with McLuhan's *The Mechanical Bride* the effort to make visible advertising's hidden operations. *The Hidden Persuaders* introduced into the public imagination the idea that Madison Avenue advertising firms were manipulating public opinion and consumer desire at the subliminal level.[26] Packard describes advertising "tak[ing] place beneath our level of awareness; so that the appeals which move us are often, in a sense, 'hidden.'"[27] Packard excavates this "depth approach" in advertising and urges readers, as McLuhan did before him, to consider advertisements as worthy of serious attention.[28] Poundstone draws upon this cultural history, using it as a framing device for *Project*, a work that is chock-full of icons appropriated from consumer culture and the visual language of advertising. He does so, I argue, in order to elicit the type of reading practice that both McLuhan and Packard promote: deep, close, and excavatory reading of multimodal, mass-market images.

Before the narrative begins, Poundstone primes his reader to approach the piece. When the reader moves her mouse toward "START," a circle of icons pop up onscreen and frame the word. Clicking any of these icons opens a static screen that contains expository text and that situates the work in a very specific historical context. (See Figures 2.3 and 2.4.) One such paratextual entryscreen states, "Subliminal advertising is coeval with concrete poetry."[29] Poundstone gives a specific date for their co-origin: 1957. This is the year *The Hidden Persuaders* was published, but it is also the year of the most infamous use of subliminal advertising in American culture. "In September 1957 ad man James M. Vicary announced that he had used a device called a tachistoscope to flash spilt-second ads during movies," Poundstone writes on the prefatory screen titled "The Subliminal Con." The ads, too fleeting to be perceived consciously, supposedly worked. "One that said 'Drink Coca-Cola' increased sales 18.1 percent," while, "A similar ad for popcorn boosted sales 57.5 percent."[30] Vicary's famous stunt has been identified as the first public

 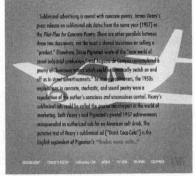

Figs 2.3 and 2.4 Screenshots of entry portal for William Poundstone's *Project for the Tachistoscope*. (Used with permission from the author.)

experiment in subliminal advertising, even though Vicary later denounced his experiment as a hoax.[31] Poundstone includes a disclaimer from Vicary (from his 1962 admittance to *The Advertising Age*), "This was a gimmick." This text is displayed in large, bold, red letters and produces a visual parallel with the only other sentence composed of large, bold, red letters on the screen: "Drink Coca-Cola." These are the words Vicary supposedly superimposed onto frames from the movie *Picnic* (dir. Joshua Logan [1955]) that he projected onto the screen in a New Jersey movie theater. But these are also the words from Decio Pignatari's famous concrete poem "bebe coca cola," also dated 1957.

In 1957 Augusto de Campos, Decio Pignatari, and Haroldo de Campos published *Pilot-Plan for Concrete Poetry*, a manifesto for a new, visual poetics. More than anything, concrete poetry is a poetics in which visual form and linguistic context are inseparable. Johanna Drucker explains that a poem is "concrete" if "the work has a distinct shape on the page and loses a part of its meaning if it is rearranged or printed without the attention to the typeface and form which were part of the poet's original work."[32] The same is true of electronic literature like *Project*, for such work is distinctly digital in its design; it cannot be printed out or transferred across media formats without a significant loss of meaning. Concrete poetry is also, like some digital literature, often regarded as avant-garde poetics. But, in these prefatory entryscreens, Poundstone places Vicary's advertising ploy on par with concrete poetry, describing both the lowbrow and the highbrow as "pivotal 1957 achievements."[33] Poundstone locates a shared origin and conjoined genealogy for these seemingly antithetical cultural practices. He thereby invites his reader to consider the characteristics shared by the unlikely grouping of these three textual genres: subliminal advertising, concrete poetry, and digital literature.

What subliminal advertising and concrete poetry share is a premise that reading happens on multiple levels *through* specific media. In the case of concrete poetry, text is a visual medium and the poem is a thing to be seen. The reading surface is understood to be a medium that can be employed purposefully for aesthetic effect and meaning, so reading concrete poetry demands deriving meaning from the visual arrangement of text on the interface of the page or screen.[34] In concrete poetry, the blank space of the page is never empty. Rather, like the pit at the center of Poundstone's narrative, its void is full of potential. Similarly, subliminal messaging is a text-based act (particularly in the conceptual experiment of Vicary's hoax which used words to increase vendor sales) that exploits the void between the visible and hidden, the conscious and unconscious, as the site for communicating meaning. What differentiates Vicary's subliminal messaging from print concrete poetry is the fact that subliminal messaging depends upon the high speed of the reading machine for its communicative, and possibly poetic, effect.[35] Poundstone's *Project* constructs a parallel between concrete poetry and subliminal messaging, and this parallel serves to illuminate the role of reading machines in both textual practices.

In *Project*'s introductory paratextual screens, Poundstone describes Vicary's experiment as a type of technotextual poetics related to another family of experimental poetics that inspires his own digital poetry: potential or combinatorial literatures such as Oulipo. In such constraint-driven poetry, the algorithm for producing a text effect is as important or more important than the end result.[36] Vicary's claim that he conducted a successful experiment in subliminal advertising became itself a kind of generative algorithm: it stimulated the American cultural imagination in wide-reaching ways to consider, fear, and produce narratives about potential machine-based subliminal messages. One can easily imagine how Vicary's claim to have subliminally stimulated desire for Coke and popcorn in the minds of innocent moviegoers generated hysteria in Cold War America. Indeed, in January 1958 the FCC held a session open to Congressmen, members of the press, and other regulatory bodies to investigate Vicary's claims of media-based persuasive power. The fear that such technology-based communication practices could be used to brainwash American citizens for political ends was powerful and palpable. As a result, Stuart Rogers for *Public Relations Quarterly* writes, "The National Association of Broadcasters boldly banned the broadcast of that which had yet to be proved to exist."[37] The ban on subliminal advertising attests to the success of Vicary's potential poetics.

Although Vicary did not intend for his experiment to be understood as poetry, Poundstone prompts us to read it that way, and doing so elicits the following questions: What are the implications of identifying poetry as something that escapes consciousness and close reading? How can concrete poetry—that genre of experimental poetics that is decisively visual—be subliminal? Since *Project* is a case of digitally produced poetics, the machine reader, rather than the human reader, is the only one capable of accessing the entire text. Does this fact alter the role and relevance of poetry? Elsewhere, in a collaborative book written with Mark C. Marino and Jeremy Douglass, I argue that works like *Project* invite comparative approaches to close reading digital literature by approaching its various medial components.[38] In this chapter I make a smaller and more concrete claim: *Project* makes apparent that some part of reading always operates unconsciously and through our reading machines. The work foregrounds the fact that reading machines are media that mediate. These machines not only enable access to content but also shape how we process and understand it. Poundstone makes this point by drawing a conceptual parallel between subliminal advertising and concrete poetry but also by adding a layer of subliminal text into his machine-based visual poetry and then calling his reader's attention to it.

Throughout the animation, white and black words flash at unreadable speeds in between the text of the main narrative. Poundstone informs his readers of the presence of this hidden text, both in the expository entryscreens that encircle START and also in the following authorial statement: "The piece is, as far as I know, the first to use subliminal effects in a work of electronic literature."[39] Unlike Vicary, who subjected unsuspecting moviegoers to his experiment in subliminal messaging, Poundstone primes readers of *Project* to focus on the vortex at the screen's center and bore down into it, to read by digging deep in order to access the hidden text it. But regardless of how carefully you read *Project*, its deepest layers of text remain inaccessible for media-specific or, more precisely, for reading machine-specific reasons. The human reader simply cannot access the programming and computer codes that enable the computer's operations. (That is, unless you hack the program or are able to acquire the programming files.) This inaccessibility is heightened because the work is built in Flash, a proprietary authoring tool for creating animations that hides its operational code from author and reader. Flash is also shrouded in a layer of copyright laws that renders its technical operations illegible at yet another level.[40] The sense of hidden depth in this particular work thus penetrates from the level of software up to the screenic aesthetic and narrative content about a bottomless pit.

Additionally, Flash actually functions in a way that furthers the sense that this software program operates in a subliminal way. Flash is a vector-based tool that produces animations by creating visual transitions called "tweens" between two locations or "keyframes"; keyframes are the unit of measurement and programming into which authors insert content into the Flash's interface. The tween (hear "between") is the software-produced animated transition that sutures keyframes to produce a fluid animation. The tween is the invisible stitch, the registered but not recognized code at the heart of Flash and works produced in it.[41] The tween is thus akin to the subliminal message flashing onscreen in-between the primary, visible words of Poundstone's narrative in *Project*. The operations of Flash's tween not only technically enable but also metaphorically support the poetic of Poundstone's digital literature.

Poundstone's *Project* promotes recognition that literature, and our means of reading it, is dependent upon reading machines and, thus, analysis of these technologies assists and rewards literary analysis. I pursue this point in the next part of this chapter by pushing against Poundstone's claim that 1957 is the origin point for *Project*'s poetics. I excavate a nearly forgotten reading machine from the 1930s and position this earlier, modernist project as the foundation for the Flash-ing poetics of Poundstone's digital literature.

Part III. Excavating the Readies

"The written word hasn't kept up with the age," so claims Bob Brown in his manifesto, "The Readies," published in the international avant-garde journal *transition* in 1930. "We have the talkies, but as yet no Readies."[42] To remedy this situation, Brown proposed to build a reading machine that would produce "a moving type spectacle, reading at the speed rate of the day with the aid of a machine, a method of enjoying literature in a manner as up-to-date as the lively talkies."[43] The Readies was never built, but its excavation and consideration as a conceptual project for machine poetics has renewed significance in a contemporary digital culture fascinated by digital reading machines and flashing poetics such as Poundstone's. In what follows, I present Brown's modernist literary experiment as a predecessor to *Project*'s Flash-ing animation, both in its aesthetic and its ambition to imagine how a reading machine can influence new poetics and new reading practices.

Literary scholars have begun the archaeology of Brown's Readies machine. In *Black Riders*, Jerome McGann describes Brown as "The visual tradition's most important modernist practitioner and theorist."[44] He places Brown in a tradition of visual poetics that anticipates experiments like concrete poetry and, as I argue, digital literature. Craig Dworkin also situates Brown in the tradition of experimental poetry, specifically such poetics that engage with technology.[45] Dworkin, more than any other scholar I know (and as I will discuss later), reads carefully the collection of poetry created for Brown's Readies machine. Michael North's seminal excavation of Brown's archive (in UCLA's Special Collections) situates the Readies in relation to the modernist media arts of photography and cinema, claiming that Brown saw the reading machine as "a sort of modernist movie constructed of type."[46] But the connection between the Readies and contemporary forms of digital reading machines is overdue. The importance of Craig Saper's recent republication of many of Brown's publications (through Rice University Press) cannot be overstated, particularly since his informative afterword introduces Brown as both a modernist writer and a media innovator. But despite this handful of scholarly reevaluations, there is much work to do. Brown was a central node in the modernist matrix and in the history of modern media, and reconsidering him through digital literature illuminates the convergence of those two trajectories. My approach to the Readies builds upon the efforts of these other scholars and adds a twist, for I read the Readies in relation to digital literature programmed to perform on a reading machine (the computer) in ways that illuminate the parallels between modernist and contemporary literary efforts to produce machine poetics.

Bob Brown's Modernist Reading Machine

Brown was a concrete poet before the term existed. Augusto de Campos, leader of the international movement in concrete poetry, described Brown as a such, as "truly striking his own footpath among the calligrams of Apollinaire and the typograms of Cummings, like those, his own manupictograms interpenetrating text and illustration."[47] de Campos even republished some of Brown's "optical poems" in an anthology titled *A Margem da Margem* (1989). Brown focused attention on the visual nature of poetry in works such as "Eyes on the Half-Shell" (1917) and in *1450–1950*.[48] But it was in his self-published pamphlet, *The Readies* (also published in 1930), that he dedicated himself to pursuing a visual poetics based in and inspired by the new media of his time. The book's dedication page reads, "DEDICATED TO/ALL EYE-WRITERS/AND/ ALL READERS/ WHO ANY AN EYEFUL."

"Writing has been bottled up in books since the start," he writes, "It is time to pull out the stopper."[49] Pulling out the stopper meant allowing words to spill across the eye, to speed by in ways that would, he hoped, "breed a new kind of writing direct to the mind through the eye."[50] Brown writes, "I wanted a reading machine to carry my words faster and farther into the minds of others."[51] Carrying words "faster and farther into the minds of others" is the ambition of subliminal messaging—the particular type of machine reading that inspires Poundstone's *Project*. Although Brown is technically nondescript about how the Readies will actually operate, it is clear from his letters that he intended his machine to produce a reading experience like that produced by the tachistoscope. He writes, "to get the idea of the reading machine you won't have to roll your eyes at all, just hold them still and imagine the following stream of words passing before them."[52] The human reader would focus on a single spot at the center of the Readies's interface, and upon this spot, the machine would flash a stream of words in a tachistoscopic manner. Brown explains, "microscopic type on a moveable tape running beneath a slot equipped with a magnifying glass" would be "brought up to life size before the reader's birdlike eye."[53] Brown's language echoes Alfred W. Volkmann's 1859 description of the tachistoscope, which he invented.

Volkmann was a physiologist who conceived of the tachistoscope in order to solve the problem of measuring stimulus-response in a laboratory setting. Volkmann describes how the tachistoscope presents an object "drawn on a strip of paper" that becomes visible to the seated viewer who "fixate[s]" "at the exact point where the drawing is" and where the next image will appear.[54] Jerome Rothenberg recognized the similarity between the Readies and the tachistoscope. In an introduction to Brown's Readies essay that Rothenberg republished, Rothenberg introduces the Readies as "a tachistoscope-like reading machine."[55] He then uses Brown's own words to describe how the Readies would present text, "'run[ning] on forever before the eye without having to be chopped up into columns, pars, etc.'"[56] Brown's conceptual machine shares certain characteristics with the tachistoscope and also, as I argue, with Poundstone's digital adaptation of it. But the Readies is very much of its own medial and literary moment.

Brown presents the Readies to address the needs of a specific moment in the production and reception of literature. The modernist moment is, he writes, "more optical, more eye=teasing, more eye=tasty," so "modern word=conveyors are needed now."[57] He writes these words as an author of experimental literature but also as a reader of it. "I love every loveable Dublintender word James Joyce ever wrote and I gurgle with delight in the joyous jugfuls of Gertrude Stein."[58] Yet Brown identifies a gap between writing and reading, between the avant-garde practices of Joyce, Stein, and his fellow writers in the pages of the journal *transition*, where "The Readies" essay version was published. This discrepancy separates literature from her sibling art forms. While the other arts kept up-to-date by incorporating the new media technologies of the time, literature remained stuck in the proverbial mud of the static page. "In our aeroplane age . . . All the arts are having their faces lifted, painting [Picasso], sculpture [Brancusi], music [Antheil] . . . Only the reading half of Literature lags behind."[59] The brackets are Brown's, and, as he continues, he uses them to identify the modernist writers he most respects for their innovation. According to Brown, "writing [Joyce, Stein, Cumming, Hemingway]" has kept pace with innovation, but "Present day reading methods are as cumbersome as they were in the time of Caxton."[60] The problem lies not with literature but with modes of accessing it: "all I hold out for is more and better *reading* of the words we've got" (emphasis added).[61]

Implicit in Brown's discussion of the Readies machine is a feedback loop between literature and its technologies of transmission, specifically between words and reading machines. He maintains that changing the way we read would in turn change what we write: "With written matter moving before the eyes new forms of expression will develop naturally and surely more expressive ones."[62] For example, Brown anticipated that presenting text at technologically heightened speeds would purge literature of conjunctions and filler text, such unneeded words as Ezra Pound sought to excise in the first rule of Imagism:"Direct treatment of the 'thing.'"[63] Brown writes, "My reading machine, by its very existence, makes a need for new words and demands the deletion of some worn-out ones."[64] For example, "The up=to=date eye scarcely sees the 'thes,' 'ands,' 'ofs,' 'as,' 'ins,'" Brown writes, "it picks out meaty nouns, verbs and qualifying words so placed as to assume importance; only essential words ever get over to the practiced reading eye, the bulky residue is overlooked."[65] *The Readies* ends with a chart showing the words most often used in English texts, prepositions and predicates that should waste away through the Readies's mechanic speed.[66] His survival-of-the-fittest attitude toward language expresses an understanding that literature is materially grounded in media ecologies and, as a result, literature and reading practices are entwined with and dependent upon media. Seventy-five years after Brown self-published *The Readies*, Poundstone explores and aestheticizes this very argument in *Project*.

Poundstone and Brown share the conviction that a mechanized reading machine bridges—literally mediating between—avant-garde and mass culture. In the narrative he presents describing the origin of the Readies, Brown locates the Readies at the heart of capitalistic culture: "The Wall Street ticker is a reading machine."[67] He came to see this fact after a stint working on Wall Street. He explains, "We read the tape. Is passed before our eyes jerkily, but in a continuous line. Endlessly, at any speed, jerk, jerk, jerk, when the Market's pulse was fast; click, click, click when it was slow."[68] The joint experiences of reading modernist literature and reading Wall Street's ticker tape inspired the Readies. "I had to think of the reading machine later," he writes, "because I read Gertrude Stein and tape-tickers on Wall Street."[69] Stein and Wall Street are not usually aligned in modernist criticism, but Brown saw their convergence through a focus on machine-based technopoetics.[70] Before Poundstone could claim that subliminal advertising and concrete poetry are coeval, Brown asserted something similar about modernist poetry and ticker tape. The Readies was born of this realization and of the hope to rectify a situation wherein "The low-brows are presently reveling their Movies and Talkies while the almost extinct high-brow is content to sit at home sipping his thin alphabet soup out of archaic volumes of columns."[71]

An article from the *Chicago Tribune* dated January 13, 1930, and titled "Left Bankers Believe Bob Brown's Pill Box Book Reading Machine Will Help Them Absorb Dozen Gertrude Stein Novels in Afternoon," sardonically suggests that the reading machine will make difficult modernist works absorbable by speeding them up.[72] If a speed-reading machine can make Stein easy to read, then technology inarguably transforms literature. Brown certainly believed that changing the reading speed would in turn alter the reading experience. When considered in relation to Poundstone's *Project*, Brown's Readies can be seen as part of a lineage of experiments in technopoetics that focus critical attention on reading machines and reading practices. Brown and Poundstone each experiment with how technological speed pushes the liminal boundaries of perception in ways that challenge our understanding of what it means "to read" literature. They invite us to consider how reading has a medial history that is part of literature and literary history.

Readies for Bob Brown's Machine

Brown produces a volume of experimental writing for the Readies, and it is in this collection that he makes his case for considering the transformative effect that reading machines can have on literary innovation. Brown published *Readies for Bob Brown's Machine* in 1931. This anthology contained short literary works by members of Brown's (and Stein's) modernist circle. Comprised of nearly 200 pages of poems and short fiction, *Readies for Bob Brown's Machine* included works by prominent modernists such as William Carlos Williams, Gertrude Stein, Filippo Marinetti, Eugene Jolas, and Ezra Pound, as well as lesser-known writers. In the preface to that volume, Hilaire Hiler writes that all of the works were "contributed by experimental modern writers [and have] been expressly written to be read on the reading machine."[73] Each work strives to capture the speed and movement of the machine through print typography and grammar but in different ways. For example, Gertrude Stein's "We Came: A History" uses equal signs to indicate anticipated movement by the Readies machine: "=History is made by a very=Few who are important=And history is what that =One says. History is"; Eugene Jolas uses dashes in his "Faula-and-Flona," which begins, "The-lilygushes-ring-and-ting-a-bilbel-in-the-ivilee"; and James T. Farrell uses ellipses in "Sylverster McGullick": "Alarm clock shrieks . . . seven a.m. . . . last night's sheik . . . to-day's sheep . . ." (see Figures 2.5 and 2.6).[74]

The grammatical and visual icons represent imagined movements that the Readies machine might make, such as sliding shifts between screens or quick flashes in the style of the tachistoscope. These visual marks are an integral part of each text's poetic. Taken together they represent a collective literary effort to express the notational form for producing potential technological action. In other words, these poems are textual acts of programming; they are code. The pages of is history because it is accompanied by reluctance. Reluctance is not necessarily history nor is decision.

I like white because dahlias are beautiful in color. Tube roses come from onions, in every sense of the word and the way of saying it is attractive to her.

How do you like what you have heard. = History must be distinguished = From mistakes. = History must not be what is = Happening. = History must not be about = Dogs and balls in all = The meaning of those = Words history must be = Something unusual and = Nevertheless famous and = Successful. History must = Be the occasion of having = In every way established a = Precedent history must = Be all there is of importance = In their way successively = History must be an open = Reason for needing them = There which it is as they = Are perfectly without a = Doubt that it is interested. = History cannot be an accident. = They make history they = Are in the place of it. = II = History leaves no place = For which they ask will = They be made more of = In case of the disaster = Which has not overtaken = Any one. Historically there = Is no disaster because = Those who make history = Cannot be overtaken = As they will make = History which they do = Because it is necessary = That every one will = Begin to know that = They must know that = History is what it is = Which it is as they do = Know that history is not = Just what every one = Does who comes and = Prefers days to more = Than ever which they have. = History must again be = Caught and taught and = Not be that it is tiring = To play with balls. = It is not tiring to go on = And make the needle = Which goes in and out = Be careful not at all = History is made by a very = Few who are important = And history is what that = One says. History is = This it is the necklace = Which makes pansies = Be made well of stones = Which they are likely = To be. This is not = History history is made = By them they make history. = III = One who was remarkable = Addressed them as follows. = Come when you like and = Leave when you

---

Fig 2.5 From Gertrude Stein's "We Came: A History" in *Readies for Bob Brown's Machine.* ed. by A. Lincoln Gillespie, Jr., et al. (Cagnes-sur-Mer: Roving Eye Press [1931], p. 100. Yale Collection of American Literature, Beinecke Rare Book and Manuscript Library.)

ringa bell rollup the . . . . . . - - - - - THICK-
FILM - - - - - - - COWCROWD   faces
- - - - - hate detest detest - - - - - - - you too you - you
red   dry   glassskin   lizards   insolentbeautynone
- - - - - huwarm - - - - - smoke - - - - - jerknecks
over   horn   rim   periscopettish   hotlate   cackledotes-
i-l-e-n-tover £ ✦ s ✦ d ✦ % % % 1,000,000 a
somuch sosososomuch nod-wise-dotty-acres good-
man & & talkrustle newssheets - - new wars whores
W-H-E-E-L-S-W-H-I-R-R-E-V-O-L-V-O-V-E-R ——
—————————————————————— s.mile-
ing-flatcoil-carrails-snakeshine-nonstop-ecstasies ——.
—————— SPINESPLINTERSTOP

                                topumble ig
foolhat ✦ knock offside seats 2 small for 2 jerk humid
windowrain / / / slantslope-arizona-mountain-oon -
(coldawmorning) - - aridry————————calm unhum
a n s a n dryf l e s h - - - - - i v e r————————
skysh imm e r   - - - -airpurain - - - -banking a.
SUDdnd e s c ent puff - - - - - arcclear edges- - - - - -
(rubbd) - - - - - - - -. - - - C l e a n s p a c E - - -
- - - f a i n t   pane   race - -
lips c u r v e c l e a r   (vast   plain)
steeltrack————————————————— horizontal
copface pops up props up p r o n e girlclearsmile
i l e i d e w i d e n s a w a y s l o w slick
i k - liquid brilliant e e t h e r s . a ✦ w a ✦
youngbodyvasespass float ✦ distant ✦✦✦ coming
here going   distant ▰→ vanish-E-E-Ns m o o t-
h o o l o o k s l o wkwik p a s s ing gazeflat ✦
up ✦ pass ✦ float ✦ clouds ✦ even ✦ drift ✦ after-
even vaporedges ✦ shred ✦ shedd ✦ light ✦ march
✦ tune ✦ unison ✦ even seen moon pulse ✦ silent
punctuate * ✦✦✦ on   * ✦✦ on moon ✦ loom
o o m s evenlunar ✦ unison on ✦ on ✦ whitetorn
black endless shrededges ✦ shedding tornevenever
white irregular moment gone ✦ liquid light
momentumurmurregu larrevolve wheels whirrune
a s y t r i c kle of.   blissombrake wave brain

Fig 2.6 From Sidney Hunt's "MORNINIGHT CAR" in *Readies for Bob Brown's Machine*,
ed. by A. Lincoln Gillespie, Jr., et al. (Cagnes-sur-Mer: Roving Eye Press [1931], p. 147. Yale
Collection of American Literature, Beinecke Rare Book and Manuscript Library.)

Readies for Bob Brown's Machine display modernist writers imagining how literary technologies might transform literature and readings of it. Dworkin insightfully describes the poems as self conscious about their status as media objects, arguing that they "situate themselves in the uncomfortable position of a belated prolepsis: a presentation in book-form of the imagined literary effect of a technology that had yet to be produced and which would ultimately make the book obsolete."[75] Brown's *Readies for Bob Brown's Machine* has been out of print since its first publication. It is a captivating text that deserves to be resurrected. Excavating this anthology of fascinating, mostly forgotten poems prompts reconsideration of these modernist writers and of modernism more broadly in the newfound light of these experimentations with reading machines and machine poetics.

To illustrate my point, I will take just one example, a poem by a canonical writer that has been republished since its appearance in Brown's anthology: William Carlos Williams's "Readie Pome." Reading this poem in the context of the Readies, however, might encourage a different interpretation of the poet's famous statement, "A poem is a small (or large) machine made out of words."[76] In 1944, over a decade after the publication of *Readies for Bob Brown's Machine*, Williams writes, "As in all machines its movement is intrinsic, undulant, a physical more than a literary character."[77] These statements are usually read within a lineage of Imagism, wherein every semiotic mark works economically, concretely even, to produce a working machine of words that stimulates vision and presents visual poetry. But Williams's claim that poetry is a machine takes on more than merely metaphorical meaning when considered in relation to the Readies; it becomes a mission statement. Here is Williams's entire contribution to Brown's volume, "Readie Pome": "Grace-face: hot-pot: lank-spank: meat-eat: / hash-cash: sell-well: old-sold: sink-wink: deep- / sleep: come-numb: dum-rum: some-bum."[78] Even with the ambiguous technical descriptions Brown provides for the Readies, one can imagine how Williams's poem might be read on the reading machine. "Grace-face" would appear onscreen before being replaced by "hot-pot"; the same sequential replacement would happen with "lank-spank," "meat-eat," and so forth. The colons separate the text pairings into discrete poetic units, each of which occupies nearly the same amount of space on the page and makes them, in a sense, visually interchangeable. The colons also demarcate possible movements of the reading machine, particularly changes between screens, so that the poem's text-units would flash before the reader's eyes in a series of montage-like replacements. Rhyme supports this sense, for the word pairs operate through an internal serialization of phonemes: "gr" is replaced by "fa," while "ace" remains. The result is an aural and visual act of textual montage that breaks up the poem into a flashing series of linguistic elements. I hope my description triggers comparisons to Poundstone's *Project*, for the way Williams presents his poem invokes a similar aesthetic to the flashing, tachistoscopic-like effect of Poundstone's digital work. As its title suggests, "Readie Pome" makes the reading machine its premise and subtext. The poem presents itself an instance of machine poetics and of programmable poetry.

Reading Williams's "Readie Pome" within the context of its original publication exposes it to be exemplary of the content in *Readies for Bob Brown's Machine*. Like other texts in that volume, Williams presents the reading machine as integral to his poem, both to accessing and understanding it. However, when Williams's "Readie Pome" is plucked from the medial context of *Readies for Bob Brown's Machine* and republished in print (as in *The Collected Poems of William Carlos Williams: 1909–1939*), it is a very different fruit indeed. The example provided by Williams's poem serves to remind us that media matters in the creation, presentation, and reception of literature. Specifically, my reading of "Readie Pome" suggests that literary texts can promote media-specific analyses that propel critical acts of media archaeology on forgotten reading machines. Such work, in turn, prompts reconsideration of the literary texts they inspire. This recursive project also lies at the heart of Poundstone's *Project*, a work that, as I've argued, performs and promotes media archeology in order to present that activity as a strategy for close reading digital literature. Excavating *Readies for Bob Brown's Machine* and reading it in relation to Poundstone's digital literature illuminates the modernist text to be an experiment in machine poetics that, like the digital work, depends upon and refers back to the reading machine that inspires it. These works thus represent a literary genealogy of machine poetics that continues from modernism to digital literature, one that takes inspiration from the ways in which reading machines shape literature and approaches to reading it.

Part IV. Conclusion

By way of concluding, let me offer up one more little gem from Brown's treasure trove. The following short poem appears at the beginning of *The Readies*, and Brown introduces it with a challenge: "Here's a poem, believe it or not."[79] Brown's poem is comprised nearly completely of printer's marks, annotations used to format the appearance of the poem during the publishing process (see Figure 2.7). These markup tags signify the procedures for formatting, page layout, typesetting, etc., which produce and are usually overlooked by readers of the final printed product. But Brown turns this hidden text, the programmatic language of print

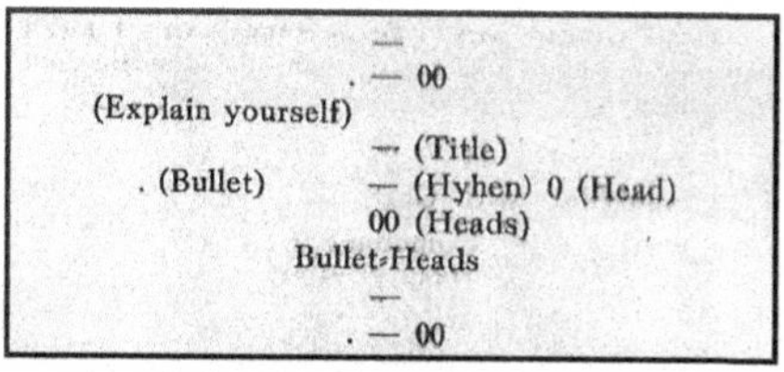
—
. — 00
(Explain yourself)
— (Title)
. (Bullet) — (Hyhen) 0 (Head)
00 (Heads)
Bullet-Heads
—
. — 00

Fig 2.7 Bob Brown's "Untitled Poem" in *Readies for Bob Brown's Machine*, ed. by A. Lincoln Gillespie, Jr., et al. (Cagnes-sur-Mer: Roving Eye Press [1931], p. 2.)

publishing, into the semantic and visual content of his poem. He thus opens *The Readies* with a poem that visually acknowledges literature to be mediated by technological processes.[80]

Reading this poem eighty years after its publication and through the lens of digital textuality illuminates another way of reading the technological protocols it encodes, one that Brown could not have foreseen. The visual marks that to modernist readers would have suggested the technical backend of print publishing bears a striking resemblance to HyperText Mark-up Language (HTML), the language that marks up web pages on the Internet.[81] Although it was published more than sixty years before the development of HTML, Brown's poem uses parentheses and language in a surprisingly similar way to HTML tags such as <HEAD>, <TITLE>, and <BODY>, which are laid out vertically in HTML source code. The tags in Brown's poem and in HTML both serve to structure the space of interface, either page or screen, so as to allow for the appearance of the literary text. In other words, by foregrounding the usually unseen mark-up codes, Brown figures the page as an interface through which the poem appears. The layers of technologies involved in producing the text become the content of Brown's poem, and he illuminates the printed book to be a reading machine. His "believe it or not" statement challenges the reader to understand that technological protocols (or codes) constitute literature and thus deserve formal analysis.

Reading Brown's Readies in relation to Poundstone's digital literature provides an opportunity to consider the connections between these writers and the literary periods and poetic practices they represent. As I have tried to show, the primary point of intersection between Brown and Poundstone is a shared effort to imagine literary revolution *through* the new media of their respective moments and, in particular, through new reading machines. These exemplary cases remind us that reading machines not only enable access to literature but also inspire its creation and critique. Recognition of the recursive relationship between literature and reading machines opens up new directions for writing literary history.

3. Speed Reading

SUPER-POSITION AND SIMULTANEITY in
Young-hae Chang Heavy Industries's Dakota *and Ezra*
Pound's Cantos

The screen flashes black to white through shades of grey as Art Blakey lays down a strong, steady drumbeat that simultaneously soothes and stimulates. The music grows into a frenzied drumroll as a numerical countdown appears onscreen (see Figures 3.1–3.3). The countdown harkens back to early cinema and situates the digital work in the context of modernist media.[1] Then the introduction, paced to tantalize: Young-hae Chang Industries presents (see Figure 3.4). Finally, the title appears onscreen. "DAKØTA" pulses for a few moments before the work begins, unleashing its speeding narrative.[2] The screen explodes with words and sounds. Sleek black text in Monaco font, capitalized and unornamented, flashes in speeding synchronization to the blaring beat of Blakey's "Tobi Ilu." *Dakota* (2002) is programmed in Flash to produce a sophisticated, minimalist aesthetic: individual words and phrases flash at center screen to take dominion over the stark white background before they are replaced by more flashing text. The work hits you forcefully. The bold text, the charged prose, and the blaring beat produce an aesthetic of flashing literature unlike anything you've seen before and yet also so very familiar. Glued to the screen, unable to look away in fear of missing something, you feverishly follow the fleeting text. You find yourself speed reading and spellbound by Young-hae Chang Heavy Industries (YHCHI). You are not alone.

YHCHI is one of the most popular and critically acclaimed collaborations in the world of new media literary art. Their work generates buzz on blogs and

10 NINE 8

Figs 3.1, 3.2, and 3.3 Consecutive screenshots from *Dakota*'s opening animation sequence. (Young-hae Chang Heavy Industries, 2002. Used with permission from the authors.)

bulletin boards; it is taught on university syllabi and inspires scholarly articles; and it has been exhibited in numerous museums worldwide.[3] This success can be attributed to its simple, minimalist and, indeed, modernist aesthetic. This aesthetic, I argue, has the effect of compelling viewers to close read. The flashing text promotes speed-reading while its literary content demands an opposite response. The resulting paradox is the cornerstone of YHCHI's digital literature and my interest in it. YHCHI's *Dakota* promotes both speed reading and close reading; and, in so doing, it demands that we adapt critical close reading practices to incorporate both modalities in order to analyze digital literature. Whereas my previous chapter pursued this effort by addressing the role of the reading machine in machine poetics, this chapter considers the role of speed—speed produced by the reading machine and enacted by the reader as part of her reading practice—as a technopoetic element that serves digital modernist literature in adapting literary forms across media formats and cultural periods.

Whatever method or pace one adopts to approach it, reading *Dakota* is not an easy task. *Dakota* does not allow its reader to control the work's pace: there is no button to stop, pause, or slow the text. Unable to control the reading pace, the reader can only sit back and try to absorb the stream of text flashing before her eyes. The experience is similar to that of reading William Poundstone's *Project for*

Fig 3.4 Screenshot of introductory title screen from *Dakota*. (Young-hae Chang Heavy Industries, 2002. Used with permission from the authors.)

the Tachistoscope {Bottomless Pit} (discussed in Chapter 2); but whereas Poundstone frames his visual flashing literature as machine-oriented, as a "project"
inspired by and for the tachistoscope, YHCHI begin by aesthetically invoking a
different visual technology as the source of their remediation: cinema. The numerical countdown that loads and introduces *Dakota* suggests that its flashing
performance produces an experience closer to viewing film than reading literature. *Dakota* is, in fact, built in a software program for creating animations that
uses the metaphor of film as its operational interface and calls its end-products
"movies": Flash. I will have more to say about Flash later, but for now the point
is that *Dakota* demands attention to the medial aspects of the literary and even
invites a comparative textual media approach to literary analysis.[4] In particular,
the Flash-based onscreen performance presents a montage-like aesthetic remix of
modernist poetry that challenges conceptions of what it means to "read" literature.
In the previous chapter I argued for the importance of considering the reading
machine as part of the literary experience, and this chapter builds upon the claim
by showing how a digital work exploits the computer's speed to promote the slow,
careful reading practice of close reading. It might seem counterintuitive to close
read in a chapter called "Speed Reading," yet this operational paradox is *Dakota's*
well-wrought urn (to invoke Cleanth Brooks), its central motivating and meaningful tension. Following the New Critics (who, as I argued in Chapter 1, are central to
the history of media studies), I pursue this paradox as a means of approaching and
analyzing *Dakota*. The work serves as my case study for showing how traditional
modes of critical analysis change along with their objects of study and, moreover,
how literature itself promotes this change.

Part I. Strategic Alignment

Young-hae Chang Heavy Industries is the name of the collaborative duo comprised of Young-hae Chang, the self-proclaimed chief engineering officer, and
Marc Voge, its self-styled chief information officer. Adopting the language of the
capitalist marketplace to describe their artistic collaboration, YHCHI suggest that
their work is a merger of high art, with its serious "heavy" affect, and also a product of the "industries" of mass-production and popular culture. YHCHI refuse to
say much about their work—"we can't and won't help readers to 'locate' us"—and
revel in a guise of anonymity that they see as constitutive of the medium in which
they work: "Distance, homelessness, anonymity, and insignificity are all part of
the Internet literary voice, and we welcome them."[5] This is not the model of the

Internet that we have come to know with the advent of Web 2.0 (around 2004), wherein the web is used as a vehicle for self-promotion and social networking. Yet YHCHI continue to maintain their minimalist aesthetic, distanced authorial persona, and approach to the Internet that they articulated in this interview from 2002. They artfully present themselves by refusing to employ the web as we might expect and saying little about themselves and their art. So what they *do* say acquires particular significance. In the few interviews and artist statements they have admitted over the years, YHCHI repeat the claim that *Dakota* "is based on a close reading of Ezra Pound's *Cantos* part I and part II."[6] This pronouncement is both a declaration and an invitation: a declaration of alignment with a canonical work of literary modernism and an invitation to read *Dakota* through Pound's first and second cantos. This chapter addresses both aspects of YHCHI's statement. I read their claim as an assertion of literary lineage linking the digital work to a tradition laden with cultural capital and then analyze how this connection serves *Dakota* and renders it an exemplary case of digital modernism.

YHCHI's consciously crafted attempt to situate *Dakota* in relation to Ezra Pound's *Cantos* and to modernism more generally is particularly intriguing because *Dakota* exists on the mass media marketplace technology of the Internet and because *Dakota*'s narrative seems to have no immediate relation to Pound's first two cantos. Yet, as I will show by accepting YHCHI's invitation and performing a close reading of the work, *Dakota* is a nearly line-by-line adaptation of the first cantos. Its remix not only revamps the modernist opus for a digital readership but does so in ways that illuminate the medial nature of that earlier text. *Dakota* presents multiple levels of address and signification that defy simple categorizations as modern or postmodern, high or low, cinema or literature. By asking readers to approach *Dakota* through the specific framework they provide, YHCHI invite examination of these critical concepts and promote a cultural repositioning of them as literature enters the post-postmodern period and electronic literature adopts a strategy of digital modernism.

Dakota is exemplary of digital modernism because it adapts a literary text and technique from modernism in order to challenge the status quo of electronic literature and our assumptions about it. YHCHI's minimalist aesthetic presents a conscious resistance to the central characteristics and expectations of mainstream electronic literature. Works like *Dakota* (as I discussed in the Introduction) resist the alignment of electronic literature with hypertext, evade reader-controlled interactivity, and favor the foregrounding of text and typography, narrative complexity, and an aesthetic of difficulty. Young-hae Chang, of YHCHI, states, "My Web art tries to express the essence of the Internet: information. Strip away the interactivity, the graphics, the design, the photos, the banners, the colors, the fonts and the rest, and what's left? The text."[7] The statement is a conscious act of defiance, a rejection of that central feature of the web and electronic literature—interactivity. "In my work there is no interactivity," Chang states, "no graphics or graphic design; no photos; no banners; no millions-of-colors; no playful fonts; no pyrotechnics. I have a special dislike for interactivity."[8] This rejection of interactivity distinguishes YHCHI's work from mainstream digital art and literature. After all, interactivity has been central to electronic literature since the early days of hypertext, when hypertext writers and critics proclaimed the reader's interactive participation as a form of authorship.[9] Forsaking such central characteristics of electronic literature as reader-controlled navigation and an extensive use of multimedia, YHCHI instead foreground the text-based nature of their digital work. They do so with a clear intention. It is not simply a "dislike for interactivity" that motivates YHCHI's electronic literature and their desire to connect *Dakota* to modernism. YHCHI see the current state of electronic literature as one in which literature is "not taken very seriously."[10] To rectify this fact, they align their digital literature with a work in a literary canon that is taken very seriously.[11]

YHCHI identify Pound as their modernist persona, adopting his practice of using personae, masks through which to speak to a new age about and through its new literature. Attaching their work to a central figure—or the central figure, for, as T. S. Eliot claims, Pound "is more responsible for the XXth Century revolution in poetry than is any other individual"[12]—YHCHI induce critical reconsideration of both digital literature and of modernism. As we will see, *Dakota*'s adaptation is both an ironic and an earnest attempt to "make it new" by rearticulating the past. Its text reads as both a simple story about a youthful road trip, complete with colloquial language and allusions to mass culture, but also as a faithful retelling of Pound's first two cantos, the first of which is itself an adaptation of book 11 of Homer's *Odyssey*. YHCHI pursue the modernist practice of renovating an ancient past as inspiration for modern literature, just as Pound did in the opening to *The Cantos*. As a result, *Dakota* not only rereads cantos I and II but also repositions them in a contemporary, digital milieu. It thus invites reassessment of "the XXth Century revolution in poetry" that Eliot identifies and whose impact is visible in contemporary electronic literature.

The cantos that YHCHI reread are, it should be said, an anomaly in Pound's magnum opus. The rest of *The Cantos* veer away from *The Odyssey* and the clear, linear narrative that serves as its opening. Because of this, YHCHI's selection of these particular poems, and my focus on them, might seem to be a misrepresentation of the connection between electronic literature and modernism via

Pound's *Cantos*. However, these particular and anomalous cantos are crucial for understanding YHCHI's exemplary digital modernist employment of modernism. YHCHI adapt the first three cantos to recuperate a central aspect of Pound's *Cantos*—their focus on media and materiality. Jerome McGann reminds us that the first edition of these first cantos displayed a print design that drew heavily from medieval manuscript ornamentation and Pre-Raphaelite adaptations of this medieval, handmade aesthetic (in particular, William Morris's Kelmscott Press). Decorated capital letters printed in red and black ink open the cantos, and this detail is important, McGann explains; "The pages of these books recollect at the design level the epochal (bibliographical) events of the fifteenth century and the late nineteenth century" and, thus, "The *Cantos* project locates itself within that historical nexus."[13] McGann continues, "Canto I launches the Cantos project in explicitly bibliographic terms: the voyage of Odyssey's is a matter of linguistic translation and book production."[14] "Canto I" can thus be understood to be a poem about media and mediation. YHCHI pursue and further this interpretation. They adapt the first canto in ways that engage with it in order to address the materiality of their own medium and moment.

Dakota enacts and aestheticizes the constitutive fact of digital textuality—that, as Katherine Hayles points out, content is composed of "flickering signifiers"—by literally flickering or flashing onscreen. *Dakota*'s narrative text thus formally turns attention to the effect that this flickering has on the way we read. This ambition is also evident in the authors' typographical decision to substitute the zero sign for the letter "O." The choice extends beyond *Dakota*, permeating all of YHCHI's *oeuvre*. This signature aesthetic move serves to visually highlight the digital nature of YHCHI's texts by showing its screenic content to be thoroughly interwoven with the numerical base of binary code that penetrates and enables it flashing performance. YHCHI thus promote awareness of the distinctively different, digital nature of their work even as they pursue a connection to modernism. The result of this strategic effort is an affective dissonance that I will explore in this chapter: the readerly experience of attempting to close read *Dakota*'s close reading of cantos I and II is one of difficulty. YHCHI's authorial assertion of a connection between *Dakota* and high modernism—rather than cinema or the more contemporary popular culture associated with digital media and online art—provides a focal point: the text. But focusing on *Dakota*'s text is quite hard to do.

Close reading as we know it, a practice of slow examination focused on the text and tensions its language produces, is something that *Dakota*'s performance elides. Its text flashes so fast that it is often impossible to read, let alone close read. Yet, framed by YHCHI's authorial claim, *Dakota* promotes two seemingly opposed reading strategies: it prompts the reader to sit back and passively consume streams of flashing text but also incites the critical reader to reread the work, transcribe the words, and compare its content to Pound's modernist epic. *Dakota*'s content calls for a reading strategy of careful interpretative comparison while its formal presentation challenges such attempts. Yet, as we will see, this fast-flashing aesthetic is also part of YHCHI's adaptation of modernism. In what follows, I examine *Dakota* as both an adaptation of Pound's first two cantos and a remediation of a central formal technique from Pound's poetics—super-position—in order to illuminate the media-specific ways in which this digital work challenges traditional reading practices in ways that promote updating of them. We begin by focusing on content, close reading *Dakota* as it close reads the first two cantos.

Close Reading *Dakota*, Close Reading Cantos I and II

Both Pound's *Cantos* and YHCHI's *Dakota* begin with a classic journey: Odysseus's visit to the Underworld during his journey back to Ithaca and a teenage cross-country road trip. The first line of "Canto I" begins midsentence and midaction as Odysseus's ship enters the Underworld. The reader joins the action through a conjunctive fragment in the first line: "And then went down to the ship, / Set keel to breakers, forth on the godly sea, and / We set up mast and sail on that swart ship."[15] *Dakota* also begins midsentence and midaction, with the shock of obscenity in large, capitalized letters: "FUCKING." The black letters sit at the center before being swallowed up into the white screen. The action continues with words and phrases flashing consecutively, replacing the previous text and following the action of Pound's canto: "WALTZED—ØUT—TØ THE CAR—PUT THE KEY IN—THE IGNITIØN—READY TØ HIT THE RØAD."[16] The sun is out, the car is packed, and beers are in the trunk: "THE SUN—HIGH ABØVE— PØURING—DØWN ØN—ØUR HEADS." A group of friends head out "CRØSS CØUNTRY— - - - -." *Dakota*'s lucid, linear presentation follows the opening canto as Odysseus's ship pierces the boundaries of the Underworld: "Came we then to the bounds of deepest water / . . . /Nor with stars stretched, nor looking back from heaven / Swartest night stretched over wretched men there."[17] While Odysseus continues into the depths of the Underworld, *Dakota*'s characters enter an American Underworld haunted by ghosts. Signs for "BLACKFØØT RESERVATIØN" and "BADLAND, SIØUX FALLS" flash quickly onscreen, and an oppressive tone creeps into the music. The characters have consumed too much alcohol and penetrated territory marked only by a "DEAD MØTEL" and an impenetrable darkness that "NØT A STARRY NIGHT—NØR A LØW FLYING JET-LINER—CØULD PIERCE." The earlier atmosphere of youthful frivolity dissolves as the text begins to flash faster, mirroring the act of reading signs from a moving car.[18] The screen becomes a physical space to be read like South Dakota's stark landscape, and a parallel is invoked between *Dakota* and the first canto as well as between the readers of both texts who struggle to make textual fragments cohere. As *Dakota's* youthful road trip enters the Badlands, the land lending its name to the work's title, the happy but hapless characters intrude into the realm of the Dead as the narrative continues to follow the plot of book 11 of the *Odyssey* on which Pound's first canto is based.

The beginning of *Dakota* is relatively easy to read. The audiovisual perfor-mance of numbers, text, and music sets a slow, steady pace that establishes a solid rhythm for the narrative. The selection of jazz furthers the connection to modern-ism, since jazz is the musical and historical counterpart of literary modernism.[19] The centrality of music in this work also furthers the connection to Pound, who perceived an intimate connection between poetry and music. Pound worked as a music critic in London, and he admired the ancient traditions of Homer and the provençal troubadours, for "both in Greece and in Provence the poetry attained its highest rhythmic and metrical brilliance at times when the arts of verse and music were most closely knit together."[20] He supposedly even envisioned *The Cantos* as following the musical structure of a fugue.[21] Soon after its opening, after the reader has settled into a pace for reading *Dakota*, something changes. Blakey's drums quicken and the narrative begins to flash at heightened speeds. The shift in pace and sound produces a frenzied affect and sense of information overload that stuns the reader. *Dakota* runs nearly six minutes, and, like the opening cantos in Pound's work, the beginning of *Dakota* does not prepare the reader for the experimenta-tion that comes next.

Whereas Pound's alterations to his source material are mostly formal—remaking the ancient epic into a decisively modern poem—YHCHI alter the content in such dramatic ways that the literary parallels are visible only to the reader willing to carefully compare the texts and tease out the intertextual allusions. In this digi-tal remix,[22] the characters start drinking, pounding beers until the word "BEER" covers the screen and shakes for a few seconds while the screen flickers between white and black. Then, a visual reprieve: "(BURP.)." In the midst of the joys of drinking, smoking, talking about sex, and insulting each other's mothers, anxiety seeps in. The "WHØØPIN'—N'—HØLLERIN'" from the beginning of the road trip shifts to "FEELING—LIKE—HELL." "BEER" becomes "BEER—IN—ØNE—HAND—BØURBON—IN—THE—ØTHER." Violence erupts in recollections of an accident and a dead friend: a guy from the old gang was "SHØT—DEAD," and the narrator "DIDN'T—EVEN—GØ—TØ—HIS—FUNERAL." The narrative describing cruising under a "HØT SUN" transitions into tragedy with deepened drumbeats. All of this follows the canto, wherein Odysseus, while in the Underworld, encounters dead soldiers, friends from war: "Men many, mauled with bronze lance heads,/Battle spoil, bearing yet dreory arms,/These many crowded about me; with shouting."[23] The dead men are bloody reminders of the wars that shaped Western civilization. Similarly, *Dakota*'s narrator stands in a dark American landscape riddled with a bloody history of battles to "win" the West and "civilize" its native peoples. In the land of the Dead, Odysseus is visited by Elpenor, "our friend Elpenor, / Unburied, cast on the wide earth, / Limbs that we left in the house of Circe, / Unwept, unwrapped in sepulchre, since toils urged other."[24] *Dakota*'s narrator also encounters a forgotten ghost from his own past. The shade of Elie (hear "Elpenor") appears, "ALL BLØØDY" like the last time the narrator saw him. Elie speaks in a series of quick frames: "I—DIDN'T—EVEN—HAVE—THE—GUN—BUT—I—TØØK—THE—BULLET." Like Elpenor, who suffers "Ill fate" and begs of Odysseus, " 'O King, I bid remember me,'"[25] Elie also fears being forgotten: "NØBØDY—LIKE—ME—AND—ALREADY—FØRGØTTEN." He attests, "NØW—I'M—IN—HELL." Then, faithfully following Pound's (and Homer's) text wherein Elpenor's visit is followed by the appearance of Odysseus's mother—"And Anticlea came, whom I beat off"[26]—so too, in *Dakota*, is the text describing abject Elie replaced onscreen by, "THEN—MY—MØM—SHØWED—UP—BUT—I—TØLD—HER—TØ—LAY—ØFF." *Dakota*'s plot carefully overlays book 11 of the Odyssey and Pound's revision of it, and the comparisons are extensive and ripe. However, *Dakota* does not easily divest itself of these intertextual connections. It is through careful close reading and rereading that the palimpsestic layers emerge.

Reading this way illuminates the decisive transformations in *Dakota*'s contemporary remaking of the modernist text. Consider, for example, the shift in the identity of Tiresias, the seer Odysseus travels to the Underworld to see. In *Dakota*'s adaptation Tiresias is reinvented into a twentieth-century cultural icon: Elvis. The name, displayed in oversized letters, throbs hypnotically at the center of the screen, occupying more screen time than any other word in *Dakota*. It is a sentence in and of itself. Just as Odysseus gives Tiresias a bloody elixir to drink to elicit his instructions on how to return to Ithaca, *Dakota*'s protagonist saves his last swig of beer for "ELVIS." Elvis appears "HØLDING—HIS—GUITAR," just as Tiresias holds his scepter. He is still "The King," not yet the bloated figure of wasted youth whose humanness tarnished the icon. This is the young Elvis,

"ELVIS—ØF—MEMPHIS," and the distinction is important to *Dakota*'s narrator who is himself conscious of "GETTING—ØLD—FAST" and obsessed with the being one of the "LØST—SØULS—ØF—LØST—YØUTH." The insistent figuration of the young Elvis, whose metamorphosis the reader (now in the role as seer) foresees, personifies the narrative's sense of wastedness: a wasted landscape (full of "TUMBLE- / WEED TRASH"), occupied by wasted (drunken) characters, cursing their wasted futures ("SMASHED—BØTTLE—AFTER—BØTTLE, —BRØWN—GLASS—ØN—ASPHALT. —THREW UP, —CURSED—FATE"). The sense of being wasted is furthered by the presentation of the text, which speeds by in a steady stream and wastes the reader's opportunity to catch all the words. *Dakota* depicts this wastedness not as a symptom of that which has been completely destroyed but rather, as in T. S. Eliot's *The Waste Land* (on which Pound's editorial contributions earned him the dedication *il miglior fabbro*), as the ashes from which new literature, phoenix-like, arises.

The transformation of Tiresias into Elvis and, indeed, the entire adaptation of the Homeric journey into an American road trip, is a playful and poignant adaptation that begs the question: is *Dakota* parody or pastiche?[27] *Dakota* presents itself as high art and mass media, remediation and retro-chic, and it reveals in these convergences. The single words and phrases—written in simple, colloquial language—are digested easily, but they are also layered with allusions that ask to be deeply mined. The clichéd scenes of male bonding and Americana can be read as simple stereotypes or complex critiques of the globalization of consumer culture. *Dakota* provides for and provokes multiple forms of address, and YHCHI enjoy the confusion their work presents: "some see it as poetry, others as pornography."[28] Evidence of the challenge *Dakota* poses to traditional aesthetic categorization is apparent in the various types of venues and exhibitions that have displayed the work. Aside from its availability (for free) on YHCHI's website, *Dakota* has been exhibited as visual art at the Whitney Museum in New York and the Museum of Contemporary Art in Athens, as part of film series at the Getty Museum in Los Angeles, and as literature in THE *Iowa Review Web* and *Poemsthatgo.com*.[29] YHCHI position their art at the cusp of high and low culture where it straddles the boundaries between modernism and postmodernism just as it challenges generic distinctions between literature and film, prose and poetry.

After all, *Dakota* is both prose and poetry. Its linear narrative is a flashing performance set to music that produces a poetic rhythm; its onscreen presentation of single words, phrases, and multiple lines of text create line breaks and enjambment while also presenting a linear narrative. *Dakota* can also be considered cinema by virtue of the fact that it is built in Flash. Yet YHCHI resist such medium-based designations: "At first, we didn't realize we were creating an animation. But it seems that by a certain new-media-art definition of things, when you use Flash you're doing animation."[30] Expressing their distrust of easy categorizations, YHCHI are aligned with Pound, who viewed genre distinctions as "rubber-bag categories" that academics use to "limit their reference and interest."[31] Part of YHCHI's strategy is to disturb the ability to limit *Dakota*—to unsettle the hinge on which rests the door dividing literature from film, reading from viewing, modernism from contemporary, digital literature.

Super-Position

YHCHI not only adapt a modernist text but also a formal technique, and they take both from Pound. *Dakota*'s formal aesthetic is not solely located in the speed of its flashing animation but also in the ways in which this animation operates through the cinematic technique of montage. Words and phrases flash onscreen, serially replacing previous text to produce multiple and layered meanings through juxtaposition. This montage aesthetic is normally attributed to Sergei Eisenstein's innovation in cinematic montage. In 1929 Eisenstein explains that in montage "each sequential element is perceived not *next* to the other, but on *top* of the other" (emphasis in original).[32] The resulting effect, he writes, "comes not from the simple sequence of the film strips, but from their actual simultaneity, resulting from the impression derived from one strip being mentally superimposed over the following strip."[33] In Eisenstein's explanation, montage creates from discrete elements something "*qualitatively* distinguishable from each component element viewed separately" so that "*two film pieces of any kind, placed together, inevitably combine into a new concept, a new quality, arising out of that juxtaposition.*" (emphasis in original).[34] But, Eisenstein's writing appears nearly fifteen years after Ezra Pound articulated a similar poetic effect.

In 1912, Ezra Pound described the central dictum of his poetics (and of the early Imagist movement), the "image," as "an intellectual and emotional complex *in an instant of time*" (emphasis added).[35] But by 1916, Pound has transitioned from a poetic practice described as Imagism to Vorticism, and he named his new poetic method "super-position."[36] "The 'one image poem,'" he explains, "is no longer just an image or object but, "is a form of *super-position*, that is to say, it is *one idea set on top of another*" (emphasis added).[37] This "super-position" is an accumulation of images, a "ply over ply" technique, to extract a quote from "Canto IV."[38] Laszlo Gefin calls this effect "the most important methodological achievement of modernist poetics."[39] Pound's "super-position" is the literary equivalent of cinematic montage, and this recognition serves to link Pound to YHCHI's experiments in textual montage[40]

As I discussed in Chapter one, Marshall McLuhan wrote to Pound (in 1948) to observe, "Your *Cantos*, I now judge to be the first and only serious use of the great technical possibilities of the cinematograph. Am I right in thinking of them as a *montage* of personae and sculptured images? Flash-backs providing perceptions of *simultaneities*?"[41] McLuhan's inquiry provides insightful keywords for understanding the poetic of textual montage that appears in Pound's poetry, in Eisenstein's writing about new cinematic techniques, and in YHCHI's digital works: "montage" and "simultaneity." Recall that "simultaneity" is a central concept and term in McLuhan's media theory; it describes the affect of the electric age and the aesthetic produced by modernist literature. Pound experimented with ways of capturing an aesthetic of simultaneity in printed poetry, and the result became a cornerstone of his poetic practice: super-position. Super-position is exemplified in Pound's most famous poem, "In a Station of the Metro," particularly as it appears in its first published version (in *Poetry* 1913). The poem juxtaposes lexical units in both aural and visual ways to create poetic tension. The two lines that comprise the poem operate through a montage effect: the second line replaces the content of the first in ways that reframe the first line and promote reconsideration of it. The semicolon that sutures the lines does so in a cinematic sense, for, in film theory, "suture" describes the act of masking the mechanical apparatus involved in producing the imaginary (and the desire and aesthetic it presents).[42]

YHCHI adapt super-position and simultaneity into a software program that remediates the filmic medium but does not actually operate through the replacement of photograms or similar units. The authors build all of their digital works in the popular proprietary authoring tool Flash by Macromedia, a program for producing animations. YHCHI uses Flash to pursue minimalistic simplicity, even though Flash is a medium that enables extensive, multimedia animations. Flash is marketed as "the industry's most advanced authoring environment for creating interactive websites, digital experiences and mobile content."[43] YHCHI employ this software extolled for enabling "mobile content"—meaning that Flash makes it easy to adapt and interact with content across various media forms and technologies—to create an aesthetic of difficulty through an experience of visual illegibility. Although YHCHI's works are textual animations, they do not utilize the platform's trademark functions: seamless animations of moving, multimedia images and interactive effects. Instead they employ Flash to focus on text and typography in a performance of cinematic, textual montage.

Flash is part of a family of animation software or 3D modeling programs that uses a timeline-and-scene cinematic paradigm. The authoring tool employs the metaphor and methodology of film to remediate this analog medium into the creation of web-based animations. Its interface depicts a timeline of cells that collectively comprise the "movie." But this act of backward-remediation only serves to facilitate the ease of its use, for Flash is technically noncinematic. The authorware distinguishes itself from bitmap-based programs like Director that create images through the composition of discrete, cell-like pixels because Flash is a vector-based tool. In other words, the comparison between film and Flash stops at its mediating metaphors. Flash uses the metaphor of film as an approachable interface for the creation of digital animations, but these movies are not based on the serial replacement of the photogram. YHCHI use this vector-based software against its will to highlight the role of the nonexistent frame in their textual montages. In so doing, they use Flash in a fashioned act of resistance to counter enthusiasm for the latest and newest through a retroaesthetic that resituates our readings of electronic literature in a literary tradition extending back to modernism and its mass media. Reading *Dakota* in this context exposes a formal genealogy of artistic acts connecting Pound's super-position to Eisenstein's montage to YHCHI's flashing digital poetics and thus provides a way to reading between text, film, and digital art.

The effects of YHCHI's digital super-position become particularly apparent after Elvis enters the narrative action. *Dakota* follows Pound's first canto and then quickly transitions from a linear narrative to something decisively different. The text shifts from Canto I to Canto II and moves toward an aesthetic more akin to postmodernism or, more appropriately, post-postmodernism than modernism. Blakey's drum solo is pierced by voices, applause, and other sounds of "liveness."[44]The work turns toward self-reflexive performativity. The text reaches heightened speeds, and the story of a teenage road trip frays into fragmentation. The screen flashes "WHAT THE?" The audience begins to cheer, and its chant is folded into Blakey's drumming. Blakey is now playing not only on the narrator's car radio but also in a live studio, and this performance is captured in a media recording to which the reader listens and in a photograph that the narrator describes: Blakey "WØRE A / WHITE SHIRT—WITH / RØLLED UP / SLEEVES—AND A TIE / THRØUGH- / ØUT." These quick, ekphrastic phrases flash while voices shout out in response to Blakey's jam session, seeming to propel his improvisation. Even in the midst of this mediatized performance, ties to Pound's *Cantos* remain visible. Pound's second canto begins "Hang it all, Robert Browning, /There can be but the one 'Sordello.'"[45] In *Dakota*'s second half, the address to Browning is supplanted by one to Blakey: "GØDDAMMITT, / ART BLAKEY" and continues, "IT MAKES / YØU THE /—ØNLY ART / BLAKEY."[46] And then, in this eruption of simulated liveness enabled by real-time media, there is a reflexive shift: the narrator and the reader both listen to Blakey's performance "NØT IN DETRØIT—ØR IN A / RECØRDING / STUDIØ—IN NEW / JERSEY, BUT—RIGHT—HERE!" Speed complicates the last monosyllabic word: "HERE!" is followed by, "I—MEAN—HØNESTLY,—IN PALPAN- / DØNG!" Palpan-Dong is a street in Seoul, South Korea, the home of YHCHI. The sequence opens up *Dakota* to narrative interpretations not previously apparent: is the narrator located in Seoul and listening to Blakey while fantasizing about an American road trip?

Identifying the journey as a mental one of cultural "passing" might explain the references to clichéd Americana—besides Elvis and Marilyn Monroe, beer and the Badlands, the narrator and his buddies "ATE—SØME—HAM—AND— CHEESE—SANDWICHES"—but such a reading simply swaps one subject identity (American) with another (Korean) in a replacement that does not allow for the cumulative construction and complexity of *Dakota*'s layered aesthetic and super-position. Indeed, although the text supplies support for locating the narrator in Seoul, the details are stereotypical Orientalist tropes that balance out the American ones. For example, "WHILE IN / THE STREET / BELØW" the narrator catches glimpses of "SØUSED / EXECUTIVES—FRØM / KANGNAM" and "GISEINGS—(KØREAN / GEISHAS)—WHØM THE /EXECUTIVES—PAY A LØT / TØ LAUGH—AT THEIR / EVERY—LAME / JØKE." An earlier narrative detail further complicates the conclusion that the narrator is watching Korean executives from a window by hinting at another way to locate the speaker. The following lines are dumped into a sentence as a narrative aside and are nearly eclipsed by the speed at which they appear: "LIKE AT A / BARBECUE—BACK IN—SIØUX FALLS, —WE DUMPED—ØUT —GARBAGE—AND BRØKE—BØTTLES." The text describes a time when the narrator was in South Dakota, a fact that complicates the identity, and particularly the racial identity, of the narrator: is he Native American, living on the "BLACKFØØT/RESERVATIØN" rather than just driving by it? *Dakota* refuses to divulge clear answers, leaving the narrator's identity and location ambiguous because "RIGHT—HERE!" is where the narrator hears Blakey play, and in a world of mobile media and streaming data, "HERE" cannot be confined to either South Dakota or Seoul, for "HERE" also refers to the computer on which the Blakey and *Dakota* play.

In the age of computers, when discrete media forms such as music and photographs are subsumed into a digital format, "HERE" means that Blakey's recording and the digital work for which it provides the beat is actually happening "RIGHT—HERE!" on the reader's networked computer. *Dakota* performs in real-time through a series of interactions across programming and binary code, authoring software and hardware. Wherever the reading machine is, that is where the work is happening and where Blakey's recording is playing. As *Dakota* nears its end, the work abandons any sense of a linear narrative and the lyrical voice presenting it. The individual speaker becomes multiple, "WE—BLARE—THE—TUNES—TØ—RØUSE—NØ—ØNE—BUT—ØURSELVES." *Dakota* moves away from the modernist model of an individual, alienated consciousness to a post-postmodern or posthuman model in which identity is distributed across and informed by network technologies.[47] Its protagonist is neither American nor South Korean but constituted by both places and both cultures simultaneously *through* the networked computer.

In *Dakota*'s digital present, which the narrative describes as "RIGHT—HERE!," identity is constructed through media technologies. This is true for the narrator and also for his gods. *Dakota* supplants Aphrodite, who appears at the end of Pound's first canto, with the screen goddess "MARILYN," whose domain is not the heavens but celluloid: "YØU ØWNED / THE—SILVER / SCREEN—CLØTHED / ØR NAKED, —. . . ØR / STANDING / ØVER—AN AIR- / SHAFT / GRATE, — MAKING / LØVE—TØ THE / CAMERA—IN TECH- / NICØLØR- -." The theme of metamorphosis concludes Pound's second canto with the biological mutation of men into porpoises carries over into *Dakota*. But the digital work presents a transformation of the human through media technologies. "MARILYN" is constituted by the camera just as Blakey plays through recorded "liveness" and is made visible because of an image captured in a photograph. Media also construct and enable the narrator's consciousness in constitutive ways. Regardless of whether the narrator actually drives across the Badlands or fantasizes about doing so from across the ocean in Seoul, the journey that *Dakota* describes is one that crosses cultural, ethnic, and geographic spaces in a manner that is indicative of and enabled by the technology through which *Dakota* operates. YHCHI adapt the Homeric quest for a reader trained as a web surfer rather than warrior, whose contemporary consciousness is shaped by global, transnational economics and digital technologies.

With the climax of the final drum roll, *Dakota* twists into a reflexive loop to address the reader for the first time and include her in the digitally-induced location of "RIGHT—HERE!" In an imagistic style of which Pound would be proud, *Dakota* concludes with words flashing faster than ever before, indeed pushing toward illegibility. The reader's engagement with the text is then brought into question:

BLACK—SAUCE—THAT—CAN'T—BE—NAMED—NØR—
IDENTIFIED—WHEN—TASTED—JUST—MIXED—INTØ—THE—
NØØDLES—WITH—DISPØSABLE—CHØP-STICKS—THEN—
WØLFED—DØWN—WITH—*YØUR*—HEAD—TILTED—TØ—THE—
LEFT—IF—*YØU'RE*—A—RIGHTY

(emphasis added).

As the reader struggles to absorb the text being hurled at her, she is implicated in the act of consuming the work. She is figured as literally eating a foreign substance speedily without identifying the food she ingests. The scene of consumption depicts the reader ingesting streams of noodles just as she absorbs flashing text streaming through the bandwidth of her computer. Interspersed in this final sputter of speeding text, the screen flickers with a grey background. The detail is a quick reference to the loading sequence at the beginning of *Dakota*. John Zuern reads the return of the grey screens as an intertextual reference that, appropriately for *Dakota*, conveys multiple levels of meaning: it loops back to the opening moments of *Dakota* and to its proclaimed source material but also serves as an "invocation by the reader's browser and its entry into the data-stream."[48] The barely noticeable, flashing grey screens situate *Dakota* in relation to its primary source material and its subject matter, Pound's first cantos, but also to the networked computer and its user/reader. Whereas the undulation of flashing grey in the opening screens served to veil the material fact that the Flash work needed time to load, the grey screens at the end are purely aesthetic. Their purpose is not only intertextual but also metaphoric: rather than load the work, they load the reader into the work. *Dakota* identifies the reader as participating in the convergence of "HERE"-ness and real-time-ness that is part of the digital work's material processing and networked poetics.

While *Dakota*'s narrator "wolfed down" images of Elvis and Marilyn Monroe, the reader "WØLFED—DØWN" the flashing text. All of this happens "RIGHT—HERE!" where Blakey plays on "YØUR" computer, before which the reader sits far back in her chair struggling to read *Dakota*'s large font flashing onscreen. In its final flashing moments, *Dakota* reminds the reader that digital literature is a performance happening across codes and platforms in the moment of interaction and that she is part of this process. Mark B. N. Hansen argues that digital art depends on the reader's body for emergence because the digital "'image' has itself become a process and, as such, has become irreducibly bound up with the activity of the body."[49] *Dakota* flashes onscreen and all over the reader's eyes; it consumes the reader's unblinking attention as the reader consumes the work. The final lines of *Dakota*'s text address not only the reader but also the kind of reading experience she has practiced for 5:56 minutes. The work concludes with the mention of "BLACK—SAUCE—THAT—CAN'T—BE—NAMED—NØR—IDENTIFIED" and the "DISPØSABLE—CHØP-STICKS" that help one to eat by "WØLF[ing]—DØWN" the food rather than savoring it. The effect ends *Dakota* by fostering an uneasiness about the kind of eating practice the work depicts and the kind of reading practice it demands. Specifically, is this active or passive reading? "Active" is an adjective often used to qualify close reading, while "passive" is its opposite; so the question of whether *Dakota* promotes active or passive reading is part of determining why and how YHCHI assert a connection to modernism. With its last screens, *Dakota*, which its authors ally with high modernism, is now depicted as fast food that the reader consumes. This begs the question: should *Dakota* be aligned with lean, mean modernism or mass culture's fast food? To answer this question, I return to YHCHI's claim that *Dakota* is based on a close reading of Pound's first two cantos, ready to recognize it as a framing device rather than a fact and, thus, a strategic act of digital modernism.

Part II. Reading against the Grain of YHCHI's Claim

For a reader who does not transcribe the text or choose to compare it to Pound's cantos I and II, *Dakota*'s blaring manifesto visual style, jazz soundtrack, and narrative ethos might invoke a very different literary lineage than the one claimed by its authors. In particular, its narrative about a youthful road trip across the United States might bring to mind Jack Kerouac's *On the Road* (1957). *Dakota* recounts such Kerouacian subject matter as male friendship, drunken hallucinations, and sexual exploits. The work presents the tone of beatness that John Clellon Holmes describes in his manifesto "This is the Beat Generation" (1952): "A man is beat whenever he goes for broke and wagers the sum of his resources on a single number."[50] *Dakota*'s protagonist wagers his resources on a road trip that will take him away from his own demons, but this effort leaves the narrator and his buddies "FEELING—LIKE—HELL,—SØRRY/ FOR—ØURSELVES." Blakey's drums lay down the beat of this beaten-down tone in a recording whose date, 1962, is contemporaneous with the period of the Beats and Hard Bop rather than Pound and modernist jazz. In the second half of the work, when the soundtrack registers the sounds of a live audience, the music unleashes further connections to the characteristically oral and improvised performativity of Beat poetry.

The road trip narratives of *Dakota* and *On the Road* share a tone of hyper-masculinity and its failure. The shocking profanity that opens *Dakota* and is sprinkled throughout its text expresses dissatisfaction with the constraints of gendered stereotypes and their expectations. For example, when the narrator fantasizes about Marilyn Monroe, the text registers an overt showmanship of sexual desire that expresses a forced and performative display of masculinity. The screen flashes "NØRMA—JEAN,—EXCUSE MY / FRENCH—WHAT A / PIECE / ØF ASS." Instead of sexual potency, however, the narrator recalls that he "FAILED TO SHØØT—A BIG WAD." Similarly, Elie laments not only his premature death and being forgotten, but that he "NEVER / EVEN—GØT / LAID—JUST—A—HAND—JØB—BUT—A—GØØD—ØNE." The presentation of Elie's lament distinguishes his admission that he never got laid from his claim about the value of his single sexual experience. The first part, "NEVER / EVEN—GØT / LAID," presents enjambment on screen, denoting connection between the words that is supported by the fact that the first screen is replaced by the second at a leisurely speed and in a shared beat. In contrast, the text that follows sputters out single words at a time at heightened speeds. The animation of textual ejaculation undercuts the hyperness of the language, revealing it to be just hype.

Throughout *Dakota* the speed of flashing text modulates to complicate moments of macho bravado that the text depicts and in ways that update Pound's super-position. For example, when "I CRIED" rests on screen, emotive despair is presented as a visual sigh. The words settle onscreen for a momentary reprieve. But consecutive screens confuse this initial sense of self-expression and release. "I CRIED" is followed by "TØ THE GUYS" and then, faster, "TØ GET SMASHED." The speeding, textual montage of these phrases generates a variety of meanings: is the narrator crying or yelling, expressing vulnerability or evading it through drunkenness? Is this a moment of male bonding and connection or its refusal? Later, another important narrative moment from the protagonist's memory is similarly obscured and opened to interpretations. "GANG" is followed by "BANG," and the juxtaposition provokes disturbing and unanswered questions about the violent event: does it describe an onomatopoetic shooting or a group rape? These instances depict the doubleness that is constitutive of the definition of "Beat," the energetic rhythm that propels the poetry and the voices of the discontent that the beat down tone registers. Additionally, the poetic effect of replacing words onscreen registers a sense of layered meanings and palimpsestic connections, from modernism through the Beats and beyond. This layering serves figuratively and formally, as in the technique of super-position, to associate *Dakota* with multiple intertextual possibilities and perspectives for interpretation.

Rather than aligning their work with Sal Paradise's bohemian wanderings, however, YHCHI assert a connection to Odysseus's journey back to Ithaca through Pound's recasting of the classical epic into modernist poetry. YHCHI use *The Cantos* similarly to how Pound uses Homer's *Odyssey*: to lay claim to an ancient cultural past as scaffolding to support a contemporary literary moment and recuperate the relevance of literature in it. For YHCHI, this past is not located in the literature of ancient Greece or the songs of medieval provençal troubadours but in the writings of the first electric age, the modernist period. As I argued in this book's Introduction, the modernist period has been identified as the origin of a new media epoch by a diverse array of scholars, including Stephen Kern, Friedrich Kittler, Lev Manovich, and Marshall McLuhan. By identifying a modernist source as the inspiration for their digital creation, YHCHI draw upon a past that, although not ancient, is the origin of their aesthetic and technological present.

YHCHI articulate a connection with literary modernism in spite of, and indeed because of, *Dakota*'s more obvious connections to Kerouac and postmodernism. They do so, I argue, in order to invigorate the current state of electronic literature. YHCHI's authorial claim encourages readers not only to approach *Dakota* in relation to Pound's adaptation of classical antiquity but also to examine the reasons for this pursuit. Doing so exposes how such acts of return prove relevant, both to modernism and to digital modernism. Carroll Terrell offers an explanation for the reason Pound's modernist epic opens with the particular scene from Homer's ancient text, and the interpretation elucidates YHCHI's similar selection of *The Cantos* as its source of inspiration. Terrell identifies the reference to Ithaca in Pound's first canto as a counterbalance to Troy, the city that Odysseus helped to destroy. "The epic 'nostos' ['return journey'] of *The Cantos* is," Terrell writes, "polarized between the destruction and the rediscovery of civilization and sovereignty."[51] Pound employs this epic situation of historical tension as a metaphoric parallel to his own cultural moment, recuperating it as a means of producing such influential, lasting literature as Homer's *Odyssey*.[52] A similar moment motivates YHCHI and digital modernism more generally, and it inspires YHCHI's balanced relationship to Pound and Kerouac. *Dakota* is poised at a balance of "destruction" and "rediscovery" in relation to its literary past and present. Instead of the cataclysmic end of print that many prophesied the digital age and electronic literature would induce, *Dakota* exposes how digital literature can follow modernism to rediscover a canonical past through contemporary media and reclaim an investment in the power and potential of literature. It does do by inviting and rewarding close reading.

The Difficulty of Close Reading and the Purpose of Difficulty

Dakota is supposedly based on a close reading, but close reading is something that the work strives to subvert. *Dakota* uses speed to produce difficulty through illegibility. In its pursuit of difficulty, the digital work follows its source material; for *The Cantos* are also famously resistant to interpretation. Donald Davie writes, "Pound seems to have had before him, as one main objective, the baffling and defeating of commentators and exegetes."[53] Pound's famous line from "Canto CXVI," "I cannot make it cohere," has become a tagline of sorts for the experience of reading *The Cantos* (and other works of high modernist literature). It is a mantra that YHCHI take up. Just as Pound claims that "the work of art which is most 'worth-while' is the work which would need a hundred works of any other kind of art to explain it," so too do YHCHI state, "We present our work the way we do to make it indeed more difficult."[54] As is particularly and painfully obvious to *Dakota*'s dry-eyed and unblinking reader, speed is used as a technical tool to enhance the work's difficulty.

The intentional use of difficulty as an aesthetic strategy bonds *Dakota* to modernism and the kind of reading practices its literature fostered. John Guillory explains that the canonization of modernism by the New Critics depended on the difficulty of these texts, so that "difficulty itself was positively valued in New Critical practice, that it was a form of cultural capital."[55] Leonard Diepeveen identifies difficulty as "a litmus test" not only for the literary work but also for the reader, a test through which "one could predict both a given reader's response to modernism by his or her reaction to difficulty, and a writer's place in the canon by the difficulty of his or her work."[56] The difficulty of these modernist texts served to create a particular class of readers, professionals who could produce interpretations of these texts through the structured methodology of close reading.[57] In this book's Introduction, I discussed the role of close reading in the New Criticism and in the emergence of literary criticism as a discipline. I also commented on the fact that the New Critical method has rightly been critiqued for its insular focus on the text as an isolated object and the conservative politics endemic to such a perspective, but that these critiques themselves deserve consideration. It is worth repeating these points in order to clarify that by arguing that YHCHI promote close reading, I do not seek to claim that this international, multiethnic partnership created by an American and a South Korean, whose work exists at the margins of traditional literary culture and often explicitly engages with issues of contemporary politics and race, should be read in the vein of the New Criticism as it developed in the 1930s and '40s.[58] Instead, I am suggesting that YHCHI's claim that *Dakota* is based on a close reading serves to focus attention on the literary nature of their text—its intertextuality and inherited poetics—rather than on other possible elements of the work, including design, programming code, music, etc. Moreover, such a focus promotes the renovation of close reading to attend to digital, networked literature like *Dakota*.

To reproduce a quote used earlier in this chapter, Young-hae Chang articulates her artistic mission as an attempt to illuminate the role of text in digital art: "Strip away the interactivity, the graphics, the design, the photos, the banners, the colors, the fonts and the rest, and what's left? The text."[59] But, *Dakota*'s text cannot be stripped away from its design, font, animation, and music. Further, because it is programmed in Flash, its source code remains inaccessible to the reader, so its narrative text cannot be easily cut and pasted into a Word document. And, because it exists online, *Dakota*'s speeding aesthetic is determined by the networked configuration of the reader's computer and Internet connection. The work's multimodal performance depends upon the specificities of hardware, software, and network settings to make it run. As I showed, YHCHI exploit this media-specific situation to produce a formal poetic that is decidedly digital. This work, and others like it, exploits the affordances of digital media in order to insist on the importance of their textual poetics. Close reading the media-specific aspects of such works means approaching them through not only technological but also cultural, historical, and political perspectives. *Dakota* thus promotes and complicates the practice of close reading that has been passed down from modernism through postmodernism and poststructuralism, and it does so in order to focus critical attention on how this central literary activity must evolve and adapt.

YHCHI's statement that *Dakota* is "based on a close reading" demands that we read *Dakota* in relation to *The Cantos* and at the same time reflexively reassess our own close reading practices. Specifically, YHCHI's challenge presents an opportunity to consider the efficacy of applying the print-based standard of literary criticism, close reading, to electronic literature. *Dakota* provides a subtle piece of support for this interpretation in its final seconds. As the text races toward its ending, it finally drops the name of its modernist persona, Pound. The name appears in the midst of a collage of fragments flashing at nearly illegible speeds: "FUCK—YØU, — ELLMANN, — THAT'S / RIGHT, —RICHARD—ELLMANN— NØRTØN, —NEW YØRK—1973,—ØN—PØUND." Pound is named in an affront on Richard Ellmann, the literary scholar and famous biographer of James Joyce, who, along with Robert O'Clair, edited the *Norton Anthology of Modern Poetry* (1973), which contained Pound's cantos I and II. The identification of and attack on the editor of *Dakota*'s source material continues YHCHI's adaptation of Pound's "Canto I." The first canto nears its end by invoking the medieval mediator who translated Homer into the text that Pound adapts: "Lie quiet Divus. I mean, that is Andreas Divus, / In officina Wecheli, 1538, out of Homer."[60] YHCHI's invective against Ellmann also raises questions about the acts of excerpting, explaining, and close reading, all of which Ellmann does in his introduction and explanatory footnotes to cantos I and II in the *Norton*.[61] Ellmann's first footnote to "Canto I" asserts the following: "For Pound, Odysseus is the type of enterprising, imaginative man, and this voyage represents in some sense a symbol or analogy of the poet's own voyage into the darker aspects of his civilization or the buried places of the mind."[62] Ellmann's explanation of what Odysseus represents is precisely the type of reading practice that *Dakota*'s speeding text evades: clear equations and analogies between text and meaning, type or symbol and their representation.

Dakota's defamation of the modernist scholar is a final act of paradoxical doubleness that both invites and refutes close reading. *Dakota* demands to be read by such critics as Ellmann, readers who will pursue connections between the digital and modernist texts, but it also warns against readings that derive simple correspondences and explanations. This final detail and dig at Ellmann prompts readers who recognize his name—and thus possess a certain knowledge of literary criticism and a modernist cultural cache—to closely read the text and consider why Ellmann might represent an outmoded and flawed reading practice. As this final example shows, close reading is *Dakota*'s subtext. Close reading *Dakota* illuminates how this central critical technique of literary study is being pushed by electronic literature to evolve in medium-specific ways.

Part III. "So that:"

The first canto concludes with the phrase "So that:"[63] The fragment does not lead into the second canto, which begins with a new narrator and narrative situation, but rather gestures to future additions and responses. The colon represents the act of rupture and the promise of continuation, a challenge to which *Dakota* rises. The end of the second canto similarly concludes with "And . . ." (ellipses original).[64] "And" is the first word of each preceding line in the last stanza. Its repetition creates a cycle that concludes "Canto II" with the same conjunctive word followed by an ellipsis, a grammatical mark signifying potential amendment and continuation. Instead of a colon or ellipsis, *Dakota*'s last word is followed by a period, but that is not the end of its programming. The work is programmed to reload and replay. After the last words dissolve on the white screen, *Dakota* begins again. This programming detail follows the end of Pound's first two cantos by providing a promise of continuation, but it also identifies *Dakota* as a self-contained and separate file from the hyperlinked network on which it is housed and accessed.

This assertion of autonomy aligns *Dakota* with the New Critical view of the poem as an autonomous art object and with Adorno's characterization of modernist art.[65] Yet, as I have argued, its digital and web-based nature also challenges such claims. *Dakota*'s final programming detail presents an affiliation with Michael Fried's version of this idea, in which the artwork (modernist painting, for Fried) achieves autonomy by rejecting its "objecthood" and accepting a "self-imposed imperative that it defeat or suspend its own objecthood through the medium of shape."[66] *Dakota* defeats its status as a digital "object" by refusing interactivity and rejecting instrumentality down to its very last moments. The final loop is the result of a default programming line coded into the Flash authorware; an author must designate a stop command to negate the automatic replay of the Flash timeline.[67] The fact that YHCHI do not opt out of this default and instead enable *Dakota* to endlessly replay is significant. YHCHI purposefully suspend *Dakota*'s objecthood through their final poetic decision to enable the loop and replay. They assert *Dakota*'s autonomy in this aesthetic act of insularity that happens, in Fried's words, "through the medium of shape" (i.e., the Flash software).

This act of automatic replay also posits a final connection to cinema, to modernism's new media. Lev Manovich suggests that "the loop" of the celluloid reel is the structural form that "gave birth not only to cinema but also to computer programming."[68] *Dakota*'s ending invokes this relationship to cinema, to its reel and looping operations but also to the aesthetic most associated with it—montage—which, I argued, *Dakota* remediates via Pound's technique of superposition. In a final gesture of autonomy and an alignment with a modernist aesthetic and medial genealogy it remediates, *Dakota* reloads and begins again. It loops back to remediate Pound's first two cantos and to "MAKE IT NEW" in new media.

4. Reading the Database
Narrative, Database, and Stream of Consciousness

One of the central questions facing the humanities in the digital age is the relationship between interpretation and information, between reading and data. In literary studies, this question spurs more specific questions: What constitutes literary data? What methods or modes of interpretation are literary? Can an algorithm, code, software, or hardware generate a close reading? Or, to put it in different terms, does authoring a database—curating materials, determining metadata, and programming the infrastructure—count as scholarship? These questions are increasingly posed to literature departments and their tenure-review committees, particularly as digital archives and databases become the purview not only of librarians but of literary scholars, too.[1] This chapter pursues a particular articulation of a question that has generated much discussion among literary critics: What is the relationship between narrative and the database?

Answers often posit narrative and database in opposition to one another. This view is expressed most famously and provocatively Lev Manovich. "After the novel, and subsequently cinema, privileged narrative as the key form of cultural expression of the modern age," Manovich writes, "the computer age introduces its correlate—the database."[2] Overlooking for a moment Manovich's maddening claim that the novel is outdated, his primary point has merit. He identifies the database as "a new symbolic form of the computer age," and thus one deserving analysis.[3] "As a cultural form," Manovich writes, "the database represents the world as a list of items, and it refuses to order this list. In contrast, a narrative created a cause-and-effect trajectory of seemingly unordered items (events)."[4] For Manovich, database is potential and narrative is its resulting output. "Therefore," he concludes, "database and narrative are natural enemies."[5] But the relationship between narrative and database is not antithetical. Nor is it merely "symbiotic," as Katherine Hayles describes it in her riposte to Ed Folsom (coeditor of the Walt Whitman Archive online) who, in a debate on the topic featured in the October 2007 issue of *PMLA*, builds upon Manovich's provocation.[6] Instead, the relationship between database and narrative, process and product, form and content, is intertwined and inseparable. "[I]mportant as Manovich's analysis has been in launching a productive line of inquiry," Hayles writes, "his construction of the narrative/database dyad is nevertheless plagued by certain intractable problems."[7] These problems are based in a technophilic desire to see difference wherever there's digitality, a desire to claim newness against the tradition of narrative, novels, and literature. These problems are not Manovich's alone but are paradigmatic of a certain kind of present-focused myopia that plagues digital studies. This is why, as Hayles writes, "The centrality of the narrative/database dynamic to new media, and especially to electronic literature, makes rethinking it an urgent concern."[8] In this chapter I seek to rethink the dyad by turning, yes, to literature.

As you might expect from previous chapters, I examine works of digital literature that adapt modernism in ways that provide new perspectives on the relationship between narrative and database, poetics and data. Literature, of the digital present and the modernist past, provides insights into this discourse by illuminating the structural opposition between information and interpretation, data and analysis, and by inviting deconstruction of it. While previous chapters traced the histories of specific digital poetics and critical reading practices back to modernism, this chapter explores the place where narrative and database overlap, intersect, and converge: namely, where cognition is represented as being accessible. With the help of a few works of digital literature, I trace the question about the relationship between narrative and database back to a single modernist text: James Joyce's *Ulysses*. Reading between *Ulysses* and the digital works I will introduce shortly, I focus on a topic that undergirds and connects literary experimentation and database engineering: the ambition to present and represent cognition with and through media.

Databases are not just repositories for storing data; they are structures that organize, prioritize, and shape information. Their mediation has meaningful impact on how information is processed, presented, and understood. In other words, databases are not just digital memory banks; they also influence human memory and cognition. Databases are increasingly used in digital literature, and such artistic contexts expose how the formal constraints of databases affect poetics and thus deserve analysis. It is not my intention to close read actual databases in this chapter but rather to show how literary works invite and promote such examination. I navigate between literary texts and media history, and the result may read more like a hypertext or McLuhan-esque exploration than a linear argument. But I do have compass and cornerstone for this exploration, a single modernist novel. *Ulysses* is an obvious source of inspiration for digital modernism. Joyce pursues the same strategy that contemporary digital writers take up: *Ulysses* renovates a text from the canonical literary past (Homer's *The Odyssey*) and experiments with remediating that older work into a different medial format (from oral epic to print codex) with the goal of challenging readerly expectations and changing reading practices. Recall the quote from T. S. Eliot that I cited in this book's Introduction, wherein Eliot claims, "in manipulating a continuous parallel between contemporaneity and antiquity, Mr. Joyce is pursuing a method which others must pursue after him."[9] *Ulysses* is a nexus point for this chapter's exploration of the relationship between narrative and database because it contains narrative, database aesthetics, hypertext, and stream of consciousness. Modernist literature developed stream of consciousness, one of the central tools for depicting consciousness in text, and Joyce was one of its primary innovators. In *Ulysses* and other texts, Joyce inspired other literary efforts to depict and extend cognition through literature and through media. This chapter examines digital remixes of *Ulysses* to show how representations of cognition—from digital databases to narrative's stream of consciousness—are always mediated and distributed across technologies.

I begin with a brief look at a work that remediates modernism in order to make visible and poetic the act of technologically mediating consciousness—indeed, to make it tweetable.

Twitter

One hundred years after Leopold Bloom's famous fictional journey around the city of Dublin, a new media experiment celebrated Bloomsday by renovating a section of Joyce's *Ulysses* online. Ian Bogost and Ian McCarthy took the "Wandering Rocks" section of *Ulysses* and turned it into a Twitter performance.[10] As you probably know, Twitter is a microblogging software and online social networking service that allows users to publish short statements online and in real-time. The text, known as "a tweet," is limited to 140 characters and is available to any other user who subscribes to a particular writer's Twitter feeds. Bogost and McCarthy created Twitter accounts for Joyce's main characters and then adapted selected text from *Ulysses* into tweets that they describe as "utterances in the first person."[11] For example, the account named "StephenDedalus" broadcast the following: "STEPHENDEDALUS: I see Dilly's high shoulders and shabby dress, shut the book quick, don't let see."[12] Bogost and McCarthy then "organized and timed these [tweets] and built a database for them."[13] On Bloomsday, they released the stream of tweets and broadcast the database-based performance. (see Figure 4.1.) The literary community largely overlooked this Twitter remix, but I see it as a significant experiment that illuminates digital writers using digital media to explore and renovate modernism, specifically, modernism's stream of consciousness.

As I read it, this Twitter-based remix provides an opportunity to see how Joyce's novel is deeply devoted to experimenting with the medial aspects of print literature, specifically, how media makes accessible and representable the cognitive functioning of one person's unconscious to others. "The result, we hope," Bogost and McCarthy write of their work, "will offer both an interesting and unique perspective on the novel and on Twitter."[14] Providing new ways of understanding digital media *and* modernist literature, works like "Wandering Rocks" perform the dual agenda

Fig 4.1 Screenshot from Ian Bogost and Ian McCarthy, "Wandering Rocks" (2007). (http://twitter.com/STEPHENDEDALUS (October 22, 2012). (Used with permission from the authors.)

of digital modernism. Approaching *Ulysses* and modernism through this Twitter-based experiment, we see how Twitter can be seen as part of a longer genealogy of literary efforts to record the experience of reading someone else's thoughts. For, at the level of spelling and syntax, Twitter operates through constrained poetics: 140 characters per utterance. Twitter also presents the conceit that a tweet is a direct transcription of the writer's thoughts. Tweets are written in the first-person point of view (in answer to the writing prompt, "What's Happening?") and presented as an immediate transcription of cognition in real time.[15] As a result, this digital application can be understood as updating an earlier literary practice that represented human cognition in text—stream of consciousness. Twitter distributes this stream of text thoughts to readers via the web's hypertextual network; and, as I will explain, the web has itself been understood as a structural implementation of associative cognition, a representation of the way the human mind works.

The Twitter-based "Wandering Rocks" project is an interesting conceptual experiment in employing a database to produce stream of consciousness narrative, but it really just serves as this chapter's opening hook. My primary tutor text is a work of digital literature that has already become a staple of the emergent electronic literature canon. Judd Morrissey and Lori Talley's *The Jew's Daughter* (2000) is a web-based novella that updates stream of consciousness by remediating both the printed page and electronic hypertext.[16] As I read it, this work invites readers to trace the subtle changes in literary engagements with database aesthetics between modernism and digital modernism by pushing us to explore the intersections between literary and computing history.

Part I. *The Jew's Daughter*

Remediation

Solid black text rests on a stark white screen. Formatted in a column with justified margins on both sides, the online digital work looks just like a printed page (see Figure 4.2). Remediation is the central operating strategy of *The Jew's Daughter*. The previous two chapters discussed remediation as aesthetic practice—the remediation of a reading machine (Chapter 2) and of a formal poetic technique (Chapter 3). But *The Jew's Daughter* presents one of the most intentional remediations of the printed page in all of digital literature. This feature of the work has attracted critical attention since its publication in 2000. Matthew Mirapaul reviewed the work in *The New York Times* in 2000 (when electronic literature was still a subject of popular interest and discussion in such publications, after Robert

◻

Will she disappear? That day has passed like any other. I said to you, "Be careful. Today is a strange day" and that was the end of it. I had written impassioned letters that expressed the urgency of my situation. I wrote to you that that it would not be forgivable, that it would be a violation of our exchange, in fact, a criminal negligence were I to fail to come through. To hand to you the consecrated sum of your gifts, the secret you imparted persistently and without knowledge, these expressions of your will that lured, and, in a cumulative fashion, became a message. In any case, the way things worked. Incorrigible. Stops and starts, overburdened nerves, cowardice (Is this what they said?), inadequacy, and, as a last resort, an inexplicable refusal. You asked could I build you from a pile of anonymous limbs and parts. I rarely slept and repeatedly during the night, when the moon was in my window, I had a vision of dirt and rocks being poured over my chest by the silver spade of a shovel. And then I would wake up with everything. It was all there like icons contained in a sphere and beginning to fuse together. When I tried to look at it, my eyes burned until I could almost see it in the room like a spectral yellow fire.

A street, a house, a room.

close

Fig 4.2   Screen 1 of Judd Morrissey's *The Jew's Daughter* (2000). (Used with permission from the author.)

Coover's [in]famous "End of Books" [1999]). Mirapaul writes, "At a time when hypertext authors are experimenting with video, 3-D environments and other multimedia elements in order to escape this link-chained cage, Morrissey has returned to the plain, white rectangular page."[17] Mirapaul sees the return to the page as a rebellious act that offers "escape" from the generic constraints of the "link-chained cage" of hyperlink-based hypertext literature (circa the 1990s first generation of electronic literature). Literary critic David Ciccoricco agrees. He describes the aesthetic of remediation in *The Jew's Daughter* as "a distinctly *radical* statement for an artist working in electronic forms," wherein the return to the page is symbolic of "some circuitous movement of history or, at the very least, the movement of a certain irony" (emphasis in original).[18] As I see it, this "circuitous movement of history" is part of a larger cultural artistic strategy that extends beyond this particular work but of which *The Jew's Daughter* is exemplary. For, as I've been presenting it, digital modernism is a conscious act of rebellion that returns to and remediates a modernist past in order to produce a "distinctly radical statement" about the current moment and its literature.

Even before presenting its first lines of text, *The Jew's Daughter* directs attention to the mediated nature of reading. The entry screen presents four options, all of which are active hyperlinks: in addition to clicking on the work's title (which opens to the narrative and the remediated page), the reader can choose "dedication," "colophon," and "page." The codex-based terminology frames the digital work within a context of print technology and book-based reading practices. The reader thus approaches *The Jew's Daughter* with a focus on media, acutely aware that this digital work intends to revel in the ways it is both like and unlike a book. The invocation to the technologies of print also serves as a reminder that books are media and that media shape literature and the reading practices we bring to bear upon it.

But this remediation of print is interrupted by the appearance, on every single "page," of a very unprintlike element. A single blue word stands out from the rest of the paragraph as a visual and recognizable sign of a hyperlink in an online document and an HTML-based hypertext. HTML was the programming language of early web-based electronic hypertexts (circa 1990s). *The Jew's Daughter* is not built in HTML but instead in Flash. And yet, like YHCHI (the focus of the previous chapter), Morrissey deliberately refuses the multimedia possibilities offered by the Flash authorware. He instead opts for a retroaesthetic that promotes association with the printed page or the screen of early hypertext literature. As I mentioned in this book's Introduction, before Flash and the second generation of multimedia electronic literature it inspired, hypertext ruled. It is easy to forget that hypertext, that early form of electronic literature that produced nonlinear storytelling through a link-and-node format of narrative chunks (or lexias), was once proclaimed to be revolutionary. But it was. Hypertexts, some thought, invited active interaction from readers to such an extent that readers became authors. Because readers could "author" their own narrative paths in a hypertext, they could thereby upend hierarchical relationships between author and reader, and more.[19] Such claims have since been challenged and, for the most part, refuted.[20] But *The Jew's Daughter* strategically invokes this early history of electronic literature through its onscreen aesthetic. Exploring why and to what end the Flash-based work pursues connections to print and to HTML opens up ways of seeing how digital modernism illuminates the entwined history of literature and computational media.

The Jew's Daughter looks like a hypertext but refuses to act like one, and this refusal is central to its digital modernist aesthetic. Clicking on or mousing over the blue text in *The Jew's Daughter* does not open a new window, lexia, or URL.

Instead, the screen refreshes and somewhere within the present paragraph, often within a sentence, the text changes. The change is subtle, and the effect is disorienting. When the next flashing replacement of text occurs, it happens in a different place onscreen. Expectations of reader-controlled navigation promoted by allusions to hypertext quickly fade, and the reader is left uncertain about how to proceed in reading this extraordinarily difficult text. I want to suggest that *The Jew's Daughter* produces this intentional dissonance for a specific and, indeed, strategic purpose: it illuminates expectations brought to bear on reading text online, specifically, the residual expectations that hypertext as a literary genre imparted on electronic literature.

The Jew's Daughter is no hypertext. It is strictly linear and is composed of numbered "pages" programmatically set so that each page contains specific content. Its aesthetic of mutating text produces a sense of fluidity and randomness, but the narrative is not algorithmically generated. It is neither open ended nor recombinatorial. The same page always displays the same text and in the same order. But just because *The Jew's Daughter* is not a multidirectional hypertext does not mean that it is easy to read or to understand. Despite its simple interface, *The Jew's Daughter* is one of the most difficult narratives I have ever read onscreen (or off). Its "pages" may appear in a linear order, but the narrative does not unfold clearly. There are many plot twists and narrators, and shifts in dialogue are often not denoted. As a result, it is very hard to know who is speaking, when, and to whom. There are also no quotations separating dialogue, so the narrative weaves in and out of vocalized dialogue and silent soliloquy. But the complexity really escalates when the text mutates. Since characters are often not named, the pronouns denoting them can change with the shift between screens. As a result, something as simple as identifying the subject of a sentence is often impossible, let alone knowing what is happening to whom at any one point in the work.

To cite one example, let's consider the transition between screen one and two. The sentence on the first screen appears as, "I rarely slept and repeatedly during the night, when the moon was in my window, I had a vision of dirt and rocks being poured over my chest by the silver spade of a shovel." After the mutation, the same passage has transformed to the following: "Her face is a pale round moon. She had a vision of dirt and rocks being poured over my chest by the silver spade of a shovel." The change registers a shift in perspective from "I" to "her," and alters the content of the passage from a confession to a narration. Yet the nightmare of being buried alive remains a point of connection between the screens and the two characters, and it leaves the reader with the nightmarish task of determining not only the meaning of the dream but also who dreamt it.

A personal confession: the difficulty of deciphering this work compelled me to undertake dramatic non-media-specific efforts. In order to follow the narrative, I resorted to printing out all of the screens and, on each page, highlighting in one color what text had changed and in a different color which text would change. I also kept a detailed list of notes identifying the main characters. But, even with this skeleton key, I hesitate to attribute proper names to the "anonymous limbs and parts" I collected, assembled, and discuss in this chapter. Morrissey's text is incredibly difficult, and it demands a disciplined reading practice.

The Jew's Daughter presents the reader with content that is hard to access, not because it flashed by too quickly to absorb (as in *Project* or *Dakota*) but because its context keeps changing. The narrative progresses recursively, with each refreshed screen bringing a change of text. The reader struggles to locate where the change of text took place and to read the content in its new context. Anticipating the next change, the reader tries to memorize the text she is currently reading in anticipation of change. For, when the next flashing replacement of text occurs, it happens in a different place onscreen. As the text and its context continues to change, so too does the reader's interpretation of the tale it tells. *The Jew's Daughter* demands a reading practice of constant rereading and thus posits rereading as central to close reading.

Adaptation

Reading *The Jew's Daughter* is challenging not only because of its form but also because its content presents an inspired adaptation of a complex novel from the modernist canon. *The Jew's Daughter* adapts a section from Joyce's *Ulysses*, and the parallels are palpable. Like Joyce's Leopold Bloom, Morrissey's protagonist is an "Irish-Jew" who wears a hat as he meanders, physically and mentally, through his urban landscape. Morrissey's main character is a merger of Leopold Bloom and Stephen Dedalus—he is a writer and a student of literature who walks the streets of Chicago, visiting a coffee shop, bar, library, and subway station, all the while carrying a notebook and making up little rhymes. During his ambulation he encounters people and visits places that stimulate his memories and meditation on a relationship fractured by infidelity. Like Bloom, he carries a racy novel, "the little book in a bag under my arm," for his beloved but adulterous girlfriend, and he maintains hopes of rekindling and redirecting her amorous attention.[21]

Unlike YHCHI's *Dakota*, which is, as I argued in the previous chapter, a faithful adaptation of Pound's first two cantos, Morrissey's digital work takes its inspiration from a modernist source and runs with it. The narrative action is not contained in a single day, as in *Ulysses*, although it is confined to a specific time period: "that was the year I never stopped walking."²² The first screens establish a loose connection to Bloomsday. Screen one states, "That day has passed like any other," while the following screen describes "That day" as Bloomsday (June 16) because "She flew me in on the seventeenth of June." The mention of "She" in the first sentence of the first screen identifies another narrative fulcrum shared by *The Jew's Daughter* and *Ulysses*: an adulterous woman who is only obliquely present in the text but is omnipresent in the protagonist's consciousness. The first line of *The Jew's Daughter* is, "Will she disappear?" The shift to the second screen provides more details about the woman who haunts the narrator's consciousness: "she is still here, dreaming just outside the door, her affirming flesh beached in bed as the windows begin to turn blue." The woman sleeping in bed with "affirming flesh" parallels the reclining figure of Molly Bloom, who, throughout Joyce's massive novel, remains in bed until she delivers its famous last lines of fleshy affirmation: "yes I said yes I will Yes." Like Homer's hero, while Bloom was away on his epic tour, a long day's journey around Dublin, his home and marital bed were usurped by an intruder: his wife's lover, Blazes Boylan. So too in the digital work does the woman's affair throw the protagonist into a psychological tailspin, prompting his trek around the city and the stream of consciousness depicting his scorned, spiraling thoughts. As this wandering writer reads and rereads clues about the affair, the reader follows in a parallel reading practice trying to disentangle real actions from imagined (even paranoid) conceits.

The Jew's Daughter adapts a short section of the much larger chapter, "Ithaca" (Chapter 17). In "Ithaca" Bloom asks Stephen Dedalus to stay the night, and Stephen refuses. Morrissey takes his title from a section wherein Stephen sings to his host a sixteenth-century, anti-Semitic ballad called "The Jew's Daughter."²³ The ballad tells the tale of Little Harry Hughes, a Christian boy who accidentally breaks the Jew's window while playing ball with his friends; in retribution, the Jew's daughter decapitates him.²⁴ This section of "Ithaca" (which I will hereafter refer to as "The Jew's Daughter" section) is, I will argue, centrally concerned with focusing attention on the media involved in cognition. Morrissey's digital work promotes examination of this aspect of Joyce's novel and why it matters. Specifically, "The Jew's Daughter" section of *Ulysses* presents what I'd like to call a "database aesthetic." Indeed, the larger chapter, "Ithaca," proceeds as a query and response format.²⁵ An unknown interlocutor asks a question about the scene and its characters, Bloom and Stephen in Bloom's kitchen, and receives an answer from another disembodied voice. The question, "Did the host encourage his guest to chant in a modulated voice a strange legend on an allied theme?" stimulates the following output of data: "Reassuringly, their place where none could hear them talk being secluded, reassured, the decocted beverages, allowing for subsolid residual sediment of a mechanical mixture, water plus sugar plus cream plus cocoa, having been consumed."[26] The response is both precise and decontextualized, so it answers the question even as it does not close off other conclusions. The response invites uncertainty because it reads as one of many possible answers in a vast pool of potential outcomes. I want to suggest that this section of *Ulysses* resembles a database or, more specifically, it depicts the experience of retrieving information from a database. Its formal structure of query and response, and the resulting aesthetic effect of this format, serves to focus attention on *how* information is processed.

The word "database" was not yet part of our cultural lexicon when *Ulysses* was published. It entered into use with the invention of computers (the Oxford English Dictionary [OED] places its origin at 1962), and yet the term aptly describes the structure of "Ithaca."[27] Consider the following example, wherein the interlocutor asks, "Why was the host (reluctant, unresisting) still?"[28] A wide variety of possible answers are not only possible but provoked, and their presence is visually signified on the page. A paragraph break and a white space follow the query. The void registers potential responses left unrecorded, and this empty space is followed by a very specific response: "In accordance with the law of the conservation of energy."[29] The answer appears without explanation, devoid of context and somewhat awkwardly. But to contemporary readers and Internet-users, the response recalls the experience of being confronted with surprising results while searching for specific information in a digital database. The larger point is that Joyce's formal conceit, what I am calling a "database aesthetic," serves to promote questions about how data is processed; it illuminates the operating structure of the information-processing system.

A database is a both a collection of data and also a way of structuring information, and Joyce explores both aspects in "Ithaca."[30] The database aesthetic of "Ithaca" is often described as resembling the "catechism," the pedagogical model used in Catholic education that teaches through repeated acts of memorizing and retrieving information. Joyce himself described the chapter this way. In a letter to Frank Budgen, Joyce writes that the chapter operates through "the form of a mathematical catechism."[31] His emphasis on the mathematical aspect is significant because it focuses attention on the algorithmic nature of the pedagogical format designed to program the cognitive databases of Catholic youth. Catechism depends upon the structured organization of content, which is also a precept of database architecture.[32] The idea in both is that the formal organization of data enables its retrieval. This concept is depicted in the narrative content of the particular section of "Ithaca" that inspires *The Jew's Daughter*.

"The Jew's Daughter" section is very much about how cognition works, specifically about how memory operates and retrieves stored information. Stephen sings a ballad called "The Jew's Daughter." He sings the song from memory, and we should recall that a ballad is itself a mnemonic device. Before Stephen's recitation, however, Bloom too attempts to sing. He begins reciting a song from his own heritage, "HaTikvah" (now the national anthem of Israel), but manages to sing only two lines. The interrogator queries, "Why was the chant arrested at the conclusion of his first distich?" The answer, "In consequence of defective mnemotechnic."[33] Bloom's memory—rather his specific technique for remembering—fails, and this failure is described in decidedly technical rhetoric. Rather than "Bloom forgot," the text spurts out a kind of computer-speak: "defective mnemotechnic." Bloom's mind is presented as a kind of memory machine, a database, just like the chapter displaying this content.

In addition to form and content, this section of "Ithaca" also performs one of the central roles of a database: it serves as an archive of multiple media forms. The pages of "Ithaca" display multiple, and indeed, multimedia, modes of reading the ballad Stephen sings. In so doing, these pages display how different media formats affect the presentation of content. The ballad's lyrics appear at the center of the page in italicized stanzas. The ballad is repeated below these stanzas in a handwritten transcription contained within a handwritten musical score. The juxtaposition of mechanically printed and handwritten text draws attention to materiality and mediation. This page spread presents the codex as a medium capable of holding, displaying, and archiving multiple media formats; in other words, the book is shown to be a kind of database. The printed page is presented as an interface for this database, a designed medium and point of entry that itself serves to organize different types of data. As Bonnie Mak shows in *How The Page Matters*, the page is a medial interface "standing at the center of the complicated dynamic of intervention and reception; it is the material manifestation of an ongoing conversation between designer and reader."[34] The pages of "The Jew's Daughter" section in *Ulysses* demonstrate this point. Joyce depicts a dialog between two characters (Stephen and Bloom), refracts that scene into an interaction between database and interlocutor, and then engages the reader in this investigation into the medial nature of literature.

Hugh Kenner's reading of this section of *Ulysses* is based in an understanding that the book is a technology akin to what we now call a database. Kenner employs David Hayman's concept of "the Arranger" to explain the strange query and response form of "Ithaca."[35] Kenner describes "Ithaca" as being organized around an "arranging presence [who] enjoys a seemingly total recall for exact forms of words used hundreds of pages earlier, a recall which implies not an operation of memory but access such as ours to a printed book, in which pages can be turned to and fro."[36] I cite Kenner here because his description of "Ithaca" implies that the Arranger's superhuman powers of recall are derived from a use of media. Kenner suggests that the book is a technology that extends human memory, not only by storing information (i.e., as an archive) but by serving as a database for organizing and accessing information. The book provides Random Access Memory (RAM); its pages "can be turned to and fro." "The Jew's Daughter" section of *Ulysses* exposes the materiality of its medium (the book) to be a precursor to digital databases. The novel is thus a worthwhile place to ground critical debates about how databases operate and serve literary studies.

"No database can function without a user interface," Jerome McGann writes.[37] In his riposte to Ed Folsom on the subject of databases in *PMLA*, McGann claims, "Interface embeds, implicitly and explicitly, many kinds of hierarchical and narrativized organizations."[38] Such recognition undercuts Manovich's argument that the schism between narrative and database is based upon the intentional ordering (or lack thereof) of information. For McGann reminds us that intention, ordering, and authorship are part of database construction even if their related actions are hidden from the reader/user. Reading Joyce's "Ithaca" chapter through Morrissey's *The Jew's Daughter* exposes how the modernist and digital modernist works unsettle the presumed opposition between narrative and database by merging the two formats at the level of literary design and poetics. The result reminds us that the way we approach and access information—that is, the way we read—always happens through media that mediate.

Part II. Distributed Cognition

Consciousness Mediated

The idea that consciousness is technologically mediated has become the capstone in theories of posthumanism. In *How We Became Posthuman*, Katherine Hayles argues that "a historically specific construction called the human is giving way to a different construction called the posthuman" due to innovations in computer science and cybernetics that produce "distributed cognition located in disparate parts," including computers.[39] *The Jew's Daughter* depicts a posthuman understanding of distributed cognition, particularly in moments wherein a character's thought is permeated by information technologies. For example, consider when an interior monologue is pierced by a nonhuman voice: "Butts of guns and barrels of bullets. I can't even touch them and can barely look at them. Your voice, a sweet, human voice. WHVAT? (that was no human voice). Excuse the bad writing."[40] The passage depicts the character's consciousness streaming through a word processor. It shows the technology affecting the thoughts as well as the way they are represented, in misspelled words. A more significant example of posthuman cognition in *The Jew's Daughter* occurs in a pivotal place wherein the digital work adapts its modernist source material.

Morrissey's *The Jew's Daughter* contains its own version of the Little Harry Hughes decapitation story, which it updates into digital media and into a posthuman conception of distributed cognition. Hints of decapitation emerge in the beginning of the digital work in such descriptions as "a decapitated greed"[41] and more explicitly in a unique animation that begins on screen 134. A rapid succession of individual letters appears in a linear stream, written across the horizontal reading line. When the animation ceases, a paragraph rests onscreen. (See Figure 4.3). The typewriter-like projection of single letters into a paragraph block registers a stark contrast to the fluid mutation of text that happens in unanticipated parts of the screen as the work progresses. The effect disorients the reader's sense of location in the narrative as well as, of course, her understanding of it. This anomalous moment also indiscreetly draws attention to itself; it is distinct but integrated. When the animation ceases and the paragraph rests onscreen, the passage is absorbed into the rest of the text onscreen. Yet something odd has happened, and its trace marks the digital page and reading process. The "page" numbers at the top of the screen have progressed from 34 to 134. This is a hardly noticeable detail; the page numbers are not at all pronounced (indeed, a knowledgeable reader must click on the little square icon in the upper-right corner in order to make the page number visible). Yet what this page-counter shows is that

(She had laid her head on the tracks and the train cut cleanly through her neck. Sh she had laid her head on the tracks and the train cut cleanly through her neck. e had laid her head on the tracks and the train cut cleanly through her neck. In Java she had seen a woman decapitated.)

Fig 4.3 Excerpt from Judd Morrissey's *The Jew's Daughter*, Screen 134. (Used with permission from the author.)

each letter of the animation is programmed to represent a different page and page number. This explains the jump from page 34 to 134 in the duration of the animation. The progression of pages shows the computer literally taking over the act of turning the "pages" while the reader sits back and watches. The animation thus reminds the human reader of the other reader involved in producing this literary text—the computer.

This invocation to the digital reading machine occurs in one of the most significant narrative moments; for it is in the animation that the text exposes the source of a character's deep-seated psychological trauma. The short animated sequence relates the moment when that character recalls witnessing a decapitation in Java.[42] The work reflexively displays a cyborgic reading practice, with the computer turning pages as human memory is pulled up from its latent depths. In this moment, computer and human memory are intertwined in the form and content of *The Jew's Daughter* in a truly posthuman sense. For, in this moment of extreme medial reflexivity, *The Jew's Daughter* references the specific media involved its processing-Flash. The authorware's interface contains numbered "keyframes" that represent temporal units (twelve fractions of a second), which the author fills with discrete bits of content; in the case of *The Jew's Daughter*'s animated sequence, Morrissey fills these keyframes with individual letters. The software program displays these keyframes sequentially and quickly to create an illusion of a fluid stream onscreen. The stream presents a digital stream of consciousness, a remediation of the modernist technique that I will soon discuss. The text in this stream also identifies Java as the place where the decapitation occurred and thus as the origin point for the traumatic event that haunts the character. But Java is also the programming language from which Flash originates.[43] Thus, form and content converge to subtly suggest that human and computer memory coproduce consciousness and its textual representation in literature, namely in the technique of stream of consciousness.

I want to pause here to consider the significance of this detail for *The Jew's Daughter* and for the argument I am making through it. In such a moment as that just described, Morrissey updates stream of consciousness and exposes how that literary practice is part of a genealogy of media-based experiments in memory extension. That geneaology connects modernist to digital and database-driven literature. The connection between *The Jew's Daughter* and *Ulysses* thus serves to encourage a revisiting of the relationship between media and cognition in modernist texts. *The Jew's Daughter* uses *Ulysses* to pursue posthuman cognition, and, in so doing, the digital work suggests that the modernist one might also present a similar sense of distributed cognition. As we will see, my reading of *The Jew's*

Daughter complicates Hayles's claim that a grand shift in subjectivity happened with the introduction of computing.[44] *The Jew's Daughter* instead suggests that the idea that human consciousness is distributed across multiple media formats goes back to modernism and the formal technique that supported this idea: stream of consciousness.

Stream of consciousness is a technique used to describe, mirror, and model the way the mind works.[45] From its evolution in the late nineteenth-century psychology to its employment as literary technique in the early decades of the twentieth-century, stream of consciousness has been understood as a form of mediation deeply tied to new media technologies. Recuperating this understanding of the literary form promotes a fresh way of viewing an old tool in the literary toolbox. It also suggests a different historical basis for considering current debates about the relationship between narrative and database by reconsidering the ties binding modernism to digital modernism.

Stream of Consciousness

In 1892 William James introduced the phrase "stream of consciousness" to describe the effect that renders consciousnesses visible and that also registers the fact that our access to consciousness is always already mediated. While consciousness may actually be composed of discrete units, he writes, it "does not appear to itself chopped up in bits."[46] Rather, "it flows."[47] James is careful to articulate that consciousness neither appears to itself nor presents itself to others as discrete bits; it is instead always experienced, or read, as an analog flow. "A 'river' or a 'stream' are the metaphors by which it is most naturally described," he explains, so, "*In talking of it hereafter, let us call it the stream of thought, of consciousness, or of subjective life*" (emphasis in original).[48] The term "stream of consciousness" should thus be understood as denoting a form of mediation. Consciousness may be digital, composed of bits, but, like a Flash animation (comprised of keyframes), it appears as an analog stream. Judith Ryan explains, "The 'bits' are simply not, for him [James], the important thing; for practical purposes, all that matters is the continuity we attribute to our perceptions."[49] From the start, then, stream of consciousness was understood and conceptualized in medial terms.

Writers and literary critics of the late nineteenth and early twentieth centuries understood this and approached stream of consciousness through a paradigm of media. They made parallels between the literary technique and specific media technologies. Édouard Dujardin, who Joyce identified as the inspiration and origin of stream of consciousness (most famously for his 1887 novel *Les Lauriers sont coupés*), reflects, "Most critics have compared interior monologue to all sorts of things—film, wireless, X-ray, diving bell. . . ."[50] It is worth noting that all of these comparable "sorts of things" are technologies. This fact that should remind us that stream of consciousness is not just a literary technique but also a *techne*, a literary technology. James Joyce certainly understood this when he experimented with different ways of representing consciousness and interior narrative and described these experiments as his "technics." Contemporary reviewers of *Ulysses* also commented on its experiments in representing cognition in decidedly technology-driven analogies. For example, Marc Chadourne writes in 1929, "The metaphor 'film of consciousness' has been used appropriately by certain critics; this image of the novelist unrolling layers of consciousness is especially vivid"; earlier, in 1922, Edmund Wilson describes Joyce's stream of consciousness as the "most faithful X-ray ever taken of the ordinary human consciousness."[51] Similarly, in 1925, Stuart Gilbert defines interior monologue as "an exact, almost *photographic* reproduction of thoughts according to the way in which they take shape in the consciousness of the person thinking" (emphasis added).[52] Literary criticism has examined stream of consciousness in relation to developments in psychology,[53] new concepts of time and experience (in particular Bergson's durée),[54] and experiments in interior monologue, but it rarely follows the path pursued by contemporary reviewers of *Ulysses* to approach stream of consciousness through the perspective of new media. Yet, more than anything, stream of consciousness is a technique used to describe, mirror, and model the way the mind works in and through written text and literary technologies. McLuhan claimed that we can only see the role of print in the moment of its eclipse (by electronic media), and I'd like to suggest that, similarly, the literary technology of stream of consciousness is made available for critical reconsideration by digital modernist works like *The Jew's Daughter*.

Modernist and digital modernist writers share the goal of making visible and aesthetic the idea that we have no access to consciousness except through mediating techniques and technologies. Stream of consciousness is one such tool. Following William James's explanation, consciousness appears as a stream because it cannot appear to itself as it actually is; it needs a mediating force. Aesthetics has often been identified as one such mediating force. Gertrude Stein, a student of William James, famously employed textual language toward aesthetic and medial effects. Adelaide Morris describes Stein's efforts as a point of connection and convergence between modernism and contemporary new media writing. She suggests that Stein shares with new media thinkers and writers a view of cognition as distributed. Although she does not attribute to Stein a full-fledged posthuman understanding of cognition across technologies, Morris does identify Stein as a kind of predecessor for this thinking and practice. "Where in Stein's reckoning, cognition is distributed between different centers *within* an individual," Morris writes, "since the mid-1980s, notions of 'distributed cognition' have increasingly extended *beyond* the individual to focus on circuits or systems that link human beings with each other, with their material artifacts and tools, and, most important for our purposes, with their networked and programmable machines" (emphasis in original).[55] From a retrospective vantage point, we can see how Stein's distributed cognition is part of the history, practice, and poetics of posthumanism. Moreover, so too are Joyce's database aesthetics in "Ithaca." These modernist writers use literature's print media to serve a similar purpose of distributing cognition as the digital technologies serve contemporary writers like Morrissey and Bogost.

What connects these writers is an effort to use text to depict the associative nature of cognition. These efforts achieve culmination in electronic hypertext, which, as I now move to discuss, is both a method of representing human cognition and an actual medium for augmenting memory. Hypertext is also a literary genre, one that became synomous with electronic literature in its earliest days. As I argued, Morrissey remediates hypertext in *The Jew's Daughter* in order to rebel against the expectations associated with that genre. Hypertext is thus a missing link in the trajectory I am tracing between modernist stream of consciousness and digital databases.

Hypertext

The word "hypertext" was coined in the 1960s by Theodor Nelson to describe a networked schematic for organizing information, but the concept that inspired Nelson's neologism dates back two decades earlier.[56] Before the introduction of the first electronic computer, Vannevar Bush, engineer and chairman of the National Defense Research Committee and director of the Office of Scientific Research and Development (which controlled the Manhattan Project), conceived of an extensive, technological system for linking and archiving information, a proto-hypertext. In an essay titled "As We May Think," published in *The Atlantic Monthly* in July 1945, Bush introduces the memex.[57] Bush's essay has retrospectively received newfound critical interest for its prescient presentation of the memex as a precursor to today's personal and networked computers; though, the significance of Bush's essay was also acknowledged at the time of its publication.[58]

"A memex is a device in which an individual stores all his books, records, and communications, and which is mechanized so that it may be consulted with

exceeding speed and flexibility," Bush writes, "It is an enlarged intimate supplement to his memory."[59] As its name implies, being a portmanteau of "memory
extender," the "memex" was meant to extend human memory, both individual and
communal memory.[60] It was a technological database and, to use McLuhan's term,
a prothesis that would extend human cognition. "The human mind . . . operates
by association," Bush writes, "With one item in its grasp, it snaps instantly to the
next that is suggested by the association of thoughts, in accordance with some
intricate web of trails carried by the cells of the brain."[61] He imagines a machine
that will both imitate and mediate the "web of trails" of human consciousness. As
Bush describes it, the memex would enable access to all written material and allow
users to add their own annotated links between documents. Individual users could
create their own "trails" (Bush's word) consisting of their own ideas and reading
paths through this endless database of content. Thus, as a secondary result, the
memex would produce a web of documents, a hypertext of sorts that could itself
be consulted and read.

Bush believed that this sort of technological system would inspire new
modes of associative thinking but also new ways of writing and reading. The
memex was part database and part authorware. "Wholly new forms of ency-
clopedias will appear," he writes, "ready made with a mesh of associative trails
running through them."[62] In other words, Bush saw his new media device as
serving to promote new forms of literacy; and, subsequently, he thought new
literary genres and modes of storing them would emerge. Bush was not interested in literature per se, and few have discussed his innovation in this way,
but he did share with Bob Brown (discussed in Chapter 2) the perspective that
changing the way we read would in turn change what we read. Moreover, his
plans for the memex did inspire developments in hypertext technologies that
did, in turn, enable new narrative forms. Foremost among those who sought
to apply Bush's ideas to reading and writing practices was hypertext innovator
Ted Nelson.

"I say Bush was right," Ted Nelson writes in *Literary Machines*, the book that
"describes a new electronic form of the memex, and offers it to the world."[63] Nelson
believed that Bush was right in conceiving of the human mind operating through
association and recognizing that this model could be supplemented through text-
based technological appendages.[64] Nelson (and other later innovators) upheld
and pursued this vision by seeking to technologically instantiate Bush's trails
to form, eventually, the web. Nelson coins the term "hypertext" to describe the
textual format enabled by a machine like the memex. He defines "hypertext" as
"*non-sequential writing—* text that branches and allows choices to the reader"

and, more specifically, "a series of text chunks connected by links which offer the reader different pathways" (emphasis in original).[65] He named his computer-based hypertext system "Xanadu" to capture the utopian and literary spirit of his (and Bush's) project.[66] Nelson was not alone in his effort to pursue the promise of a memory extender through digital computing. His contemporary, Douglas Engelbart (now famous as the inventor of the computer mouse), had more success in this endeavor. Inspired by "the vector [Bush] had described," to cite Engelbart's own words, Engelbart was involved in building a computer system called the "oNLine System" (NLS), the first to use links within a full-blown hypertext system.[67] NLS was also called "Augment" because it, like Bush's memex, strived to augment human cognition. But the hypertextual network par excellence is, of course, the Internet.[68]

In literature, however, the hypertext par excellence precedes the digital age. At least, so claims Michael Joyce, author of the acclaimed electronic hypertext *afternoon: a story* (1987, 1990), which is often identified as the first important work of electronic hypertext. This respected author of digital literature describes a deep-rooted connection to the earlier Joyce. "Hypertext doesn't spring out of nowhere," he claims, and Joyce's *Ulysses* is "understandably the original hypertext."[69] Michael Joyce is not alone in this assessment. James Joyce's innovations in stream of consciousness prompt contemporary critics to identify him as "hypertext's patron saint" (Mark Nunes) and to see *Ulysses* as "a hypertext novel before its time" (Michael Groden) or even an "*implicit* hypertext in nonelectronic form" (George Landow and Paul Delany, emphasis in original).[70] Morrissey makes a similar argument through in his own work of electronic literature, which, as I've shown, remediates hypertext as it remixes *Ulysses*. Though *The Jew's Daughter* adapts a specifically nonhypertextual chapter from Joyce's novel, its selection illuminates the database aesthetics of the often hypertextual *Ulysses*.

Reading Joyce's modernist literature *through* digital modernist literature, as I have been doing, exposes a genealogy that connects modernism and digital modernism by way of literary experiments in representing consciousness distributed across media. This literary trajectory complicates linear narratives about the progression from modernism to postmodernism, humanism to posthumanism, by connecting literary history to computing *before* the period of cybernetics and the appearance of digital technologies. Joyce's database literature can be read in relation to digital databases, but it can also be read in relation to experiments in predigital technological hypertexts such as Vannevar Bush's memex and also to later instantiations and conceptualizations of it, including the web. For, as I hope I showed, *Ulysses* contains both notions of hypertext: (1) a formal means of depicting cognition and (2) a technical format for distributing consciousness across media platforms. When viewed this way, the modernist novel serves to disable simple binaries between narrative and database.

The deconstructive drive at work in Joyce's novel is one reason why Jacques Derrida finds it so significant. In "Two Words for Joyce," Derrida describes Joyce's texts as part of a larger, complex machine, a type of database.[71] He writes, "you can say nothing that is not programmed on this 1000th generation computer—*Ulysses, Finnegans Wake.* . . ."[72] Similar to how Kenner focuses attention on the Arranger's use of the book technology in "Ithaca," Derrida claims that to read the database aesthetics of Joyce's novels would require an actual database, "a machine capable of integrating all the variables, all the quantitative or qualitative factors," a machine that "would only be the double or simulation of the event 'Joyce."[73] He calls this conceptual machine, the database capable of doubling Joyce's oeuvre, "joyceware."[74] I'd like to suggest that *The Jew's Daughter* is a kind of joyceware that prompts us to reread Joyce's work and thereby double the event that is "Joyce." Reading *The Jew's Daughter* in relation to the joyceware that inspires it also shows how pursuing a digital modernist reading strategy illuminates the connections linking hypertext, narrative, and database as well as modernism and digital literature.

Part III. Actual Database Literature

To conclude this chapter, I turn to one other work of digital literature that adapts *Ulysses*, but this one differs dramatically from either the Twitter-based remix of "Wandering Rocks" or *The Jew's Daughter* because it is actually a work of database-poetics. Talan Memmott's *My Molly (Departed)* (2008), formerly titled *Twittering: A Procedural Novel*, draws inspiration from *Ulysses* to explore posthuman cognition through the merger of narrative and database.[75] It shows how electronic literature actually experiments with databases to renovate literary representations of human consciousness.

My Molly (Departed) is a database-driven, generative experiment, what Memmott calls "a textual instrument designed as a performance application."[76] Its content is generated in the moment of interaction or, more specifically, when the reader presses a key that prompts the page to reload. Reloading the page causes the application script to run again and to generate a new compilation of texts from a database that contains numerous files. To "read" this piece, you play it, but not in the way you play a video game—and this is one way in which this work asserts its allegiance to digital modernism rather than to mainstream new media culture. *My*

Molly (Departed) rejects popular expectations of what it means to play new media objects in its pursuit of high modernist aesthetics.

Memmott is a respected digital writer, best known for *Lexia to Perplexia* (2000), a work that has received a fair share of critical analysis and gained a secure position in the canon of electronic literature.[77] *Lexia to Perplexia* aestheticizes posthuman subjectivity in semantic wordplay and visual-linguistic poetics. It is commonly described as "codework," a genre of literature that intersperses computer code and natural language.[78] *My Molly (Departed)* pushes beyond the postmodernist and poststructuralist inspirations undergirding Memmott's signature codeworks into the genre of generative, combinatorial performance. Intended to be performed rather than read, *My Molly (Departed)* is not an autonomous artwork; it is a database that requires interaction in order to produce poetics.

Reading this work entails approaching the keyboard as a musical instrument. Pressing a key elicits a selection from 212 different audio files and 1,500 text fragments. Each key has a number of possible audio, image, and text files attached to it, and the result is that pressing the same key twice can elicit a variety of different responses. Memmott explains, "the piece exists as a framework for potential recombinations."[79] The content of the work remains latent until appropriate play processes a recombination of multimedia files into a meaningful arrangement. Meaning here is not just textual but also visual, aural, temporal, and affective. However, there is only one way to begin the work: you must press "Return." Pressing the Return or Enter key initiates this digital, database-driven literary engagement with Joyce's *Ulysses*. This first act of engagement, pressing the Return key, serves to instantiate and represent the central act of digital modernism: returning to the past to make it new through new media.

Memmott's original title was *Twittering: a Procedural Novel*, and that title referenced two literary genres: (1) Twitter, the Web 2.0 social networking application that Bogost and McCarthy use to adapt the "Wandering Rocks" section of *Ulysses*, and (2) the novel. Despite the now-dispensed-with subtitle, this work bears little resemblance to what we might typically call a "novel." There is no stable narrative to follow and no readily identifiable or fleshed-out characters. Any semblance of narrative coherence depends upon the intertextual references that this database, procedural work offers up. What is the source material for these intertextual references? You guessed it, Joyce's *Ulysses*. Unlike the other two digital works examined in this chapter, *My Molly (Departed)* is not an adaptation of that modernist work. Indeed, the intertextual references are extremely subtle and far-between; but they are there. On the whole, these references are, as the new title suggests, centered on the character of Molly Bloom. "My Molly" is an oft-repeated text fragment in

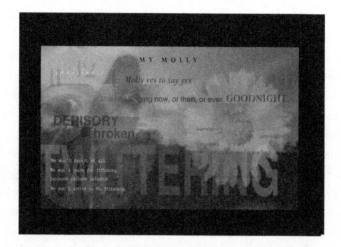

Fig 4.4 Screenshot from Talan Memmott's *My Molly (Departed)*, formerly *Twittering: a Procedural Novel* (2008). (Used with permission from the author.)

the database performance, and the line turns the tweets in this work (formerly known as *Twittering*) into something novel-like. Molly is alluded to in lines like, "Molly yes to say yes" and "We dont like books with Mollys" (see Figure 4.4). *My Molly (Departed)* relies upon these intertextual allusions to *Ulysses* to provide textual coherence and to secure a literary framework for its generative experiment in multimodal poetics.

Despite the connections I am drawing out between *My Molly (Departed)* and *Ulysses*, a narrative is impossible to decipher, particularly one based in Joyce's text. When I first started writing this chapter, Memmott still insisted on labeling his work "a novel," claiming that genre category in his work's title. I found this claim intriguing, for Memmott's insistence that this work—which seems, in every way, to challenge the category of "novel" and the concept of narrative—is a novel provided a foothold for complicating the distinction between narrative and database. The new title, *My Molly (Departed)*, implies a loss or death of something previously held dear, and one could speculate that this loss references the rejected old title, *Twittering: a Procedural Novel*, and the categories that title invoked. In other words, Memmott's work suggests that our definitions of "novel," and thus of "narrative," are outdated and "departed." They change and adjust under the influence of digital databases.

Regardless of its ultimate genre categorization, *My Molly (Departed)* is part of the literary effort I've been tracing throughout this chapter—to represent cognition in literary text. Indeed, it presents an emergent representation of consciousness on its very first screen. After pressing Return and entering the work, the reader is faced with a gray and heavily pixilated screen. This first screen displays an image of white noise, the component of communication that serves as supplement to the message and which indexes the mediated nature of communication. We can interpret this first screen as reflexively referencing the role of mediation in the work, indeed of identifying mediation as the subject of the work. But there is more to be gleaned from it. A flat, white line cuts horizontally through its surface, and its presence serves to illuminate the layers of shadow and depth behind it. With this screen as its entrance, work begins by making visually manifest a parallel between the black-box, depth models used to describe human and machine cognition. As *My Molly (Departed)* continues (or, more accurately, as the reader/user performs the work), it takes the parallel between human and computer and ties it into a complicated knot. Memmott promotes an understanding that the relationship between writing technologies and written texts—between Twitter as a platform and the "tweet" as a poetic text—constitutes a feedback loop between human mind and media format. *My Molly (Departed)* shows literature to be a real-time performance distributed across reader, computer, and programming files that operates through the structure of a database. The work also illustrates how such emergent technopoetics transform the way consciousness is depicted.

Like *Ulysses*, "Wandering Rocks," and *The Jew's Daughter*, *My Molly (Departed)* displays stream of consciousness as a process distributed across media forms. It then enacts this concept into an actual database aesthetic. The consciousness streaming through the screen's surface in *My Molly (Departed)* is a hybrid of human and machine. Memmott (human author) created a database based upon his individual specifications for arranging literary data in such a way as to elicit an anticipated aesthetic. He programmed and the computer then enacts, and the resulting cyborgic identity is registered in the work through a male voice that reads the text fragments as they are culled from the depths of the program. The voice might be understood as humanizing the machine or referencing the influence of the human on the computer's procedural logic, but what these voice clips actually depict is the interpenetration of human and machine. This is particularly evident when the man's voice is interrupted by another sound file, such as a trumpet blare or some other kind of instrument. The voice is clipped, decapitated (to resurrect imagery from the narrative in *The Jew's Daughter*), and the result is somewhat horrifying. The effect registers the fact that the human voice, and thus the human behind it, is just another data file. This programmed detail suggests that what we think to be real and analog about humanness is actually the result of digital production. The point, and Memmott's work that makes it, thus supports William James's description of consciousness; the expectation of an uninterrupted voice and a whole human being it references are illusions created by the mediated streaming of bits. Memmott's stream of consciousness provides a new media twist on this old idea and shows how literary depictions of consciousness invite reconsideration of how consciousness is—and was—understood.

Conclusion

This chapter explored a grouping of experiments across media forms and literary periods that share the goal of representing the mediated nature of consciousness. Joyce's *Ulysses* is the nexus point for this constellation of digital modernist works—Bogost and McCarthy's Twitter-based work "Wandering Rocks," Morrissey's *The Jew's Daughter*, and Memmott's *My Molly (Departed)*—which take from their modernist inspiration a desire to examine and represent the operations of cognition *through* literary technologies. The digital literary works explored in this chapter foreground generative performance, queried searches, unpredictable results, and deeply coded technological mediation as part of the practice of representing human consciousness. They renovate stream of consciousness for a digital age by expressing the intertwined relationship between human consciousness and digital computing. In so doing, they revise and revitalize our approaches to reading literary modernism and its continued influence. Such works also remind us of how early hypertext projects sought to extend human memory in ways that also connected to modernist literary techniques. Focusing on these points of intersection secure the links between literary history and computing history. Since it is Joyce's print-based database aesthetics that inspire digital and database-involved literature, such contemporary works also prompt reflection on how a database aesthetic and a sense of distributed consciousness are not located solely in the now and in the new media but have earlier roots. Tracing these roots provides a media-focused frame for rereading modernism as well as a historical foundation for approaching contemporary literature, especially literature that experiments with representing consciousness as its subject becomes posthuman and its medium becomes digital.

In an interview I conducted in 2003 with Morrissey and Talley (which was focused not on *The Jew's Daughter* but on another work of digital poetry the pair coauthored, *My Name is Captain, Captain.*), I asked the authors what they expect from their readers. In retrospect, I now understand their answer as a perfect articulation of the strategy of digital modernism, the act of renovating the modernist past in order to produce specifically timely, digital literature. I end the chapter with them:

> **JP:** What kind of responsibility do you desire and expect from the reader?
>
> **M&T:** To read. To write. To repeat. To become the ear of the poet-sleuth who excavates the poem, stirs up history, only to become implicated in a new repetition.[80]

5. Reading Code

The Hallucination of Universal Language from Modernism to Cyberspace

---

"Human beings have always been digital." So begins Erik Loyer's online digital novel *Chroma* (2001). The enigmatic first line is heard, not read, spoken by a magisterial male voice. In fact, there is no text to read in this novel's prologue, just simple but sophisticated visuals that fill the screen and dance to a haunting aural backdrop of long, plaintive chords. A starkly outlined, geometric figure floats against a forest-green background. It is a human body comprised solely of chartreuse lines for limbs and rectangles for head and chest. The reader controls the figure's movement; it is an avatar. But its movement is deeply constrained, confined to only shifting sideways across a horizontal plane. As the figure moves, solid rectangles dart across the screen at sharp angles filling the background environment with more geometric shapes. The chartreuse color and primitive design are reminiscent of early computer graphics, and the formal insistence on an angular, mathematical aesthetic visually references the programming code enabling this digital presentation (see Figure 5.1). The distinguished but disembodied male voice speaks in a calm, soothing manner. The voice belongs to Dr. Ian Anders, the lead scientist in the mission at the center of this episodic work of science fiction. As he begins his tale, Dr. Anders's words support the suggestion made by the work's interface design—*Chroma* explores the idea that mathematical code is a universal language.

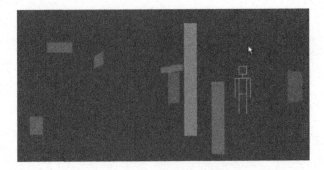

Fig 5.1 Screenshot from Erik Loyer's *Chroma* (2001) Chapter 0: Prologue (Perform Text section).(Used with permission from the author.)

Chroma depicts an attempt to access a lost Eden, one that is digital and thus mathematical in nature. As Dr. Anders explains in the prologue that opens the novel,

> Eons ago, all human beings had the ability to enter 'mnemonos'
> A natural cyberspace where the things of the mind appear
> as real as anything your five senses perceive.[1]

We were displaced from the Edenic realm of the mnemonos and have since forgotten it. Dr. Anders proposes to reclaim this ancient realm. To do so, he must remind others of its existence. This is the quest at the center of *Chroma*'s narrative: to access and communicate to others the marvels of mnemonos. But this is neither a purely scientific or exploratory pursuit; it is also deeply philosophical. Anders must expose the fact that what appears to be real and true is actually a constructed facade based in forgetting and erasing history. Hence, the name of this natural but forgotten place is "mnemonos" after the Greek goddess of memory. Remembering requires excavation, the discovery and presentation of forgotten history, and this excavation is, I'd like to suggest, the novel's subtext. It is also what renders this a work of digital modernism. The need to excavate history and read into unseen connections links up this work, and my reading of it, to earlier chapters. Chapter 1 excavated of the role McLuhan served in founding media studies upon New Criticism's close reading; Chapter 2 pursued a media archaeological approach to excavating the tachistoscope and the Readies via Poundstone's *Project*; Chapter 3 explored the hidden connections between super-position across media forms and periods; and, Chapter 4 excavated the role of media and mediation in stream of consciousness. I open Chapter 5 with *Chroma*, a work that carries an allegorical message for our own digital age. For, despite Dr. Ander's belief, cyberspace is not natural, and the ideologies that represent it as such have deep histories in need of excavation.

This chapter examines a conceptual history whose nexus point lies at the intersection of literature and computing: in the belief that universal language is possible with the right textual code. This belief undergirds ideologies that code is universal and that cyberspace (or, even, digital culture more broadly) is natural or inevitable. I read works of digital literature that challenge the idea of universal communication through digital code, and I do so by focusing on their digital modernist aspects. Namely, I trace a connection between contemporary views of digital code as rational, natural, and universal back to modernist ideas that the Chinese ideogram is a language for universal poetics. Digital modernism critiques this modernist inheritance and offers an opportunity to consider the intellectual histories shared not only between literary periods but also between literature and computing. To begin, we return to *Chroma* and consider its critique of Dr. Anders's mission to return to the lost Eden and achieve universal communication.

Part I. *Chroma*

Chroma opens with a black entry-screen. Before Dr. Anders proclaims that "Human beings have always been digital," the work presents a hypnotizing animation sequence that slowly unfurls to present its title. The animation establishes a mysterious and entrancing tone and minimalistic aesthetic that suggests some of the central ideas its narrative will pursue. It opens to a stark black screen, whose background music pulses with electronic sounds. Barely audible voices begin to pierce the aural backdrop. They whisper, interrupt, overlap with each other. Slowly, the voices rise in volume and multitude until a powerful chorus produces a boisterous surround-sound cacophony. The voices increase in volume until they achieve momentary harmony and collectively whisper the novel's title "*Chroma*." As they do so, previously illegible white shapes consolidate to form letters that spell out the title. The effect serves to render audio and visual senses inseparable and show how meaning-making is experiential and embodied. During these first few seconds, *Chroma* introduces itself as a multimodal work deeply concerned with exposing the different ways in which information is accessed and understood. Its opening animation primes the reader to notice how many voices and individual elements come together to produce something that appears whole or universal. Indeed, before its narrative even begins, *Chroma* presents an aural heteroglossia that formally critiques the idea of universal communication.

Chroma continues this pursuit in its narrative. The novel is comprised of the collected journal entries written by Dr. Anders and the three people he assembles to serve on his expedition to explore the mnemonos, who he collectively calls the "Marrow Monkeys." Each chapter is dedicated to a single author (or monkey), so the Prologue is by Dr. Anders, Chapter 1 is by Duck at the Door, Chapter 2 is by Orion17, and so on. The first-person structure of these narrative accounts disallows any sense of an omniscient or universal point-of-view. Moreover, the work strives to disable a unified or universal point of view in its formal presentation of the narrative. For, there are two ways to read each of these individual chapters—Perform Text and View Text—and this formal arrangement has significant results.

Perform Text is *Chroma*'s default option. It presents the story as an audio-visual animation accompanied by a voice-over that narrates the content of the journal entry. Dr. Anders's Prologue opens the novel in this mode. There is no text to read onscreen in Perform Text, no hyperlinks or interactive choices, and no ability to pause the animation. The reader just watches the performance. In contrast, View Text presents the journal entry as a vertical column of scrollable text. There is music but no voice-over or animation; the reader encounters the static text in silence. Though the text doesn't move, it is actually inaccurate to call it "static," as I just did. It does not move around the screen; it stays in its position in the poetic line, but it flickers (see Figure 5.2). This flickering invokes the "flickering signifier"

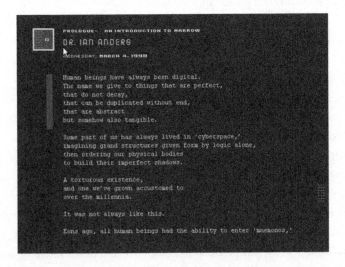

Fig 5.2 Screenshot from Erik Loyer's *Chroma* (2001) Chapter 0: Prologue (View Text section). (Used with permission from the author.)

of digital textuality, as Katherine Hayles identifies it.[2] The flickering reminds us that *Chroma*'s View Text has more in common, at a material level, with the visual but nontextual performance of Perform Text than with any kind of printed text. The experience of moving between View Text and Perform Text also exposes how the same story told in different ways, that is, in text or in a voice-over on a visual animation, produces starkly different reading encounters. Loyer substantiates this point by refusing the reader the ability to open Perform Text and View Text simultaneously; only one window and one reading mode is accessible at one time. This programmatic decision forces the reader to compare the two reading registers, recognize the differences between them, and translate the narrative content across them. The result is an acute awareness of the fact that medial format informs and transforms content; and, that something is always lost in the translation of content across media platforms.

This lesson is brought home by an unintended consequence of *Chroma*'s specific medium. *Chroma* was built in Shockwave, a multimedia platform released in 1995 and used to create web-based animations, and it no longer has strong compatibility with many web browsers and Apple products. By virtue of this technical fact of media specificity, *Chroma* suffers from increasing inaccessibility. *Chroma*'s formal structure of Perform Text and View Text reminds us that communication is multimodal, multisensory, and dependent upon specific media and materialities. The novel engages with these topics aesthetically and in ways that make disturbingly ironic, and perhaps even retrospectively poetic, its possible obsolescence. Dr. Anders believes he has "found the key/ that can unlock the ancient realm."[3] He recruits three researchers, the Marrow Monkeys, to enter and reclaim the mnemonos. He selects these assistants because they "demonstrate a strong affinity for marrow," the substance that comprises the mnemonos; marrow is a medium that "transmits information just as the air transmits sound," and it injects materiality and embodiment into the otherwise virtual and transcendental realm of the natural cyberspace.[4] The fact that this space is filled with a matter named after that substance which fills human bones is significant because in this original cyberspace, materiality matters.

Chroma narrates the quest to achieve universal communication in the mnemonos and to "safely reveal its intricacies to the public."[5] But there is a problem. While Anders's team is successful in entering the digital Eden, they cannot communicate in it. They erroneously "assumed that this world's marrow/ would somehow provide instantaneous translation/ between our myriad intimate tongues."[6] The implicit allusions to Babel are made manifest in Dr. Anders nightmares. He has "Visions of some hell in which/ their self-absorption continues until/ none of us share a language in common."[7] The Marrow Monkeys remain trapped "in our own separate worlds," unable to communicate with each other in the mnemonos.[8] They are perfect representations of Leibniz's "windowless monads," and I will later explore the relevance of this particular allusion.[9] The image of the Marrow Monkeys drifting in a prelapsarian cyberspace displays the failure of Anders's mission. As I read it, *Chroma* is an allegory about the necessary failure of efforts to seek universal language through computer code and within cyberspace. The necessary part of this argument comes from *Chroma*'s implicit critique of the ideologies involved in identifying computer code as a universal language.

Because the Marrow Monkeys are unable to communicate in the mnemonos, one of them, Orion17, devises a solution. They will build avatar bodies and use these bodies as mediating interfaces for communicating in the natural cyberspace. Orion17 explains, "I've been thinking about our own DNA,/ our genetic code, as a kind of program/that describes a human body. What if we could write programs that would make/ bodies for us in marrow?"[10] In a gesture that becomes central to contemporary science and the cultural discourse surrounding it, Orion17 maps computer code onto genetic code and thereby depicts actual, physical, marrow-filled bodies as chains of alphanumerical, discursive signifiers. Orion17's language slips from "describe" to "make," and this substitution enables him to describe bodies as something one dons like clothing. "We'll design avatars, virtual bodies for us/ to wear while we're in marrow," Orion17 states.[11] The idea that one can separate body from self or soul is certainly not new, but *Chroma*'s digital narrative updates this transcendentalism into a contemporary version of this ideology in order to critique the cultural enterprise it supports.

Orion17's plan presents a clear example of what Alan Liu describes as "the governing ideology of discourse network 2000: *the separation of content from material instantiation or formal presentation*" (italics in the original).[12] Reframing and appropriating Friedrich Kittler's language and extending his media-based history, Liu describes the operational logic of the twentieth century as a belief in the ability to separate content and form. This separation, of course, is the foundational concept of information and communication theory. Communication theory, which intersects with and influences the development of digital computing, dictates that a message must be capable of being separated from its material instantiation in order to be transmitted across channels and distances so that it can reach the intended receiver. In its current digital manifestation, Liu explains, the "ideology of division between form and presentation" becomes "a religion of text encoding and databases."[13] This religion supplies the governing belief of Orion17's plan; namely, the idea that specific bodies don't matter. Only one character, Duck at the Door,

refutes the underlying assumptions of Orion's solution and exposes the computational logic behind it. The novel gives her the last word.

Duck at the Door is the only character in *Chroma* identified in gendered and
racial terms. Of the four characters in the novel, three are men, and their races are
undisclosed. This lack of information is actually quite significant. Writing about
the construction of avatars in MUDs (Multi-User Domains), the text-based social
networking spaces popular in the early days of cyberspace, Lisa Nakaumura argues
that "the choice not to mention race does in fact constitute a choice; in the absence
of racial description, all players are assumed to be white."[14] Unlike the undisclosed
characteristics of her fellow Marrow Monkeys, *Chroma* identifies Duck as biracial and female. Through her dissenting response to Orion17's plan, we come to
see how these personal factors ground her critique of the ideological scaffolding
enabling Orion17's belief in transcendental data and the larger discourse network
2000.

Duck's journal entry in Chapter 6 refutes Orion17's assumption that creating
avatar bodies will provide a simple solution to the failure of communicating in the
mnemonos. Orion believes and builds his plan upon the following if/then statement, "If we agree in advance on exactly how these [avatar] bodies/ will function,
and exactly what they can look like, / I think we'll finally be able to see each other,/
talk to each other, while we're in the mnemonos."[15] Orion17 attributes the failure
to communicate in the mnemonos to an inability to see one another, which is
akin to identifying a technological problem of inefficient interfaces. He seeks to
fix this technical issue by creating a better protocol for describing avatar bodies in
the cyberspace. But Duck responds by pointing out the cultural, not just technical, aspects of the situation and the political ideologies that undergird Orion17's
plan. She does so by drawing a parallel between real and virtual worlds, showing
how in the real world, and not just in the mnenmonos, she is already an avatar
of sorts.

Duck describes herself as "invented body," a racial hybrid of her parents's dis-
regard for the rules of "a game they were playing/ A role-playing game" wherein
"[e]very character could also belong to/ one and only one racial group,/ a rule my
parents chose to subvert."[16] In an "American/ variation on this kind of game/that
was all about race" Duck's biracial body threatens the rules and operations of the
system.[17] She upsets the default option by requiring that two racial categories be
checked off on her identity card instead of one. "And this is viewed as cheating, be-
cause/ belonging to a particular race/ gives your character special abilities."[18] The
results of her particular infringement of checking off two identity boxes instead of
one causes Duck to experience many "unsettling things" in her real life outside of

the mnemonos: "Unjustified love/ unjustified hate/ constant misunderstandings/ and all because of my invented body,/ my avatar."[19] Her personal narrative shows how the virtual realm is not the only place where bodies are read in accordance with normative guidelines and codes. In both real space and cyberspace, interfaces mediate and shape meaning. Duck experienced this firsthand in the real world, and she is fully aware of the irony of her situation wherein she is asked to create an avatar for the virtual environment of the mnemonos.

The Perform Text version of Duck's chapter, which is, recall, the default way of reading the work, demonstrates her critique of this situation and does do in visual and visceral ways. It is designed to appear as a videogame. The screen is divided horizontally in thirds, and the upper-level displays a scoreboard and a labyrinth-like city permeated by a single yellow dot. The dot is the reader/user's avatar, and it corresponds to a red dot in the bottom part of the screen. Unlike the yellow dot situated in a dimensional, spatial environment of a cityscape, the red dot at the bottom slides upon a blank, olive-green background. As the dot moves, it draws, and it leaves behind the traced outline of a minimalist maze. As the maze grows, it begins to take the shape of a human body, one comprised of geometric lines and internal networks. The red dot—ink, blood, marrow—is the reader's avatar through this bodied space. As the reader/user moves the dot and writes the limbs of a body in cyberspace, she participates in playing the type of game that Orion17 devised to save Dr. Anders's mission—one based on designing avatar bodies. In order to move through the chapter and hear the narrative, the reader must participate in drawing the avatar. Formally, then, Duck's chapter shows how easily one can be made to submit to the ideological underpinnings of a cyberspace game that builds human bodies and is programmed by human beings.

In the voice-over that accompanies this chapter's gameplay, Duck describes her experience as an avatar in the American game of racial politics. She calls the programmers of the game "caste masters," implying that they, rather than the players of the games, are the powerful agents. Writing code to create a gameworld encodes biases, cultural hierarchies, and power structures that remain unseen but present and powerful. Duck's testimony exposes this fact and stands in stark contrast to that of her male colleagues. Where the Marrow Monkeys see a technological glitch and, in response, optimistically focus on solving it through technical and utilitarian tasks—that is, building avatars—Duck sees an ideological agenda. The third of the Marrow Monkeys, Grid Farmer Perry, derides Duck for choosing "her politics" over her friendship with Orion: "That's Duck, always taking a/ stand against whatever the majority thinks."[20] But Duck makes clear that being a minority (either by way of the appearance of her body or the content of her ideas) is not a choice. The form and content of her chapter suggests that her location on the gameboard of American cultural politics is preprogrammed. As she watches her fellow Marrow Monkeys design a plan to create avatars and navigate the mnemonos, she recognizes a similar power dynamic at work. "Perry and Orion are coming up with a new game," she claims, "They're coming up with new rules, right now."[21] With the white men constructing the rules of the game, Duck concludes, "I can already tell I'm going to have to cheat to win."[22] This is the novel's last line.[23]

Dr. Anders's mission fails. The Marrow Monkeys remain unable to communicate in the mnenonos. The pre-Babel language of the natural cyberspace remains inaccessible, and *Chroma* is clear about why. Whether they are built of flesh, code, or text, bodies exist, perform, and operate within specific networks and systems of protocols. Universal language is not possible—even in cyberspace—because languages are codes programmed by human beings. And these humans, like Orion17 and Grid Farmer Perry, infuse specific ideological positions into their protocological endeavors. These biases might be unconscious but they are powerful. Moreover, they are taken from the experiences and positions on the rule-bound grids of the metaphorical gameboards they occupy in real life. *Chroma* thus posits a trenchant critique of the ideology of universal language and the belief that it can be achieved through digital technology.

Now let's see what Loyer is responding to and how his web-based novel is part of a longer genealogy of intellectual and aesthetic concerns that goes back to modernism. To do so, I turn to a specific node in the intersection of computing and literary history, one situated in the modernist period.

Part II. The Quest for Universal Language

Efforts to discover a universal language reach back to ancient times and to the biblical story of Babel, but contemporary pursuits to construct a universal language through a set of manmade, linguistically programmed rules converge around the last decades of the nineteenth and early decades of the twentieth centuries—the period of modernism. Esperanto, Solresol, Volapük, and others emerged in the same period with the same goal: to achieve universal communication in a world rapidly becoming global and feeling the effects of colonialism and the industrial revolution. Experiments in universal language and in literary modernism developed contemporaneously and converged in significant ways.

One such example is Ezra Pound's view that Chinese ideograms served as a kind of universal language and a code for modern poetry. The idea that ideograms are code for universal communication did not originate with Pound. He is part of a longer line of thinkers going back to the philosopher and mathematician Gottfried Leibniz. Pound and I. A. Richards, Leibniz and Warren Weaver: these names aren't usually considered together, but they all sought the means to pursue universal communication. Exploring how they did so illuminates historical and ideological parallels and important convergences between media history and literary history around the topic of universal communication.

In "The Genesis of the Media Concept," John Guillory traces a prehistory of media studies to early studies of rhetoric in the seventeenth-century, and he focuses on universal language projects. He describes these projects as "nothing other than attempts to grasp the idea of communication" and claims that they can be understood as suturing the fields of media studies and literary studies.[24] "[T]hese projects," Guillory writes, "already approached language as a medium of communication, while falling short of formulating a coherent conceptual object."[25] Viewed in this way, universal language projects are part of media studies and media history. In a footnote to his essay, Guillory explains why, as a literature scholar, he finds himself interested in the history and prehistory of media. "As a discourse of writing and of print, works of literature are also indisputably media," he writes; "Yet literature seems to be less conspicuously marked by medial identity than other media, such as film, and that fact has tacitly supported the disciplinary division between literary and media studies."[26] It is my ambition in this chapter to confront "the disciplinary division" by approaching universal language projects from a different perspective than Guillory does, but for a similar purpose—to expose the intersection of literary and media studies.

Modernist poetic-political efforts in universal language emerged along with a structuralist understanding of language in which linguistic signs are understood as having not inherent but ascribed meaning. This understanding was disseminated through the posthumous publication of Ferdinand de Saussure's lectures (which were published in 1916). For my purposes—as I move to consider Pound's view of the Chinese ideogram—it is important to note that Saussure differentiates between ideogrammic and alpha-numeric languages, and he focuses on the latter. Saussure claims that ideograms reflect a "mental substitution of the written word for the spoken word" that results in "the substitution [that] is absolute," whereas in phonetic languages, that relation is arbitrary.[27] Hold onto Saussure's distinction between ideogrammic and phonetic languages for a moment, while I bring into the fold the influence of structuralism on computer science.

The influence of structuralism on computering is evident in the way the computer scientist and artificial intelligence innovator Terry Winograd describes the computer: "In the popular mythology the computer is a mathematics machine; it is designed to do numerical calculations."[28] "Yet it is really a language machine," he continues, "its fundamental power lies in its ability to manipulate linguistic tokens—symbols to which meaning has been assigned."[29] Winograd thus presents the computer as operating through a structuralist understanding of alphanumeric language. The "linguistic tokens" that the computer processes are meaningful only within the constructed system that assigns on/off, negative/positive values to binary digits; moreover, this meaning is not natural but arbitrary. Yet the actualities of computer processing challenge a strictly structuralist logic, for meaning is not derived from a simple relationship between sign and signifier in computational operations. Instead, the computer translates content across multiple levels of languages and layers of programs. And yet the fact that its linguistic operations remain unseen and unknown to most human readers inspires imaginative narratives, theories, and mythologies about the natural and universal power of digital code. *Chroma* is one such example.

Much important scholarship has addressed the individual topics I examine here—the role of the Chinese ideogram in literary modernism, the history of the search for a perfect language, the universal nature of computer code and machine translation, and so forth- and I do not aim to recapitulate this work. This is not a chapter about computer code or universal language per se. I use those keywords as modalities through which to explore the intersections that emerge when they are placed in conversation with each other and when computing and literature are approached as sharing a historical and ideological core. Rather than explain the actual, technical, and linguistic operations of code and language, this chapter strives to illuminate the interconnected histories that *continue* to foster a cultural imagination that universal communication is possible through computers. The digital modernist works I examine in this chapter exploit the nexus between universal languages, the Chinese ideogram, and computational code. They exemplify the entwined histories I trace, and they critique the fantasy that universal language is made possible by computational notions of language as code. These works thus provide a lens through which to revisit and reconsider discourse about universal language, both from the distant and immediate past.

Computationalism

In one of the foundational essays in the history of computing, "Computing Machinery and Intelligence" (1950), Alan Turing describes the computer as a "universal machine" because it translates other media formats into digital code. Digital code is thus posited as the universal, default language for mimicking all other media forms. Turing's essay was conceptual rather than technical. It introduced a way of viewing the computer as a machine capable of universal translation and thus as a universal language machine. The idea that computers and, more precisely, that the digital code that makes computers run can enable universal language lies at the heart of computationalism. In *The Cultural Logic of Computation*, David Golumbia describes the underlying logic of computing as "overlap[ping] with the most influential lines in the history of modern thought, namely, the rationalist theory of mind."[30] Computationalism depends upon the idea that rational calculations can describe the world; moreover, that these descriptions can be understood as generative of that world. In other words, the understanding that computer code can describe other media forms and then reproduce them supports the idea that computer code is a universal language. But, as Duck pointed out in her critique of Orion17's plan to construct bodies out of code, such rationalist logic and rhetoric do more than build digital objects—it supports "the rhetoric of computation," as Golumbia argues, "and the belief system associated with it, [that] benefits and fits into established structures of institutional power."[31] Duck at the Door would certainly agree. The lesson *Chroma* imparts through Duck's final chapter is that rational and computational projects might be technical but that does not mean they are devoid of human and cultural biases.

One place to see the intersection of computational logic, rhetoric, and programming is in the computer-based universal language projects that have been part of computing from its inception. Golumbia describes such projects as machine translation as "ideological programs driven by a furious need to show that computers can take over language, that language can be formalized."[32] Conversely, he identifies "the main intellectual program in these areas—namely, the desire to show that human language is itself computational."[33] In other words, efforts in machine translation inform the way we think about language and communication more generally. "There is little more to understanding computation than comprehending this simple principle," Golumbia writes, "mathematical calculation can be made to stand for propositions that are themselves not mathematical, but must confirm to mathematical rules."[34] Describing the world in mathematical terms imposes a human logic, order, and power structure. Hayles also critiques computationalism or "The Regime of Computation," as she calls it, for similar reasons. She finds fault with such thinkers as Stephen Wolfram, Edward Fredkin, and Harold Morowitz, who claim that "the universe is fundamentally computational" and identifies the intellectual slippage that occurs when "code is elevated to the lingua franca not only of computers but of all physical reality."[35] In this computational

logic, code is deemed a perfect language (to invoke Umberto Eco's distinction between universal and perfect languages), for it mirrors nature in ways that can be
thought to also generate nature.[36]

We can understand Orion17's plan to build avatars in *Chroma* as exemplifying
this computational view of code. Likewise, Duck at the Door's fictional commentary serves to critique it by pointing out that computer code is neither natural nor
universal. Code, like the technologies that employ it, is constructed and shaped
by human beings; it is thus also informed by cultural history, and, as we will soon
see, the poetic imagination. Recall that Winograd identified the computer as a
language machine, but it is also a metaphor machine. As Wendy Chun explains,
computers "both depend on and perpetuate metaphors."[37] "Because computers are
viewed as universal machines," she writes, "they have become metaphors for metaphor itself: they embody a logic of substitution, a barely visible conceptual system
that orders and disorders."[38] The way computers operate and are perceived to operate is grounded in a logic of substitution, and this logic undergirds Orion17's plan
as well as the rationale behind the Regime of Computation that the novel allego-
rizes. Recognizing the role of metaphor in these intellectual paradigms should also
illuminate the importance of approaching computing from a literary background
and perspective.

Literary critics thus have a significant role to play in unpacking and explaining
the ways in which metaphors about computing influence the cultural imagination
of digitality. This chapter is one such attempt. More than anything, I seek to excavate a historical and discursive parallel between modernist and contemporary *understandings* of code. The benefits of reading across connections between literary
and computing history are particularly evident when we examine an exemplary
case of computational logic *in* literature. The view that code is natural and that
nature consists of code motivates Ezra Pound's approach to the Chinese ideogram
and his use of it in modernist poetry. And it is to this particular computational
(and poetic) substitution that I now turn.

Ezra Pound and the Chinese Ideogram

When T. S. Eliot introduced *Cathay* (1915), Pound's volume of translated Chinese
poems, he called Pound the "inventor of Chinese poetry for our time."[39] Eliot's
grandiose title for this fellow Anglophone poet is problematic for many reasons,
not the least because Pound could not speak, read, or write Chinese, nor had he
ever visited China.[40] The fact that Pound could not read Chinese did not stop him
from taking on the task of editing the manuscripts of American sinologist Ernest

Fenollosa on the subject of the Chinese ideogram.[41] Indeed, as I will show, it is precisely because he did not read Chinese that Pound could claim, as he did, that the Chinese ideogram is a universal medium for poetry.

Pound extracted the ideogram from its service as a medium of communication and turned it into a new medium for modern literature. This repackaging of Chinese into a literary medium depended on a confluence of events, many of which are known to modernist scholars but bear repeating here. When Pound arrived in London in 1908, that city was abuzz with the Orient. The British Museum's oriental art expert, Lawrence Binyon, had just published *Painting in the Far East* (1908), the first serious study of Far Eastern pictorial art in English.[42] Binyon would come to serve as Pound's mentor in Chinese art (and Pound called him "BinBin" in personal letters home).[43] In 1912, when Pound met with H. D. and Richard Aldington for tea in the British Museum to draft the Imagist rules for poetry, he also had regular lunches with Binyon.[44] In 1913, in a moment now mythologized in literary history, Binyon introduced Pound to Mary Fenollosa, widow of Ernest Fenollosa. Mrs. Fenollosa handed the young poet a sheaf of her husband's papers, which included translations of Chinese poetry, dissections of Chinese ideograms, and the unfinished manuscript of *The Chinese Written Character as a Medium for Poetry*. She asked Pound to edit her husband's unfinished work, and in so doing, presented him with the means through which he would remake modern poetry.

1913 is a turning point in modernism because the Imagist manifesto, "A Few Don'ts," was published in the March issue of *Poetry* and because it is the year Pound discovered the Chinese ideogram. In this foreign textual sign system, Pound found the manifestation of the first and most important Imagist rule: "Direct treatment of the thing." Hugh Kenner describes Pound's discovery of the Chinese character as a pivotal point in his career, for, within "a few months the Image became the Vortex; in the late spring of 1914 pages were added to the bindery sheets of *Blast* already printed, to introduce the term 'Vorticism.'"[45] Pound's poetic trajectory from Imagism to Vorticism—from a poetics centered on the static, concrete image to one focused on dynamic force—finds its inspiration in Fenollosa's text. Critics generally regard the influence of Fenollosa's manuscripts on Pound as significant for both the poet and for twentieth-century poetry more generally.[46] The culmination of this influence is evident in *The Chinese Written Character as a Medium for Poetry*, Fenollosa's manuscript, which Pound edited and published in 1918.

Pound wrote a short foreword to Fenollosa's book that considerably reframed it into a treatise in general aesthetics. But, in its manuscript form, Fenollosa's text had no such aspirations. Pound's foreword states, "We have here not a bare philosophical discussion, but a study of the fundamentals of *all* aesthetics" (emphasis added).[47] Despite Pound's introductory description, Fenollosa's text asserts a different emphasis. Fenollosa focuses on literature as a means of addressing larger, political issues. He begins by stating, "The Chinese problem alone is so vast that no nation can afford to ignore it."[48] He writes, "An unfortunate belief has spread both in England and in America that Chinese and Japanese poetry are hardly more than amusement, trivial, childish, and not to be reckoned in the world's serious literary performance."[49] In contrast to this view, Fenollosa recognizes literature to be a cross section between national and poetic registers, and he presents his manuscript accordingly—as both a poetic and a political enterprise. Fenollosa's introductory framework presents his text as an ambassadorial act to understand "the other" through their language and literature. From the beginning of his text, Fenollosa insists on the political poignancy of poetry, and he turns to this claim again in the text's conclusion: "We have been told that these people [the Chinese] are cold, practical, mechanical, literal, and without a trace of imaginative genius. That is nonsense."[50] Bookended by such politically minded statements, *The Chinese Written Character as a Medium for Poetry* resists Pound's classification of it as a general or universal study of aesthetics. Recognizing this fact illuminates Pound's purposeful hand as editor. Turning Fenollosa's manuscript into a treatise with universal aspirations took effort. Indeed, as Yunte Huang has shown, Pound excised much of the political tone from the original manuscript in order to foreground the aesthetic aspect of the text.[51] The editorial expurgation of these passages transforms the essay from one addressing a particular period, people, and political climate to a general treatise on poetics that Pound then employs for his own purposes.

In Fenollosa's depiction of the ideogram Pound discovered a visual medium for universal communication. Fenollosa presented the ideogram as "based upon a vivid shorthand picture of the operations of nature."[52] This closeness to nature stood in sharp contrast to the alphabetic system of English, which, we recall from the beginning of this chapter, Saussure contemporaneously defined as arbitrary in its semiotic operation. Earlier I pointed out that Saussure distinguished between ideogrammic and alphanumeric language, and he pursued his structuralist theory only in relation to alphanumeric text. According to Saussure, the other term ideogrammic language, operated in stark contrast to alphanumeric text. Chinese ideograms supposedly depicted a direct visual correspondence or otherwise logical relationship between the linguistic sign and the natural world it signified. The relationship between this text and the world it described was thus visible and understandable. Fenollosa understands Chinese in a similar manner. For him, ideograms express the dynamism of the natural world. He writes, "A true noun, an isolated thing, does not exist in nature."[53] Therefore, "The verb must be the primary fact of nature, since motion and change are all that we can recognize in her."[54] Pound reads and reacts to this particular point in Fenollosa's manuscript. For him, the direct and universal aspects of the Chinese ideogram render it the natural medium for universal poetics.

In a fascinating note that he adds to the margin of Fenollosa's text, Pound suggests that the ideogram is a medium akin to other media forms that artists use to express the natural and universal. He relates how Vorticist sculptor Gaudier-Brzeska was able to read Chinese without any training in the language but simply by relying on his artistic ability to see into nature:

> Gaudier-Brzeska sat in my room before he went off to war. He was able to read the Chinese radicals and many compound signs almost at pleasure. He was used to consider all life and nature in the terms of planes and of bounding lines. Nevertheless he had spent only a fortnight in the museum studying the Chinese characters. He was amazed at the stupidity of lexicographers who could not, for all their learning discern the pictorial values which were to him perfectly obvious and apparent.[55]

The anecdote expresses Pound's view that Chinese is a natural and universal language, one that is particularly discernible to the artist, a person skilled in seeing in visual terms ("of planes and of bounding lines"). With this note about Gaudier-Bzeska, Pound inserts two points into Fenollosa's manuscript. First, he presents Chinese as a universal sign system, a medium that records and projects the natural world. Second, he identifies the artist as being more attuned to nature's frequencies.[56] Thus, as an artist himself, Pound is not only an editor but also a kind of medium through which messages flow and are transmitted.

Pound turns Chinese into a kind of medium. In *Ideographic Modernism* Christopher Bush examines the idea that the ideogram is a medium, a kind of modern invention akin to many other types of new technological media of the modernist period. "The ideograph is a modern Western invention," he writes, "one contemporaneous with, and related to, such other modern inventions, such other forms of writing, as the telegraph, the phonography, the photograph, and the cinematograph."[57] Bush identifies the ideograph as a central discursive and technical element of Western modernism that emerges "at the intersections of three critical discourses: Orientalism critique, grammatology (the study of writing), and media theory."[58] We can see this dynamic at work in Pound's editorial interaction with Fenollosa's manuscript, and when we do, we recognize Pound's own interest in mediality. As Bush suggests, "we can think about modernism's China as not just something thought *about* but also something thought *with*" (emphasis in original).[59] It is ultimately as a poet dealing with literature's medium, rather than a translator dealing with linguistic content, that Pound approaches Fenollosa's manuscript. To this understanding of Pound's use of the ideogram, we can add Eric Hayot's point: "it was as though something in the Chinese permitted, or gave birth to, the Poundian unveiling of the universal."[60] In other words, Pound sees Chinese as a universal code, and he reframes Fenollosa's text accordingly. He turns it into a treatise on universal poetics that can then serve to validate his own developing literary practice. It is in this way that Pound "invents" Chinese as a new medium for modern poetry.

Despite the importance of Pound in the genealogy I am tracing between modernism and digital modernism, the idea that Chinese is a medium for universal language far precedes him. It reaches the modernist poet via a lineage of thinkers in America that includes Fenollosa's major influence, Ralph Waldo Emerson. In *American Hieroglyphics,* John Irwin shows that an interest in Egyptian hieroglyphics pervaded nineteenth-century American poetry. Although the written character of interest to the transcendentalists was the Egyptian hieroglyph rather than the Chinese ideogram, they are, in certain ways, interchangeable. Hieroglyph and ideogram both represent and serve the efforts of Western thinkers to extract a foreign, textual character from its communicative service and become a transcendental medium for new poetic possibilities. A motivating factor in the American Renaissance, Irwin states, was "an Adamic task" of learning to "call objects by their right name," which implies an ability "to call them by their original names."[61] This "task" assumes that objects have "original names," and, thus, that there is a forgotten past to discover. Recall *Chroma*'s tale of a search for a lost Eden, the "natural cyberspace" of the mnemonos. The digital work presents a contemporary configuration of this tradition (although, as I argued, the digital novel critiques the intellectual tradition upon which its narrative depends). But an earlier, modernist version is evident in Pound's engagement with the Chinese ideogram. "Chinese for Pound," Ira Nadel writes, "meant the recovery or reinvention of Adamic speech."[62] Pound inherits a vision of the ideogram from Fenollosa (and Emerson) that is imbued with the potential for written language to recapture Edenic speech and thus repair the ruptures of Babel.

Babel is, of course, the Biblical story that explains the chaos and confusion of human communication across multiple languages. Babel also becomes the source of many metaphors through which this ambitious quest to recuperate and employ an ancient, universal language is described. This quest connects twentieth-century poetry to the parallel trajectory to which I now turn: the early history of computing.

Universal Code

We can trace the Western idealization of Chinese as a universal language beyond Pound and Emerson back to the seventeenth century and the origins of binary code. Jesuit missionaries exploring the East sent reports back home to Europe describing Chinese as *lingua univeralis*, and, as a result, Huang writes, "Europeans believe[d] that they had finally found in Chinese the prototypical human language."[63] Philosopher and mathematician Gottfried Leibniz fantasized about Chinese, and he funneled these ideas into his philosophical writings. Leibniz supplied "the initial germ for the birth of computers," claims Michael Heim.[64] This origin, he writes, "started with the rationalist philosophers of the seventeenth century who were passionate in their efforts to design a world language."[65] Specifically, Leibniz created a rational universal code or universal character set, *characteristicia universalis* that, Heim explains, "rests on a binary logic" similar to the binary logic that eventually enables digital code.[66] In 1679 Leibniz outlined plans for a calculating machine based in binary numbers, a protocomputer of sorts. He grounded his efforts in mathematical computing upon ideas about Chinese language and philosophy, specifically the conceptual correspondence between Yin/Yang. The idea that a binary operating function underlies a universe of dualities becomes the foundation for the mathematical structure of binary states in digital computing.

Like Pound, Leibniz believed he had found in Chinese a precedent for his own theories and a medium for their expression. Where Pound saw universal truth residing in the "one-image poem" of the haiku, Leibniz discovered it in the sixty-four hexagrams of the *I Ching*.[67] But both Western thinkers shared the idea that Chinese is a medium that, rather than just serving interpersonal communicative efforts, can enable larger philosophical and poetic goals. Following in Leibniz's wake, philosophers and poets alike have fantasized about Chinese as a universal code. On this point, Jacques Derrida identifies "the *function* of the Chinese model in Leibniz's projects" as a cornerstone in Western philosophy (emphasis in original).[68] Derrida describes Leibniz's use of Chinese as a tool or technology that "functions" or serves a particular ideological enterprise. He writes, "all the philosophical projects of a universal script and of a universal language . . . invoked by Descartes . . . Leibniz, etc., encouraged seeing in the recently discovered Chinese script a model of the philosophical language thus *removed from history*" (emphasis added).[69] When extracted from communication and "removed from history" or the historical moment of its employment, language is no longer context driven. It becomes instead a rarefied, artificial system of empty signifiers. This presentation of the ideogram as a universal medium, Derrida writes, "arbitrarily and by the artifice of invention, wrenches it from history and gives it to philosophy."[70] Such extraction has decisive ramifications for Western thought and also for this chapter's argument.

"The concept of Chinese writing thus functioned as a sort of European *hallucination*," Derrida writes (emphasis added).[71] I italicize "hallucination" and employ it in this chapter's title in order to emphasize how poets and philosophers—and, as we'll soon see, computer scientists—use the ideogram to serve their own, individual ideals. They use the ideogram in order to hallucinate about supposedly universal truths. Leibniz and Pound shared this hallucination, and versions of it continue into the contemporary computing age. Its digital counterpart is the "consensual hallucination" known as cyberspace; and "a mass consensual hallucination" is how novelist William Gibson famously described the vision of cyberspace he presented in his novel *Neuromancer* (1984).[72] Cyberspace was thus introduced to the popular imagination as a "consensual hallucination" before the technological network and its virtual realm even existed for the masses to access.

We have seen that the parallel histories of computing and poetics, that I have been tracing here via Pound and Leibniz, share a view (or hallucination) of the Chinese ideogram as a universal medium. The Western hallucination that turns Chinese into a universal language supports the idea (or ideology) that cyberspace is a realm of transcendental information and disembodied communication (a "discourse network 2000," as Alan Liu called it). This hallucination renders code natural, universal, and true. The idea that code is a natural language (and thus, as *Chroma* proposes, that cyberspace is a prelapsarian Eden) turns computer code into a contemporary equivalent of the Chinese ideogram (as we saw it described by Leibniz, Fenollosa, and Pound). This concept is built into the computing machines from Leibniz onward and into the cultural understanding of them. Indeed, as I now venture to show, these parallel histories of poetics and computing intersect in the mid-twentieth century when computer science comes into its own. The specific point of convergence: the shared effort to achieve universal language through technological efforts in machine translation.

Machine Translation and Basic English

Machine translation uses computers to produce universal communication through digital translation, and it has been an essential aspect and ambition of digital computing from its inception. "Universal language is not a project to which the computer has been applied," David J. Gunkel explains, "it constitutes the very genetic structure and fundamental program of the technology itself."[73] Computing pioneers Warren Weaver and Norbert Wiener shared a vision of a super-computer that would apply cryptographic techniques (acquired during WWII) to all translation.[74] In July 1949, Weaver, the father of Communication Theory and Cybernetics, wrote the now historic memorandum in which he introduced the idea of computer-based universal translation. Titled "Translation," this memo employs allusions to Babel as the pillars upon which to build his vision for computing:

> Thus may it be true that the way to translate from Chinese to Arabic, or from Russian to Portuguese, is not to attempt the direct route, shouting from tower to tower. Perhaps the way is to descend, from each language, down to the common base of human communication—the real but as yet undiscovered universal language—and then re-emerge by whatever particular route is convenient.[75]

Weaver identifies universal language as an Edenic quest, one that is "real but as yet undiscovered," and he invokes the tower of Babel as the central trope to describe the computer-based effort to achieve it. He continues to use this trope in later talks and publications so that Babel thus becomes a central metaphor of computing as Weaver becomes part of a genealogy reaching back to Leibniz as well as to Pound and Fenollosa. In a collection of essays on the topic of machine translation, published six years later, Weaver employs the analogy to Babel to describe the shared goal of computer scientists: "the logicians who design computers, the electronic engineers who build and run them . . . are now engaged in erecting a new Tower of Anti-Babel."[76] Babel is thus presented as the backdrop for a computing initiative that will build upwards toward the heavens in the pursuit of a universal language. Ironically, the construction project to build a universal language is based in a single, foundational language: English. Rita Raley points out that "machine translation tries to posit a kind of universality and transparency to translation," even though the computer "operates around and with English as a pivot language."[77] Efforts to repair the ruptures of Babel through the digital computer thus depend upon a substitution of English for universal language. The sleight of hand replaces the universal—identified as Chinese by Pound, Fenollosa, and Leibniz—with English, and it enables the fantasy of universal language to continue into the digital realm.

Before we leap to the contemporary era, however, we should pause to register the fact that a similar substitution of English for Chinese as the base language for universal communication was attempted in the period just prior to Wiener and Weaver's computing efforts and just after Pound's publication of Fenollosa's manuscript. In the period bookended by modernism and early electronic computing, Charles Kay Ogden introduced Basic English.

Basic English is an International Auxiliary Language constructed to enable universal communication through a simple but potentially global language. It is a pared-down version of English comprised of 850 words, eighteen of which are verbs, and simple rules for their organization and use. The acronym for BASIC (British American, Scientific International and Commercial) expresses its universalizing agenda. Ogden published a series of books in the 1930s delineating Basic English and advocating its usage. Such books include *Basic English: A General Introduction with Rules and Grammar* (1930) and *Debabelization* (1931), whose title situates Basic English in the constellation of efforts to achieve universal language and also the metaphorical tropes used to describe them. In fact, Pound reviewed *Debabelization* for *New English Weekly*.[78] In a short piece titled "Odgen and Debabelization" (1935), Pound claims to be "Ogden's ally" although "probably the last one he looked for";[79] this is because Pound supports Basic English not for its communicative potential but for its ability to foster poetic skills. "For three decades," Pound writes, "I have believed, taught and practiced that translation is the absolute best among all forms of writer's training."[80] Basic English "offered as a second and supplementary language," Pound writes, could serve as a mode of "training and exercise" for writers.[81]

Another figure that keeps popping up in the various constellations I am tracing throughout this book is I. A. Richards, and again he takes a prominent role in advancing Basic English. Richards (who, as I showed in Chapter 1, inspired Marshall McLuhan's adaptation of close reading toward media studies) was actively involved in the Basic English movement. He wrote a book, *Basic English and its Uses* (1943), that presents the invented language as a medium for achieving peace in a war-torn world. In 1950, he took Basic English abroad—to China, in fact—in an educational effort that occupied his later career, as Rodney Koeneke documents.[82] For Richards, Basic English could not only assist in teaching English but also improve language skills for English natives, particularly those not equipped with the translation skills acquired from elite universities.[83] He also shared Pound's view of Basic English as furthering literary, not just literacy, skills. Richards describes Basic English as a means of "conceiving a world language in a truly planetary spirit—as a universal *medium*" (emphasis added).[84] When conceived as a medium, Basic English is a tool that can be updated and reconfigured to serve purposes unforeseen by its inventors and early advocates. One such extension of Basic English was into the realm of cybernetics and computer science.

Lydia H. Liu identifies Basic English as a precursor to "one of the most significant biocybernetic inventions since World War II"—Claude Shannon's Printed English.[85] Printed English, as Shannon describes it, is a method for statistically determining "how much information is produced on the average for every letter of a text in that language."[86] This concept produced a correspondence between text and numerical symbols which, Liu writes, "laid the foundation for what would become the ASCII code" and which would "achieve its ultimate ideographic embodiment in the mathematical figuring of 0/1 binary oppositions."[87] Recognizing the connection between Basic English, Printed English, and their derivatives should remind us that the heart of these foundational computing projects is an English-based effort to achieve universal language. "With the English code being named the original code," Liu writes, "Printed English was poised to become the first universal ideographic system with respect to which all other languages of the world would turn into translations."[88] In other words, English was poised to become universal—and, indeed ideographic—by virtue of the digital computer.

Having pursued the relationship between Printed English and Basic English, through the long backstory of efforts to pursue universal language, we now have a foundation for approaching and historicizing contemporary discourse about the computer and the World Wide Web.

The World Wide Web and Global English

As its name proclaims, the World Wide Web employs a global rhetoric to express the sense that this technological network of interlinked computers offers a global communication system. Uniform Resource Locators (URLs) denote specific addresses on a network that allows computers in different locations to share information, but for these computers to communicate, they must share a language. Thus, the central precept of networked computing, the underlying vision of a global network supporting the digital global village, is the belief in a programmable universal language. The technical details of Internet communications are not my subject here. You can read about how code and Internet protocols actually operate in many other venues.[89] Rather I continue to trace the historical and discursive parallels between modernist and contemporary *understandings* of code as enabling universal language. To do so, I now turn to the World Wide Web.

The Internet has gone through many linguistic renovations. For example, when the web was introduced in the early 1990s, its hyperlinked, networked structure was supported by HTML (HyperText Markup Language). This hybrid of English and machine symbols derive from the SGML (Standard General Markup Language), which has a predecessor in GML (General Markup Language); but that is another digression and discussion. The significant point is that these markup languages annotate (or mark up) text to identify how it will be laid out on the screen. These markup languages helped to foster the success of the web, and, importantly, they are all based in English. When the web developed into Web 2.0 (in the mid 2000s), its content and user base grew exponentially and deepened in complexity, and the meta-language XML (eXtensible Markup Language) emerged to encode this diverse information. As its name suggests, XML also retains its English "base," to use Weaver's term for describing how to build a universal language via computers. Writing about the protocols that define and enable communication between computers across the network known as "the Internet," Laura DeNardis points out, "There is nothing preordained about these communications norms. They are socially constructed protocols."[90] Alexander Galloway has convincingly argued that it is precisely *through* protocols that the Internet inscribes technological control into its decentralized network.[91] Further, Wendy Chun has shown that the mutually constitutive relationship between control and freedom online is not just technological but cultural; it has been built into the idea, image, and use of the web from the earliest advertisements promoting computers and web access.[92] In other words, the cultural and technological layers of digital computing are neither separate nor discrete. The traffic between them operates in a feedback loop, what Lev Manovich calls "transcoding":[93] "The result of this composite [of cultural and technological layers] is a new computer culture—a blend of human and computer meanings, of traditional ways in which human culture modeled the world and the computer's own means of representing it."[94]

Transcoding offers a possible paradigm for understanding the role of English in computers. For English is not only the base for high-level markup languages; it is English all the way down into the layers of programming that enable computer processing and Internet communications. HTML sits on top of an Apache web server that sits on top of C++, which sits on top of assembly language. All of these programming languages include or are structured by English, and the specificities of this fact permeate even the lowest levels of programming languages, such as first-generation (which uses English letters interspersed with numbers) and second-generation assembly language (which uses English-based commands such as "mov" and "int"). Even hexadecimal machine binary code includes English alphanumeric text. The objection could be raised that these English signs are arbitrary since the language of code is mathematical rather than linguistic, even electric or technological. Indeed, Kittler puts forth this argument in his famous essay "There Is No Such Thing as Software" (1995) wherein he claims that at its base, computing is but a series of electrical impulses.[95] Yet the fact remains that

English signs, abbreviations, and transcriptions permeate computer operations in fundamental ways. Recognition of this fact might cause us to pause before identifying the computer and its code as universal.

It is also worth remembering that English is the language of the web but not of the world. English is used as the language of capitalistic commerce and is studied as a mode of communication, but Chinese is the language of daily communication in the most populated country in the world.[96] There is a "mismatch," Joe Lockard writes, "between the net's lingua franca and the overwhelmingly non-anglophone world," and this situation "has been so widely overlooked as to become a comment in its own right on a willful mass blindness that characterizes cyber-english culture."[97] I quote Lockard here because his rhetoric, particularly the language of "willful mass blindness," echoes Derrida's depiction of the "interested blindness" that supports Western philosophical views of Chinese as a universal language.[98] The concern that cyber-English or "Global English" (as it is often called) is hegemonic and has the potential to serve as a colonizing force inspires much backlash in both popular and scholarly discourse. For example, postcolonial theorist Gayatri Chakravorty Spivak writes, "I am deeply troubled by claims to global English," for, "it is sometimes claimed that the Internet can go Chinese."[99] Note Spivak's suggestion that for the Internet to incorporate Chinese it must take a turn and "go" in a different direction. Spivak continues, "I think for that to happen Chinese will probably have to go beyond simplified characters and confine itself to the twenty-six letters of pinyin, make its tonal system contextual."[100] Spivak implies that not only would the Internet have to change to fully engage with Chinese, but so too would Chinese also have to change.

Chinese may have inspired early Western thinkers to fantasize about the possibilities of binary code, but the actual translation of ideograms into digital code has proven a technical challenge. The particular challenges Chinese poses to the Internet and its operational protocols serve to disable the paradigm of willful or interested blindness that identifies Chinese and computer code as universal. Encoding Chinese characters into digital code is difficult due to the sheer number of characters (Chinese contains more than 71,000 characters and over 4,000 syllables in standard Chinese pronunciation) as well as the numerous possible phonetic effects that alter meaning. The scale of transcription poses a stark contrast and challenge to the limited character set of the English alphabet, upon which digital programming is based.[101] Because of the difficulties involved in transcoding Chinese and other ideogrammic-based languages into the English-based ASCII system, a new standard was created in 2003: Unicode CJKV (Chinese, Japanese, Korean, Vietnamese). Innovations in translation software (such as Babelfish) and coding standards are intended to enhance the transmission and transcoding of information online by extending the potential number of languages used, but such additions do not address the larger ideological implications about the systems of power that support digital infrastructures and the interactions they enable. Sandy Baldwin writes, "As with the ASCII standard, Unicode is easily critiqued for the way it inevitably re-maps geopolitical concerns and contentions."[102] Even if Unicode does not exactly "re-map" real-life politics onto the virtual realm, such technical solutions do point to the ideological, political, and economic forces that promote and serve to benefit from attempts at universal language. The need for constant emendations to translation software and machines only expose the problematic nature of this quest and attest to the fact that this situation is as much a technical challenge as an ideological one.

Ironically and with a sense of poetic justice, then, it is Chinese—the language that Pound, Leibniz, and others perceived to be universal—that disables contemporary hallucinations about universal language. This is why digital modernist literature employs the ideogram in its onscreen poetics to critique ideological undercurrents inherited from modernism and computer science. Armed with an understanding of the historical, ideological, and technological backdrop that motivates them, we now turn to back to the literature to consider how digital writers engage the idea of achieving of universal language through digital code.

Part III. Digital Modernism's Critique

Young-hae Chang Heavy Industries's *Nippon* (2002) displays ideograms onscreen as part of its formal aesthetic in ways that complicate translation and transcoding.[103] The ideogrammic language in use in this piece is Japanese, not Chinese, but YHCHI juxtapose English and Japanese onscreen in ways that visually represent and poetically confront the ideological issues I have been discussing in this chapter. In *Nippon,* Japanese and English occupy opposite sides of a horizontally divided screen. (See Figure 5.3). The interface presents a perfect opportunity for translation. But

Fig 5.3 Screenshot from Young-hae Chang Heavy Industries's *Nippon* (2002). (Used with permission from the authors.)

Nippon thwarts efforts to translate across the languages. Like all of Young-hae Chang Heavy Industries's (YHCHI) works, *Nippon* is built in Flash to produce a fast, flashing performance choreographed to a jazz soundtrack. (I discussed this poetic in my reading of *Dakota* in Chapter 3). But there is an added element of complication here. When *Nippon* begins, the two languages flash in synchronicity to the same beat and tell the same story. But with the introduction of syncopation into the jazz track, the dance of the languages across the dividing line begins to diverge. Each language starts to flash to a different instrument: English to the trumpet, Japanese to the piano. As the music accelerates, so does the text. The visual dialectic is strengthened by the contrasting colors of the screen. In the upper part of the screen, Japanese appears as red text against a white backdrop; in the bottom register, English is presented in white against red. The languages dance and clash against the colors of the Japanese flag in a performance that aesthetically depicts the traffic of translation happening between, across, and through them. The effect is an audio-visual dialogue between two languages and the cultures they represent, two nations who are central players in advancing global technology and the technoculture of the World Wide Web upon which *Nippon* is accessed.

But there is another aspect of *Nippon*'s poetic that only becomes evident when approached through the perspective gained by the efforts of this chapter, by tracing the role of the ideogram as a site of deep intersecting interests and histories shared between literature and computing. This perspective illuminates *Nippon*'s central aesthetic feature—its juxtaposition of alphanumeric and ideogrammic text—and shows it to be part of a much longer history. We need only compare a page from Ezra Pound's later cantos (particularly Canto LXXVII) wherein he uses Chinese ideograms and a screenshot from *Nippon* to see how YHCHI adapt Pound's use of the Chinese ideogram to present universal poetics. Japanese is, of course, a different language system than Chinese (although it does incorporate Chinese ideograms), and it possesses a distinct cultural history; nevertheless, the juxtaposition of *Nippon* and Pound's canto is visually striking.

The Cantos places Chinese ideograms on a vertical axis along the right-hand margin, so that they appear to the English reader as a kind of frame around the poem. In contrast, *Nippon* presents its Japanese text on a horizontal axis, above its English text so that the two are equal and inseparable. Yet, both works share an effort to use juxtaposition in order to explore the relationship between Western and Eastern linguistic signs for a poetic effect.

Pound juxtaposes Chinese and English not for translation purposes but to display, as Ming Xie writes, "the metamorphic passage or inter-traffic between them."[104] YHCHI do something similar but toward a different purpose. They use the bilingual juxtaposition to invoke the technological codes involved in producing their onscreen aesthetic. *Nippon* sets up an opportunity for translation but then dashes this possibility with the formal, animated presentation of its text. Due to the speed of the flashing words, even a reader fluent in both languages is unable to read both texts simultaneously. The reader grows acutely aware of the failure of human translation to keep up with the other reader concurrently working to translate *Nippon*'s text—the computer. *Nippon* draws attention to the computer's circuitry and protocols (particularly since it is accessed online) in ways that direct discussions away from a rarefied thing called "code." The visual opportunity for translation depicted onscreen is made possible by the layers of translation happening across protocols, platforms, and languages that remain hidden. *Nippon* thus reorients the ways in which we read to remind us that computers, their operations and codes, and the ways in which they are discussed are never separate from but always embedded in specific cultural contexts.

Nippon's narrative also supports this argument. Even though the text never directly discusses digital technologies, the Internet, or the culture of transnational capitalism, the effects of digital technoculture provide its centrifugal force. *Nippon* creates a microcosm around archetypal characters and builds a universal narrative that critiques and subtly complicates the concept of "world wide" in World Wide Web. *Nippon* narrates the thoughts, actions, and interactions of a group of businessmen and "working women" in an after-hours brothel-bar, a night amidst the "world's oldest profession." The unnamed characters are archetypes: the domineering madam, the leggy, lust-inspiring singer, the man who flirts with the prostitute while praising his loyal wife. The male characters make excuses for being out rather than at home, and the stories they tell are so common that the female listeners have "HEARD THIS— KIND — ØF — STØRY— MANY — TIMES."[105] *Nippon*'s narrative appears worlds away from critical discussions about compilation and computation. The title is the only indication of geographical location given; besides this hint, the narrative could happen anywhere (or, at least, in any urban setting). It is, in a sense, universal. The men in the bar are coworkers but not friends, and although the happenings occur after-hours and in an environment distinct from the office-space that contains their gray-suited, daytime efforts, the activities in the bar are still work. The fact that work bleeds into nontraditional working locations and hours further renders this an archetypal story for the digital, mobile, networked age.

The workers, both the male customers and also the female escorts, labor to listen to their "HØST," who is also their boss. While he speaks, they "THINK— FØND— THØUGHTS— ØF— DEATH— AND NØTHINGNESS." The narrative alternates between first- and third-person points-of-view, shifting between the perspectives of the women, the men, and an omniscient narrator. All of the characters are in the midst of on-the-job education. An experienced voice prompts the working women to turn the tables and regard their male clients as laborers who "WØRK FØR YØU, — SWEAT — FØR— YØU." Instructions follow: "LEAN— YØUR— HEAD— BACK— AND — LET—THE— SMØKE— ØUT— LIKE— A SIGH, — A— LØSS— REGRET— THAT —HE— CAN SØØTHE." The men also experience their after-hours entertainment as a form of labor: "EVERYØNE— MAKES AN EFFØRT— TØ— BE — SØCIABLE." At the end of the night and the end of the animation, *Nippon* shows that the effects of global corporate capitalism are not limited to the confines of the after-hours bar but are evident in the daytime, too. In morning light laden with ennui and isolation, the streets are filled with "TØØ MANY MEN IN DARK-GREY SUITS/ HURRY TØ TAXIS,/ AND LØØK HØW MANY— HAVE —CHAUFFERS." The various industries involved in producing this cultural effect are indicted in the judgment repeated in *Nippon*'s first and last lines, which each state, "IT'S WRØNG." Yet, *Nippon*'s last line continues, suggesting that such conclusions are never black and white (or red and white): "IT'S—WRØNG,—ALL WRØNG.—AND—YET IT'S/ ALL SØ RIGHT."

Nippon can be read as a critique of the homogenizing influence of the English-based and Western-focused web. The narrative registers hints of the negative effects of Western cultural colonization on the Japanese subject. Consider, for example, when the narrative slips into the interior consciousness of the characters: "ØUR—HØST" shared "HIS —DEEPEST — THØUGHTS —ØN — LIFE – —HIS —LIFE, — WHICH RESEMBLE A —LIVE, — UNCUT —ADAPTATION — ØF AN ØLD BLUE/ EYES' FAVØRITE." Whether the man's "DEEPEST—THØUGHTS" were actually so shallow as to resemble a sentimental Sinatra song or it is the narrator who is constrained to such descriptions, the presence of Old Blue Eyes in the inner thoughts of the narrator and/or the host attests to the infiltration of American culture into the deepest reaches of Japanese consciousness. In another example, the narrator assesses the scene at the bar and notices a set of interesting discrepancies: "THE LIPSTICK, —PEARLY— PINK,— SHØULD— BE— BLØØD—RED" and "THE— WHITE— LIGHT/ SHØULD BE — YELLØW,— A— SLEEPY—YELLØW - — NØT— HARSH— FLØURESCENT." The observations are those of a director preparing for a cinematic scene, and they express the narrator's possession of a set of preconceived notions, informed by mass media, of what the moment should look and feel like. While such moments might seem to represent a homogenization of cultural influences, *Nippon* complicates this conclusion in its formal performance. The split screen and speeding interaction between English and Japanese renders the languages and the cultural powers they represent as participating in a collaboration, a duet even, that produces the digital work and its presentation of a situation that is both "wrong" and "right."

Nippon's conceptual dichotomies of English/Japanese, red/white, East/West, work/leisure, male/female, commerce/sex, ideogrammic/alphanumeric, code/language are displayed in a performative act of deconstruction that complicates their divisions and shows their relationships to be symbiotic rather than oppositional. As *Nippon*'s long animation proceeds, the boundary line cutting through the interface separating red and white text begins to blur. The presentation of English and Japanese in contrasting colors flashing on opposite sides of a horizontal line produces an optical illusion similar to the anamorphic effect that Rita Raley identifies as essential to early electronic literature.[106] One half of the screen and one language can be read only by forgoing the other. If the reader chooses to focus on reading the narrative, she must focus on one side of the screen. If she chooses to experience the aesthetic of the two languages simultaneously, she forgoes reading for content. *Nippon* thus pursues a similar formal technique as *Chroma*, with its View Text and Perform Text options. Both digital works force the reader to choose a way of accessing the literary text that highlights the inextricability of content and form. These digital modernist works expose message to be dependent upon medium and remind us that neither are ever universal.

One way that *Nippon* draws attention to the specifics of its medium is through its interface design. The dividing line separating English and Japanese serves to reflexively allude to the role of the screen itself as a medium, one that mediates between machine and human. The invisible, executable programming code the drives the work remains hidden from the reader, but the result of this translated code flashes onscreen.[107] The performance of ideogrammic and alphanumeric text is both a metaphor and a metonym for the operational relationship between screenic text and the code compiling it. *Nippon* focuses attention on how code and ideogram are deeply dependent upon the specific contexts enabling their performance. Whether those contexts are technological, cultural, or both, the extraction of one element—code or ideogram—from them is nothing short of impossible. YHCHI thus employ the ideogram as a poetic symbol in order to resist Pound's earlier usage of it. *Nippon* counters ideas about universal translation through its use of ideograms, specifically hopes of achieving universal communication through computers and code.

Conclusion

This chapter sought to recuperate shared points of connection between the histories of literature and computing by excavating efforts toward universal communication. Exposing these shared lineages supports reconsideration of the relationship between these seemingly separate fields of knowledge, practice, and poetics. I hope it is now evident how these two fields, literature and computing, which are often posed as opposites, share certain core foundations. Moreover, this reminder should serve to illuminate the importance of literature and literary analysis in digital culture, for *Nippon* and *Chroma* are examples of digital literature that present immanent critiques of their technocultural context. Specifically, they resist ideologies of universal language passed down from earlier periods and into our own digital culture. This is a particularly vital service in a culture besieged by the logic of computation, protocol politics, and Global English.

Recuperating and asserting the importance of the literary in a digital age is the main point of this chapter and of this book more generally. And, if you agree with Derrida, it is also the main point of the Biblical story of Babel, the story that so inspired innovations in computing from Leibniz to Weaver. In "Des Tours de Babel" Derrida interprets the Babel story as a political parable and an origin point for literature. For Derrida, the Babel story depicts the Semitic people failing to build a tower to heaven but also failing to establish a totalitarian empire based on a single hegemonic language. The story of Babel depicts the failure of this linguistic totalitarianism as the origin point of translation. For Derrida, translation is a gift to humanity, for it privileges diversity over homogeneity and reminds us of the beauty of multiplicity. Reading the Babel story in this way, Derrida frames the biblical story not as a lament for a lost universal language but as an allegory that "exhibits an incompletion, the impossibility of finishing, of totalizing."[108] This incompletion is a good thing. For Derrida, the Babel story insists upon "the necessary and impossible task of translation, its necessity *as* impossibility" (emphasis in original).[109] The impossibility of perfect translation is nothing short of the impossibility of universal language.[110] In Derrida's deconstructive reading, the destruction of the Tower of Babel is not just the origin site of translation but also of literature more generally. Translation and literature are identified as inseparable, and Pound would certainly agree.

Digital literature literalizes this point, for its screenic poetics appear only through a series of processural translations across layers of languages and codes. Translation is at the heart of digital literature, despite rhetoric about the potential of digital code and computing to produce universal communication. Digital modernist literature like *Chroma* and *Nippon* employs the web to comment upon and critique the ideological undertows prevalent in discourse about machine translation and universal language that reach the present via modernism. They illuminate the cultural and historical contexts in which technical and poetic feats occur, and they invite us to excavate and follow the threads connecting literature and computing. Such works serve an important dual purpose in contemporary culture: they resist the hallucinations of cyberspace, and they illuminate the importance of literature in our digital age.

6. CODA—Rereading
*Digital Modernism in Print, Mark Z.
Danielewski's Only Revolutions*

We look at the present through a rear-view mirror, we march backwards into the future.

—Marshall McLuhan, *The Medium is the Massage*

We move forward by looking backward, McLuhan claimed, and this epigraph encapsulates the strategy of digital modernism that I have been exploring throughout this book: making it new is a recursive act of engaging with a literary past through media. The rearview mirror is a medium that enhances and distorts a driver's backward vision in order to mediate navigation and movement forward. Contemporary writers of digital modernism look in a rearview mirror of sorts in order to drive literature forward and into the digital realm. But what about print literature? How is it involved and informed by the relationship between modernism and digital modernism? By way of concluding this book, I move to show how the strategy of adapting modernist literary practices for a digital readership is not limited to digital technologies or to works of electronic literature. This is in part because digital technologies have so permeated our culture that all literature, regardless of its output platform, is impacted by digitality. This chapter explores this point by considering how certain experiments in contemporary print literature might be considered part of digital modernism. I conclude in this way in order to revisit and tie together central points I made earlier and also to extend the ramifications of my study. I focus in this concluding section on a highly experimental print novel that exemplifies digital modernism and that adopts McLuhan's metaphor of the rearview mirror as its central operating strategy.

Part I. The Bookbound Novel

Mark Z. Danielewski's *Only Revolutions* (2006) tells the story of two young lovers who venture on a road trip across the United States. Despite the linear, picaresque quality of a narrative that moves from one location to another, the novel formally insists on circularity. As its title expresses, *Only Revolutions* represents the dual and often paradoxical strategy at the heart of digital modernism: the act of recursively returning to the past to renovate contemporary literature. The word "revolution" is a noun and a verb, a spatial area and a temporal distance. It simultaneously suggests circularity and wholeness, rebellion and change. When paired with the qualifier "only," "revolutions" implodes, for a constant state of either constancy or change engenders its opposite—stasis. This circularity, expressed in the epigraph to this chapter, is metaphorically and formally enacted in *Only Revolutions*.

This is a 360-degree book. It contains 360 pages, with 180 words per page, with each page divided at its center along a horizontal axis into two sections that each contain 90 words. Each page of *Only Revolutions* contains an invisible horizon line in its middle that produces a kind of mirror effect. The first-person perspectives of the two narrators, Hailey and Sam, are printed in poetic stanzas that begin at opposite ends of the page. While the book's cover, proclaims *Only Revolutions* to be "a novel," it is also, undisputedly, a work of poetry. The intricate arrangement of text on the page pronounces it as such. In order to read this genre-breaking work, the reader must experiment with it, physically. You must turn the book around, literally rotate or revolve it 180 degrees, in order to read both sections of the page. The text on the page is further formatted for visual and poetic purpose. Where Sam's text appears in large font at the top of the page, Hailey's is printed upside-down in smaller letters at the opposite end, and vice versa. Each page can be read from either end with a simple turn of the book, and this feat of interface design and page layout becomes more apparent as the reader progresses in the narrative. For the work operates at a receding ratio between the font sizes of the two narratives, which shifts as the reader makes her way into the novel. So as you follow the tale of one narrator, the other's voice becomes visually smaller and diminished in contrast.

The novel has two beginnings, and each of the codex's covers opens to the start of either Hailey's or Sam's story. Upon opening the book to Hailey's story, the

reader encounters her narrative looming large, while Sam's text appears in minia-
ture print. All "O"s and zeroes contained in her narrative are colored gold, like her
gold-flecked eyes. Meanwhile, opening the book to Sam's side of the story figures
his narrative taking up most of the page space. Every circular linguistic character is
here printed in green, the color of his green-flecked eyes. In the middle of the book,
at page 180, both stories appear in equal sizes. The intricate page-design produces
a constantly shifting perspective that mirrors the movement of Sam and Hailey
as they cross the terrain of the United States. Moving through the pages of this
book is like moving through a physical landscape, and the effect draws attention
to the work's mediality. Indeed, the divided interface of the page space shares an
aesthetic with YHCHI's *Nippon* (discussed in the previous chapter). Both *Nippon*
and *Only Revolutions* invite a comparative reading practice of reading across and
between the two sides (of screen and page, respectively) to see what they share and
how they differ. *Nippon* and *Only Revolutions* also use their respective interfaces
to draw attention to the ways in which their poetic practice is informed by the
specifics of their medial form; the works are both about media and mediation. In
the case of *Only Revolutions*, this media is one that we use often without thinking
about it as a mediating technology: the book.

   Only Revolutions a bookbound object and a physically static text but, as we will
see, it is also a decidedly interactive work that demands significant and nontrivial
(ergodic) action from its reader.[1] Steering the book in constant circles, in a series
of only revolutions, the reader learns to see anew the well-known literary medium
of the codex. The novel fetishizes its codexical format even as it shows print literature evolving by adapting and incorporating the influences, aesthetics, and reading practices of the Internet. Moreover, and this is why Danielewski's novel serves
as my example of digital modernism in print, *Only Revolutions* formally encodes
this digital influence in ways that promote the types of literary critical reading
practices that I have been advocating throughout this book: close reading and
also comparative, media-specific, and media archaeological approaches. This is a
novel that enacts a digital modernist strategy of making it new by showing how the
old technology of the book—and the discipline of literary studies built to revolve
around it—is renovated through engagement with new media.

   As you might surmise from this brief summary of *Only Revolutions*'s formal
structure, this book makes serious demands of its reader. Its poetic content is playful and obscure; its typographical experimentation is beautiful but baffling. It requires a willingness to play, experiment, and interact with the book medium in
unexpected ways. In the process of making its reader reconsider how to engage
with the book object, *Only Revolutions* prompts consideration of what actions

constitute reading and how we go about it. How do you read this book? Do you read one narrator's story straight through or flip between them? Do you read a chunk of pages from Hailey before switching over to Sam? A publisher's note contained on the inside cover suggests a reading practice of proceeding by reading eight pages in one narrative before turning the book around to read the other narrator's story at the other end of the pages read. This suggestion enables the reader to follow the two characters as they experience the same action in different ways. Since both protagonists approach the same content from a different perspective, reading the second perspective has the sense of reloading the story and promotes a reading practice of rereading.

Unlike William Poundstone's *Project for the Tachistoscope {Bottomless Pit}* and YHCHI's *Dakota*, which are programmed in Flash to loop and reload, *Only Revolutions* employ print poetics and page design toward a similar purpose. Like those digital works, this novel demands that the reader reread in order to close read. As in *The Jew's Daughter*, wherein text mutated within paragraphs and context constantly changed, we read *Only Revolutions* by rereading. The content is set in ink, but its context changes with the 90-degree turn of the book. For each protagonist offers a different version of the same narrative story. The effect: reading *Only Revolutions* is an act of recycling. The suggestion to read eight pages at a time sets a pace and readerly movement that progresses in the narrative and the physical space of the book's pages by moving forward, then pausing, and revolving the book to begin reading again. The extraordinary formatting and constraint-driven poetics of *Only Revolutions* turns reading it into an enacted performance of its title. The novel also promotes a reading strategy that enacts the strategy of digital modernism: reading is rereading, and innovation happens by remaking the past.

The novel imparts an acute awareness that reading is a deeply medial activity dependent upon the specificities of reading technologies, even when the technology involved is that older literary medium, the book. We rotate this book in order to read its content and, in the process, are thereby forced to touch, hold, and feel the codexical object. This is how *Only Revolutions* defamiliarizes the book medium and the very familiar act of reading it. As we saw in Chapter 1, Marshall McLuhan showed that a medium only becomes visible and comprehensible when eclipsed by a newer one. Of particular interest to him was how the dawning of the electronic age brought newfound understanding of print. More recently, media scholars have dissented from the assumption underlying McLuhan's theory of media history— that history is a linear narrative of medial succession propelled by two central, revolutionary moments: the printing press and electric media. To take just two examples, scholars Bonnie Mak and Lisa Gitelman work in very different periods to expose the co-existence of multiple media in ways that complicate an evolutionary paradigm. Their research examines overlapping and often mutually dependent usage of old and new technologies, such as the contingent textual strategies of manuscript and print culture in the Middle Ages (Mak) and the interdependence on oral and inscription technologies in the nineteenth century (Gitelman).[2] *Only Revolutions* supports such scholarly reconsideration, for it challenges simple distinctions between print and digital as it also exploits the pleasures and possibilities of the codex in ways that show the book to be dependent upon digital media and networked reading practices. Indeed, *Only Revolutions* is deeply penetrated by digitality and is very much about its digital moment. But before showing this to be the case, let me step on the brakes and first attempt to describe the narrative and poetics that unfold in this bookish book.

Only Revolutions is an extraordinarily difficult work, difficult to maneuver and to difficult to understand. This difficulty is an intentional part of its aesthetic ambition and part of what positions it alongside the works of digital modernism that, I argued, employ difficulty to acquire serious attention as literary art. Attempting to summarize the narrative of *Only Revolutions* is not only a challenge but also a type of heresy of the paraphrase, to invoke New Critic Cleanth Brooks. As I mentioned, *Only Revolutions* is billed as a novel, but its pages present poetic stanzas filled with typographical and semantic play and thus refuse simply summary of content. Yet I will try.

Only Revolutions contains the stories of Hailey and Sam, two young lovers on an epic road trip across America who remain "always sixteen." Throughout the novel, Danielewski spells "always" with a double "l," as "allways." The two words, "all" and "ways" are connected without the loss of any part just as the characters are connected into a singular entity, US, while retaining their individual sides of the story (quite literally, as each one presides over one half of each page). Visually, the double "l" denotes the parallel double yellow lines that mark the roads on which the two primary characters travel. Aurally, the phonotextuality of the word "allways" invokes a keyword from Danielewski's earlier and equally ambitious novel, *House of Leaves* (2000): "hallways."[3] The visual and vocalized similarities between "allways" and "hallways" bridge the author's two books. But this novel is conceptually and aesthetically distinct from *House of Leaves*. Indeed, Danielewski has described them as conceptual opposites; meaning, they are separate but intimately related.[4] For example, whereas the majority of the action in *House of Leaves* takes place within the labyrinthine house on Ash Street, *Only Revolutions* unfolds across the network of highways and roads that constitute the infrastructure uniting the United States of America.

These "allways sixteen" characters remain frozen at the age when they receive the quintessential sign of American freedom—a driver's license. Sam and Hailey "runaway, throwaway, outtaplay" (H 97).[5] They "evade arrest, dodge the draft" (H 60) and otherwise strive to outdistance the encroaching stasis of the status quo. The stasis that spurs their flight is "A horror I should easily outrun but can't leave behind" (S 34). The novel moves constantly between states of movement and stillness, between driving or running away and staying the same age forever. These opposite states are, it becomes clear, mutually constitutive, just like the parallel lines on the road that divide but also connect the two lanes. Together, Sam and Hailey travel on roads and along a river, two great symbols of freedom and possibility in American literature (think Whitman's "Song of the Open Road," Twain's *Huckleberry Finn,* and Kerouac's *On the Road*). The novel's utopian spirit, road-trip remix, and poetic apostrophes to America's individualism invoke canonical American texts as well as, as Danielewski himself points out, films like *Bonnie and Clyde, Natural Born Killers, Badlands,* and *Thelma and Louise.*[6] But there is no other book like this one.

Hailey and Sam are two individuals pursuing American individualism, and they are constantly on the move. Each protagonist states, "We go with the/ current. Our own current. Ahead." (H219); "We go with the/ flow. Our own flow. Onward" (S219). All the while, Hailey and Sam are pursued by The Creep, an enigmatic character whose name appears in purple. This menacing figure stalks the couple and carries with him a noose, roman cord, or the like. The Creep seems to represent normative values and institutionalized roles, for his single purpose is to threaten the kids, to tie them down or worse. "Time to tie you down" (S 275) is his motivating mantra.[7] Sam and Hailey know they are being followed, so they refuse to stop too long for fear that "the World retake what we always elude when we run" (H 209). But The Creep patiently stalks the couple, unleashing violence whenever they meet. Hailey and Sam continue to move, emboldened by their sophomoric but sure sense that, as Hailey states, "Everyone wants to conquer me" (H 92). They live by the motto, "Where there's a Wheel, there's a way" (S 225) and "If you can't fix it, give it a spin" (H 245). As readers, we follow them as they outrun The Creep, and in so doing, we also creep. "There's only one person I can think of who ultimately ends up pursuing them [Sam and Hailey]," Danielewski tells Anthony Miller in an interview, "'Who makes it the whole way?' he asks, and then he points right at me."[8] With our hands at the wheel, we steer the book, hoping to catch and harness some of the couple's youthful energy.

But they can't run forever. They eventually run out of gas, literally and figuratively. Death comes at the end of the novel in the form of paralysis and stasis—poison from a bee sting and frozen ice. In an adaptation of the death scene from *Romeo and Juliet*, Sam or Hailey (depending on which narrative you read) mistakes paralysis for his/her partner's death and commits suicide by freezing to death ("And I, your sentry of ice, shall allways [sic] protect") (S/H 360). Both narratives express a version of the same sentiment. Hailey states, "Without him I am only revolutions of ruin" (H 347) while Sam similarly claims, "Without her I am only revolutions of ruin" (S 347). Far before this scene, however, a different type of paralysis sets in.

Midway through their 360-page romp (around page 180), Sam and Hailey decide to get married. Sam's text states, "we're here to get circled" (S 256), and his words express the sense that confinement is brought through the act of enclosing a finger with a wedding band. It is not the Creep's noose or roman cord but the wedding ring that finally cages these free spirits. Hailey's text expresses this sentiment couched in nature-related imagery describing suffocation: "we're married amber" (H 297). Hardened resin is beautiful but destructive, killing whatever it encloses. Marriage, that institutional act of codifying love, is the thing that seals (circles, amber-ifies) the couple's fate.[9] From then on, as if shifting gears, the novel changes its tone. "The Wheel his no more/We're stuck" (H 312). After traveling for miles on ribbony highways, Sam and Hailey stop driving and settle down. They find jobs and experience a new version of life, one scheduled around only revolutions of bill cycles and working shifts. "Hard work. The Onlygettingby/ cycle of striving. Shifts. Onshifting/ driving us apart/ Sam leaving when I arrive/ Sam arriving when I leave" (H/S 169). Things have changed. Now when they have sex, Sam doesn't pull out. The detail is significant because it suggests the possibility of laying seeds for another generation, which would effectively terminate their own status as children. For nothing marks the end of one's own childhood like having children. The characters recognize this fact, as the following line expresses; it appears verbatim in both of their narratives and thus denotes a significant point of intersection across their narratives: "we'll never again have/ the time to return for" (H/S 316). Without the time to return—that is, the ability to revolve or to only revolve—the circular path turns linear, youth turns to age, and allways sixteen is nevermore.

Despite this narrative plot, however, there is nothing linear about the novel. It revolves rather than progresses and employs the circle rather than the line as its structural model. This is evident in the icon that identifies the novel on its hardcover spine: a circle with two parallel lines inside it. The image resembles a pause symbol on a CD or DVD player, perhaps alluding to the relationship between movement and stasis that I have been exploring; the two lines might also reference the two characters, Sam and Hailey, who seem to live together in their own little bubble. Instead of a picturesque plot or linear timeline, theirs is a revolving hamster wheel or a Hegelian model of history. Consider the connotation of the primary modus operandi and refrain for its protagonists: "we're allways sixteen" (H/S 167, H/S 195). This statement renders them simultaneously time based and timeless. They are "out of time" (S/H 320), implying that they are both running out of time and also extracted from its passing into history. Thus, their narratives are both archetypal, extracted from history, and also deeply embedded in specific historical contexts. The novel depicts the same action happening again and again in different chronotropic and chronological moments and locations. The characters repeatedly drive to new places, meet people, join a party, have sex, suffer violence from strangers, depart, and move onto the next scene. These modular and repeated actions form a revolving plot of seemingly transcendental actions, but they also unfold against a historical timeline filled with specific dates and events, a formal element that constitutes another aspect of the novel's medial aesthetic and masterful page design. As we will later see, this formal aspect extends the bookish aesthetic of *Only Revolutions* out into the digital network.

The inside margins of each page are lined with a vertical column of text that abuts and figuratively reinforces the book's spine. A single date sits atop the list in bolded text, a title that situates the decontextualized content below. This timeline provides a context for Hailey and Sam's cyclical narrative. Hailey's narrative begins on November 22, 1963, and ends on January 19, 2063; Sam's begins on November 22, 1863, and ends on November 22, 1963. The dates intersect at the assassination of President John F. Kennedy and make that moment in American history the point of overlap between the protagonists. Later in this chapter I offer an interpretation about why this particular date serves as the spoke in the wheel of the novel's revolution, but for the now the point is that this timeline serves to ground and register as archetypal the road-trip narrative. The timeline along the book's spine presents historical dates that puncture the protagonists' storytelling in subtle ways. On July 27, 1969, for example, the fashion and colloquialisms of the late '60s penetrate the text so that Hailey is "Helterskeltering" while Sam is "bellbottomed" (H 79). On the page identified as April 3, 1942, the narrative in Sam's register describes "PEST CONTROL, jerking/ around, sprays Zyklon mist" (S 175), invoking the poisonous gas used by the Nazis to murder Jews in concentration camps during the Holocaust. In a more subtle example of the porosity between the timeline and narrative text, Hailey's narrative dated April 15, 1992, describes the characters driving across a "terrortory" (H 227). The misspelling of "territory" visually reflects the ever-present terror of post- 9/11 life and expresses the penetration of the timeline into the storytext.

Through the relationship between timeline and narrative, the novel explores the relationship between individual and collective. Hailey and Sam are identified as "US," and the capitalization of the word implies both the collective unit comprised of the two protagonists ("us") and also the national community to which they belong and across whose landscape they traverse. The tension between US and U.S. motivates much of the novel's narrative action and formal aesthetics. The vertical column of dates presents communal history, while the poetic text beside it displays the protagonists' individualist and even narcissistic experiences. The two textual registers represent different paradigms (individual and collective) and also reference different methods of organizing and displaying information. In particular, these two registers reference the relationship between narrative and database that I explored in Chapter 4, through a close reading of the database aesthetic in Joyce's *Ulysses* and Morrissey's digital remix of it in *The Jew's Daughter*. Joyce's influence and his "database aesthetic" (as I called it in that chapter) is also visible in Danielewski's novel. And, at this point in my examination of digital modernism, the influence of Joyce on contemporary, digital modernist writers should be of little surprise.

Before Sam or Hailey's narrative begins, Danielewski presents an intertextual reference or (if you will) a visual shout-out to *Ulysses*. The first page on each side of the codex contains a large, capital "S" or "H" (depending on which side you open the book to begin reading). The single letter takes up the entire page, just like the big "U" on the verso side of the title page in the first American edition (Modern Library 1934) of Joyce's modernist opus.[10] And, the same typography presents the letter "S," the first letter of the narrative in that edition: "Stately, plump. . . ." *Only Revolutions* is so obsessed with visual details—typography, color, design, layout— that the subtle but clear visual and intertextual detail to *Ulysses* should not be overlooked; it serves a specific purpose. It locates the contemporary novel in a genealogy that reaches back to Joyce and to modernist poetics more generally. It introduces *Only Revolutions* as operating in the strategy of digital modernism. Joyce's influence permeates Danielewski's text and the resulting allusions are ripe for the reaping. Consider how, as Hailey and Sam speed faster in their car, the spaces between words drop away: "somehowsomenow" (H/S 28), "PedaltothePas-PasMetal" (H 49), "GrowGrowling" (S 49). The words become the visual embodiment and representation of speed and its effect on reading. (They also invoke my earlier discussion of speed reading in Chapters 2 and 3). Danielewski follows the modernist master's mode of using playful and poetic misspellings to focus attention on the visual, concrete, and material aspects of words on the page. The effect serves to remind the reader that language is media and that media matters.

When these onomatopoeic representations turn to representing the sound of thunder, Danielewski directly invokes Joyce's *Finnegans Wake*. Joyce's text famously contains enigmatic and onomatopoeic thunderclaps, ten of them, one of which is one hundred letters long.[11] *Only Revolutions* contains its own thunderous lines, including the following: "Over the way the strangest looming./ Boooooooooomblastandruin./ Gathering soooooooon" (S 27) and "Over the hills the strangest crash./ Booooooooomblastandruin./ Loooooooming at last" (H 27). In *The Role of Thunder in Finnegans Wake*, Eric McLuhan—yes, Marshall McLuhan's son—makes the case for the importance of thunder in *Finnegans Wake*. The critical study is the result of younger McLuhan's doctoral research, but it is also the result of a father-son study session.[12] Eric McLuhan argues that the role of thunder in the *Wake* is, as one might expect from a writer named McLuhan, to encode and express the effects of media: "The thunders record and replay the means of human speech and the most profound effects of our technologies on shaping our culture and sensibilities."[13] For McLuhan, Joyce's *Wake* is about and structured around media theory. Steeped in his famous father's media theories (he even cowrote books with his father, including *The Laws of Media* [published in 1988, after Marshall McLuhan's death in 1980]), Eric McLuhan shares with his father a love of modernism and of Joyce in particular. In my first chapter, I argued that media studies emerges from Marshall McLuhan's adaptation of a New Critical approach to close reading modernist literature into a means of reading the mass media. I now move to conclude this project by coming full circle to end with McLuhan's critical readings of Joyce as an entrypoint to understanding how the intersection of media and literary studies informs contemporary print literature.

Coming full circle and reading in circles are one and the same in both *Finnegans Wake* and in *Only Revolutions*. The *Wake* famously prompts its reader to read in circles because it begins and ends in the middle of the same sentence. It produces a circuit that promotes a reading practice of reading in, and only in, revolutions. Danielewski copies this conceit, explaining, "The first word of Sam is related to the first word of Hailey, which is related to the last word of Sam and the last word of Hailey."[14] In Chapter 4, I explored the connections between Joyce's technopoetics and actual digital technologies (hypertext and databases); Danielewski clearly understands these connections. He tells an interviewer, "The thing about the Internet is it's just an extension of a capacity that was already understood when the encyclopedia was being written, when Joyce was writing *Ulysses*."[15] He claims that Joyce's modernist text was "already hypertext," for, "You had to click onto a certain allusion to get that it was from Hamlet to understand that Daedalus was Telemachus. All these things were there"; moreover, he concludes, "The Internet being huge now is just an extension of what was going on at its inception."[16] Danielewski hereby identifies a direct lineage, "an extension," connecting then and now, *Ulysses* to *Only Revolutions*, which also links print literature up to the Internet.

Only Revolutions begins with a reference to the Internet before its narrative even begins. Upon opening the book, the inside covers present a spectacular display of concrete poetry comprised solely of circles. Os and ovals, full and overlapping, cover the verso and recto pages of the inside covers. These pages are green or gold, depending on whether you open to Hailey or Sam's side of the book, and they are covered with circles comprised of black text. This text presents an intricate visual concordance of sorts. Its conceit references the similar concordances in *House of Leaves* (that took the shape of squares and rectangles, designating the walls and windows of the house on Ash Tree Lane) and the extensive, playful index at the end of that novel. The textual concordance in *Only Revolutions* is different, though. It is presented in circles and printed backward. One would need a mirror (and perhaps a magnifying glass) to read it; or, more appropriately to this road-trip narrative and the epigraph from McLuhan that opened this chapter, one would need a rearview mirror to read it.

There is one place in this concordance where a mirror is not needed because the words are large, bold, and clear even through they are printed backward. Centered in the outside margin, at the edge of the verso side of the inside cover (in both Hailey and Sam's version) are the following three words: Whole, Word, Write. Printed at the center of the margin and staggered across three indented lines, they comprise a minipoem. Like the rest of the text on the inside cover, these words are written backward. But the acronym that these words spell out remains legible whether the text is read backward or forward: WWW. The reference to the World Wide Web inside the covers of this book is subtle but suggestive. This is, after all, the concordance section of the novel, where every topic contained in the book is supposedly listed and accounted for. But, the web is, in fact, wholly absent from the novel's text. *Only Revolutions* seems to have no interest in digital technologies or culture. Such media forms are wholly absent from the narrative content. "*Only Revolutions* is about technology, partly because no technology appears in the book," Danielewski explains in an interview with *LAist*, "Nothing. No radios, no wires, no telegraphs. All technological process has been eradicated. There are not many books where you read and ask 'What's missing? What's NOT in here?' "[17] Although the novel contains no technologies, they permeate it. Moreover, as I now move to show, the book is deeply implicated in digital networks. We see this to be the case by exploring how the novel is addressed to readers connected to the digital network and attuned to its networked reading practices.

Part II. The Digital Network

Throughout the novel, Hailey and Sam's stories are punctuated by bold, capitalized words that interrupt the narrative flow. This highlighted text signifies plants (in Hailey's text) and animals (in Sam's text) but with such explicit detail that the words seem out of place, strange, and, even, nonsensical. Consider the following line from Sam's narrative, "bolt a hundred **Barn Swallows.**/ **Aphids** & **Gnats** panic. **Mayflies**/ too. Not me. Nothing frantics me" (S27, emphasis in original). The visual boldness of these words distinguishes them from the narrative of which it is part and draws attention to this content. Why "aphids" and "Mayflies" rather than just flies? The strange explicitness of this content might remind us of the database aesthetic in *Ulysses's* "Ithaca" chapter wherein, as I argued in Chapter 4, the overly detailed responses to questions posed by an unknown interlocutor served to provoke, for a digitally literate reader, the experience of interacting with a database or search engine. The pages of Danielewski's novel produce a similar effect, and there is a reason why.

The bold words that puncture the pages of *Only Revolutions* were, in fact, culled from a search of sorts conducted online. They were supposedly selected from emails sent to the author; I say "supposedly" because there is no available documentation of this process. Yet on August 17, 2005, at 11:27 p.m., Danieleswki sent a message, titled "THAT," to members of the *House of Leaves* Bulletin Board, a large and vibrant online discussion space established for his exceptionally popular first novel.[18] The posting began, "Yes, it's about time for something new/ but before bringing their long run to a close/ it makes sense first to turn to you." Readers and fans of *House of Leaves* dedicated enough to join the Bulletin Board and participate in the extensive threads of its conversations it housed knew that "THAT" referred to the much-anticipated work-in-progress, *Only Revolutions*.[19] In his post, Danieleswki invited readers to participate in completing *Only Revolutions* by responding to a series of questions.

"Here's what I'm after," Danieleswki wrote, and listed the following five writing prompts:

> 1—A specific moment in history, over the last 100 years, which you find personally compelling, defining or at bare minimum interesting. Necessities:

exact date, a refinement of detail, along with a reference or link. An image is also welcome. (Nix on cultural events, i.e. books, music, art, movies.)

2—A personal moment in your history which you might like to see pop up somewhere. Again: exact date, precise details. Again: no cultural references. Again: an image is welcome though definitely not necessary.

3—A kind of animal you admire.

4—A kind of plant you pause for.

5—Your favorite car.[20]

When Sam and Hailey speed through the American landscape in an endless series of cars, from "Pontiac Dual Range" to "Saab Sonett" and "Chevelle SS396," when they view a motley array of flora and fauna, including "Morning Glory" (which, by the way, was my submission!), they are interacting with content that was crowd sourced via the Internet. This content was provided, at least to some extent, by Danielewski's readers. Although *Only Revolutions* has inspired quite a bit of scholarly interpretation in the short period since its publication, the significance of this detail in the novel's publication history has been overlooked and underestimated. It seems to me that this neglect elides the opportunity to examine how *Only Revolutions* engages with the digital to produce its bookish aesthetic.

Within the context of the narrative, the highly detailed, colored, and bolded words seem strange and, indeed, estranged. This content is set apart from the narrative text by its explicitness and visual uniqueness, but there is a reason for its distinctness, a media-specific rationale, even. The results of Danielewski's interaction with his readers are represented visually in the novel in an aesthetic that sets this content apart from the rest. This media-specific detail of *Only Revolutions*'s publication history is crucial to my understanding of it as a bookbound novel with digital ambitions and, moreover, to one engaged in the strategy of digital modernism. The embellished words extracted from readers's emails serve as figurative hyperlinks connecting unseen readers of Danielewski's previous novel to this one. They also link the print codex to the Internet. In so doing, they foster connections between both media forms and the poetic practices associated with them.

"As archaic as it is, with its illuminated text and its ribbons, this book could not exist without technology," Danielewski explains.[21] The author specifically refers to his compositional practice of using "my G5 and 23-inch screen, with two pages on the screen at one time."[22] Danielewski admits to using a variety of software programs (including Adobe InDesign) and "[o]nline resources, certain archival things" to find and manage information, including Font Pro because "I had like 10,000 fonts, which is also a huge deal to manage" as well as online databases like "the *OED* online so I could race through etymologies quickly, double-check words."[23] The novel is not only beholden to digital software programs and databases but also to networked search engines. Danielewski suggests that his novel could not have been created without or before the Internet, for, as he remarks in an interview, the historical data contained in *Only Revolutions* "go[es] beyond what I can perceive when I'm looking at thousands of books."[24] The pages of his bookish novel display the use and influence of networked search engines and online reading practices. While these technologies are absent from the narrative content, each page of the novel contains a digital imprint. No textual detail is more representative of this medial interpenetration than the date that begins Hailey's narrative and concludes Sam's: November 22, 1963.

Earlier I noted that the narrative revolves around this particular date in American history, which is, of course, the day John F. Kennedy was assassinated. However, the reason why this event is the centrifugal point for narrative action is left undisclosed. I would like to suggest that the backstory of the novel's publication history provides a hint. If readers of Danielewski's first novel supplied the dates of "A specific moment in history, over the last 100 years," Danielwski's first prompt from "THAT," then November 22, 1963 represents a shared data point. To put it differently, the date signifies a point of collective consciousness for this web-based, networked readership. Like the digital interface of a tag-cloud that registers the dominance and popularity of a particular search term or keyword in relation to other words, the novel testifies to the social significance of November 22, 1963 in the imaginations of the author's data set, a.k.a his readership. Danielwski creates an "us" from his diverse and distributed readers based on their collective conceptions of U.S. history *via* the Internet. Writing about the timeline that graces the book's gutter, which also contains content supplied from readers, Mark B. N. Hansen writes, "the online solicitation of dates and events from his fanbases," serves to make "the narrative all that much less an allegory of Danielewski's own perceived sense of history and all the more an allegory of his generation's collectively experienced and collectively selected history."[25] As I read it, the crowd-sourced content in the timeline content and in the bolded names of flora and fauna in the narrative text serve to make the narrative all that more about digitality. Specifically, these details and knowledge of their media-specific production illuminates how digital networks support and inform literary poetics as well as reading practices and communities.

Understanding November 22, 1963 to be an indexical reference to online data mining and crowd-sourcing promotes recognition of how this novel simultaneously represents and critiques what media critic Henry Jenkins calls "convergence culture." Jenkins describes "convergence culture" as "a paradigm shift—a move from medium-specific content toward content that flows across multiple media channels . . . and toward ever more complex relations between top-down corporate media and bottom-up participatory culture."[26] Convergence culture, Jenkins argues, produces a new type of "prosumer" who not only consumes but also helps to produce media content within this culture of interconnected media technologies and corporate structures. This prosumer is Danielewski's reader, the "you" addressed in the opening of "THAT." But what Jenkins sees as a sociological phenomenon and reality of our digital age, Danielewski turns into an aesthetic strategy. He invites participation from his readers in order to deconstruct the very notion of participatory culture. He employs convergence toward its antithesis. For Danielewski uses his fanbase and networked media in order to uphold the traditional hierarchy of author and reader.

As we might expect from a work of digital modernism, *Only Revolutions* pursues the conceit of mainstream convergence culture in order to challenge, complicate, and subvert it. The novel plugs into the digital network to incorporate readers' web-based comments into its print pages. Its bolded words and enigmatic timeline reflects the imprint of prosumption—a feedback loop between author/creator and user/reader via the networked convergence of media. But this backstory is hidden from those readers not in the know. The information that explains (granted, only to some extent) the novel's strange formatting is not announced in the pages of the book. A reader approaching the novel without knowledge of "THAT" would have no reason to assume that its experimental typography represents the imprint of web-based participatory culture. Neither does this knowledge serve to elucidate the novel, for the effect produced by these words remains obfuscating rather than illuminating. Rather than inviting collaboration, these marks generate poetic difficulty and proclaim the author's omnipotence. Only Danielewski can explain the significance behind the words he selected from the search results reaped via the digital infrastructure undergirding participatory culture. Yet this paradox of convergence culture is precisely the point. In an age wherein literary scholarship has deconstructed the Romantic figure of the authorial genius, and the DJ is identified as the artist exemplar of the digital age, Danielewski insists on the authority of the author and on the autonomy of the literary work.[27] With its 360-degree aesthetic, *Only Revolutions* revolves around itself, turns inward, and proclaims its value as an autonomous, enigmatic work of literary art. In so doing, *Only Revolutions* joins Poundstone's *Project for the Tachistoscope {Bottomless Pit}* and YHCHI's *Dakota* in using the specificities of its media format to create a self-contained artwork within the hyperlinked network of digital culture.

Only Revolutions also offers a way of seeing the novel's print medium anew through its relationship to the digital network. The novel engages with digitality in order to fetishize its bookbound form. One need only consider the bookmarks in the hardbound edition to see how the novel works to keep its reader intensely aware of the materiality of the codex. The book contains a gold and a green bookmark, each secured at opposite ends of the spine. Each bookmark corresponds to one of the character's narratives. The yellow one marks and maps the reader's movement through Hailey's narrative; the green one helps navigate through Sam's text. A reader who follows the publisher's directions—reading eight pages from one side of the book, and from one narrator, before turning the book around—witnesses the progression of the bookmarks. Yellow and green start at opposite ends of the spine and head toward each other as the reader progresses through the text. They meet in the middle, kiss, and cross over each other at the book's midpoint and the narrative's climax, the apex of the characters' love. The bookmarks then go their separate ways to finish, once again, at opposite sides of the paper-filled landscape contained within the book's bindings. The bookmarks offer just one more example of how reading this novel is an experience in learning to see the book as a medium containing complex navigational structures and opportunities for interactivity.

Only Revolutions turns our attention back to the book. But it does so by employing and invoking digitality. The novel revolves around the Internet in order to show literature's older medium to be more multimedia than we previously thought. Or, following McLuhan, we might even say that this road-trip novel functions as a kind of rearview mirror for viewing the present medial moment as we move forward into the future.

An Open-Ended Conclusion

After cycling through a history that spans two centuries, Sam and Hailey's stories come to an end. But before they do, the historical timeline and register of dates that lines the book's spine on the inside-margin's vertical column does something strange: it goes blank. In Hailey's narrative, this historical database ends on May 29, 2005. The next date listed is June 18, 2006, which is the novel's publication date. This date sits atop a glaringly empty space. The shock of whiteness in a textspace previously filled with data registers a profound shift, and it demands attention. The blank margin beckons and invites readers to fill it in. The effect exposes and illuminates the white paper on which the novel's text is printed; it heightens awareness of the technologies and media involved in literature.

The emptiness under the date also suggests open-endedness—it is not just empty but open to new possibilities and entries. The space thereby asserts a poetic connection to the colon and ellipsis with which Ezra Pound concluded his first and second cantos, respectively (and which I discussed in Chapter 3 in relation to YHCHI's remediation of them). Such acts of concluding by refusing to end are poetic statements. They proclaim that the individual literary text is part of the present moment and that the reader is an interactive agent in fulfilling their potential. The blank space in Danielewski's *Only Revolutions* continues this poetic tradition. It suggests that there might be more content to record in the historical timeline, but it leaves such action to the reader to author. Danielewski concludes his novel by suggesting that the codex is a medium that will continue to serve the vital and poetic purpose of representing and archiving personal and collective histories into the unforeseen but increasingly digital future.

Only Revolutions displays how digitality informs, inspires, and imprints print literature by exploiting the interplay between the codex and digital networks in ways that assure the continuation of book-based literature. The novel exposes and aestheticizes the relationship between print and digital media to be a feedback loop. Its title refers to the act of reading the book by turning it around in a complete circle, to the revolutions of the protagonists' tires on the highways of America, and also to the ways in which revolutions happen (in a Hegelian model) through dialectical relationships between seemingly oppositional forces, such as print and digital, old and new, beginning and end. Through its bookbound layout, *Only Revolutions* promotes a reading practice in which the act of revolving between seemingly oppositional points produces a circle connecting them. In its narrative, form, and format, *Only Revolutions* presents the idea that literary revolution happens by looping back, by returning to the past in order to move forward. This is digital modernism.

"A return to origins invigorates," Ezra Pound writes.[28] In that vein, and by returning to the poet who helped me to begin this book, I conclude by pointing out that *Only Revolutions* confirms what we have learned across these six chapters: digital modernism illuminates how digital literature can support reflection on older literary practices and reading technologies. As a result, we are able to see the past and the present anew by way of literature that makes it new in new media.

Notes

Introduction

1. Wendy Hui Kyong Chun discusses the role of "new" in "new media," insightfully pointing out that the focus on "'making new' reveals the importance of interrogating the forces behind any emergence, the importance of shifting from 'what is new' to analyzing what work the new does." "Introduction: Did Somebody Say New Media?," in *New Media, Old Media*, eds. Wendy Hui Kyong Chun and Thomas Keenan (New York and London: Routledge, 2006), 3.

2. Qtd. in Thom Swiss, "'Distance, Homelessness, Anonymity, and Insignificance': An Interview with Young-Hae Chang Heavy Industries," *The Iowa Review Web* (2002), accessed October 17, 2012, http://iowareview.uiowa.edu/TIRW/TIRW_Archive/tirweb/feature/younghae/interview.html.

3. "The Tradition" in *Literary Essays of Ezra Pound*, ed. T. S. Eliot (New York: New Directions, 1954), 92.

4. T. S. Eliot, "*Ulysses*, Order, and Myth" in *James Joyce: Two Decades of Criticism*, ed. Seon Givens (New York: The Vanguard Press, 1963), 198–202. Originally published in *The Dial*, November 1923. For a thoughtful meditation on how Eliot's myth-based reading of *Ulysses* has served literary criticism, see Kevin Dettmar's "'Working in Accord with Obstacles': A Postmodern Perspective on Joyce's 'Mythical Method'" in *Rereading the New: A Backward Glance at Modernism*, ed. Kevin J. H. Dettmar (Ann Arbor: University of Michigan Press), 277–296.

5. Enda Duffy, *The Speed Handbook: Velocity, Pleasure, Modernism* (Duke University Press, 2009), 42.

6. See Michael Levenson's *A Genealogy of Modernism: A Study of English Literary Doctrine 1908–1922*, (Cambridge: Cambridge University Press, 1984), Lawrence Rainey's *Institutions of Modernism: Literary Elites and Public Culture* (New Haven: Yale University Press, 1998, particularly Chapter 1), and Marjorie Perloff's *The Futurist Moment: Avant-Garde, Avant Guerre, and the Language of Rupture* (Chicago: University of Chicago Press, 1986).

7. Friedrich Kittler, *Discourse Networks, 1800/1900*, trans. Michael Metteer with Chris Cullens (Stanford: Stanford University Press, 1990), 369.

8. Friedrich Kittler, *Discourse Networks*, 83.

9. Friedrich Kittler, *Gramophone, Film, Typewriter*, trans. Geoffrey Winthrop-Young and Micahel Wutz (Stanford: Stanford University Press, 1999), 14.

10. Lev Manovich, *The Language of New Media* (Cambridge: MIT University Press, 2001), xv. I discuss the ways in which my project differs from Manovich's later in this introduction; for, although Manovich and I both pursue a connection between digital media and modernism, our approaches and arguments differ in methodology and purpose.

11. N. Katherine Hayles's "Deeper into the Machine: The Future of Electronic Literature," *Culture Machine*, vol. 5 (2003), accessed October 17, 2012, http://svr91.edns1.com/~culturem/index.php/cm/article/viewArticle/245/241.

12. Eastgate published these titles in a proprietary format, disc and CD-Rom. Eastgate also produced (through the efforts of Jay David Bolter, John B. Smith, and Michael Joyce) Storyspace, an authoring program specifically designed for producing hypertexts. Many of the important early works of electronic literature were built in Storyspace. For more on Storyspace software, see http://www.eastgate.com/storyspace/index.html or The Electronic Labyrinth at http://www3.iath.virginia.edu/elab/hfl0023.html.

13. See George P. Landow's *Hypertext 2.0: The Convergence of Contemporary Critical Theory and Technology*, 2nd ed. (Baltimore: Johns Hopkins University Press, 1997) and also "Hypertext, Hypermedia, and Literary Studies: The State of the Art" with Paul Delany, which is an introduction *Hypermedia and Literary Studies*, eds. Landow and Delany (MIT Press, 1991).

14. *Poems That Go* was edited by Megan Sapnar and Ingrid Ankerson, accessed October 17, 2012, http://www.poemsthatgo.com.

15. Qtd. in Swiss, " 'Distance, Homelessness, Anonymity, and Insignificance': An Interview with Young-Hae Chang Heavy Industries."

16. Clement Greenberg, "The Notion of 'Postmodern'" in *Zeitgeist in Babel: The Postmodernist Controversy*, ed. Ingeborg Hoesterey (Indiana UP), 46. The essay was previously published in *Arts 54*, No. 6 (February 1980).

17. For example, in *After the Great Divide: Modernism, Mass Culture, Postmodernism* (Indianapolis: Indiana University Press, 1986), Andreas Huyssen argues, "Modernism constituted itself through a conscious strategy of exclusions, an anxiety of contamination by its other: an increasingly consuming and engulfing mass culture" (vii). Huyssen distinguishes between modernism and postmodernism, by claiming that contrary to modernism, "postmodernism rejects the theories of the Great Divide" (viii).

18. In May, 2001 Gonzalo Frasca founded Ludology.org, "an online resource for videogame researchers"; in July 2001, the first issue of *Game Studies.org* appeared and scholarly print publications about games studies proliferated.

19. In *21st Century Modernism: The "New" Poetics* (Oxford: Blackwell Publishers, 2002), Marjorie Perloff asks, "what if . . . there were a powerful avant-garde that takes up, once again, the experimentation of the early twentieth century?" (3–4). It should already be obvious that I argue that an avant-garde is doing just that and doing it online. Whereas Perloff charts a continuum between modernist poetry and "the unfulfilled promise of the revolutionary poetic impulse in so much of what passes for poetry today" (5–6), I am interested

in recognizing a new wave of applied practice in a new media format. Despite the title of her book, Perloff does not engage with the poetics of the new century in their new media formats.

20. See Andreas Huyssen, *After the Great Divide: Modernism, Mass Culture, Postmodernism* (Indianapolis: Indiana University Press, 1986).

21. See Henry Jenkins, *Convergence Culture: Where Old and New Media Collide* (New York University Press, 2006). I discuss this book and its central concept of convergence culture in more detail in the Coda.

22. A *New York Times* article describing the emergence of video games in the Academy, Michael Erard's "The Ivy-Covered Console" (February 26, 2004), pits games against modernism as a means of describing their cultural position and possibility. The article ends by quoting author and English Ph.D., Dexter Palmer, positioning games in relation to literary modernism: "'Maybe,' he said, 'game critics can someday explicate Arc the Lad, bringing it to a larger market in the same way that the literary entrepreneur Sylvia Beach supported Joyce and published *Ulysses*. But I don't want to draw the comparison between Arc the Lad and *Ulysses*,' Dr. Palmer said, 'because that would be very, very wrong.'" Although the works in this study are not games, they do complicate the simple conclusion that digital narratives occupy such different ends of the cultural spectrum and that to read them as you would *Ulysses*—i.e., to close read or "explicate"—would be "very, very wrong." Indeed, this book strives to complicate, if not outrightly reject, the assumption that games and other objects of digital culture should not be read with the dedication and critical reading practice one would turn to highbrow literature.

23. In "Digital Constructivism: What Is European Software? An exchange between Lev Manovich and Geert Lovink" (November 11, 1998), Lev Manovich writes, "Like you, I also believe in digital modernism or avant-gardism" (http://www.nettime.org/Lists-Archives/nettime-l-9811/msg00063.html). As far as I can tell, Manovich does not use the term again, either in that conversation or in his published work. Instead, in the rest of this net-time correspondence and in his larger body of work on new media, Manovich uses the terms "modernism" and "avant-garde," often interchangeably. For Manovich, "modernism" is a flexible category with historical dates ranging "approximately from 1860s to 1960s; or from Manet to Warhol; or from Baudelaire to McLuhan" ("Avant-Garde as Software," *Ostranenie*, ed. Stephen Kovats [Frankfurt: Campus Vertag, 1999]). In contrast, I use the term "modernism" to refer to a specific strategy employed by writers in the early decades of the early-twentieth century and adapted by writers of contemporary digital literature.

24. Lev Manovich, *The Language of New Media*, xxxi.

25. Lev Manovich, *The Language of New Media*, xxxi.

26. Lev Manovich, "Avant-Garde as Software." http://www.manovich.net/articles.php

27. See Fredric Jameson's *Postmodernism: Or, The Cultural Logic of Late Capitalism.* (Durham: Duke University Press, 1991), chapter 1 in particular. This is neither Manovich's conclusion nor his tone. He does not see the absorption of the avant-garde into the computer as a bad thing but rather as an effect of the technology: "what was a radical aesthetic vision in the 1920s became a standard computer technology by the 1990s" ("Avant-Garde as Software").

28. See Enda Duffy, *The Speed Handbook: Velocity, Pleasure, Modernism* for brilliant explorations of the role of speed in modernist culture and art.

29. John Guillory, "Close Reading: Prologue and Epilogue," *ADE Bulletin*, no. 149 (2010), 13.

30. John Guillory, "Close Reading: Prologue and Epilogue." In this way, Guillory argues that Richards's "prologue" to close reading has much in common with close reading's "epilogue," as exemplified, Guillory argues, by N. Katherine Hayles's argument about hyper-attention (in Hayles, "Hyper and Deep Attention: The Generational Divide in Cognitive Modes," *Profession* [2007], pp. 187–199).

31. Jeffery T. Schnapp, "Fast (slow) modern" in *Speed Limits*, ed. Jeffery T. Schnapp (Milan: Skira, 2009), 27.

32. Much has been written about the value judgments implicit in the distinction between slow and fast reading. "Good Reading Is Slow Reading," J. Hillis Miller claims in a section title of *On Literature: Thinking in Action* (New York: Routledge, 2002).

33. Jonathan Culler, "The Closeness of Close Reading," *ADE Bulletin*, no. 149 (2010), 3. Culler continues, "though 'slow reading' is doubtless a less useful slogan than either 'slow food' or 'close reading,' since slow reading may be inattentive, distracted, lethargic" (23).

34. Qtd. in William J. Spurlin's "Afterword: An Interview with Cleanth Brooks" in *The New Criticism and Contemporary Literary Theory: Connections and Continuities*, eds. William J. Spurlin and Michael Fischer (New York: Garland, 1995), 366. In this interview, Brooks also states that the term "The New Criticism" "was not a name we used to describe ourselves" (367).

35. Qtd. in William J. Spurlin's "Afterword: An Interview with Cleanth Brooks," 367.

36. Frank Lentricchia, "Preface," *Close Reading: The Reader*, eds. Frank Lentricchia and Andrew DuBois (Durham: Duke, 2003), viv.

37. The New Critics were not alone in pursuing commitment to form and formalism. The Russian Formalists were hugely influential in and around the same period.

38. I. A. Richards, *Principles of Literary Criticism* (New York: Routledge [1924], 2001), vii.

39. I. A. Richards, *How to Read a Page: A Course in Efficient Reading with an Introduction to 100 Great Words* (Boston: Beacon Press, 1942), 14–15. Or consider Cleanth Brooks's statement in a later essay, "The Formalist Critic" (1951), "the formalist critic is concerned primarily with the work itself. Speculation on the mental processes on the author takes the critic away from the word into biography and psychology" (reprinted in *Praising it New: The Best of the New Criticism*, ed. Garrick Davis [Swallow Press/Ohio UP, 2008]), 86.

40. I. A. Richards, *How to Read a Page*, 15.

41. See John Guillory, "Close Reading: Prologue and Epilogue."

42. I. A. Richards, *Practical Criticism: A Study of Literary Judgment* (Myers Press reprint, 2008 [1929]), 234.

43. I. A. Richards, *Practical Criticism*, 234.

44. Andrew DuBois, "Close Reading: An Introduction" in *Close Reading: The Reader*, eds. Frank Lentricchia and Andrew DuBois (Durham: Duke, 2003), 4.

45. Gerald Graff, Literature Against Itself: Literary Ideas in Modern Society (Ivan R. Dee, 1979), 129.

46. Miranda Hickman, "Rereading the New Criticism," in *Rereading the New Criticism*, eds. Miranda Hickman and John D. McIntyre (Columbus: Ohio State UP, 2012), 9.

47. Gerald Graff, Literature Against Itself, 133.

48. Gerald Graff, Literature Against Itself, 133.

49. Cleanth Brooks, *The Well-Wrought Urn: Studies in the Structure of Poetry* (New York: Reynal & Hitchcock, 1947), 8.

50. For a cogent critique of the results of this formalist focus, see Robert Scholes, *The Crafty Reader* (New Haven: Yale UP, 2001). Scholes rails against the heritage of the New Criticism: "we have lost the craft of reading poetry—lost sight of poetry's private pleasure and of its public powers—and that our methods of studying and teaching poetry for the past half-century are very much to blame for this condition" (6). The New Critical "preference for subtlety and complexity, which went hand in hand with a sustained critique of the obvious and sentimental," he writes, "had the effect of cutting off poetry they liked from the more popular poems that had functions to get many young people interested in poetry in the first place" (13).

51. T. S. Eliot, "Tradition and Individual Talent" in *The Sacred Wood: Essays on Poetry and Criticism* (London: Methuen, 1920).

52. I. A. Richards, *Principles of Literary Criticism*, 11.

53. For more on how close reading has a "scientific or perhaps quasi-scientific origin" due to how Richards "constructed a psychology of reading on the foundation of the stimulus-response model" used in contemporary scientific discourse, see Guillory's "Close Reading: Prologue and Epilogue" (11).

54. Gerald Graff, *Literature Against Itself*, 129.

55. Robert Archambeau, "Aesthetics as Ethics: One and One Half Theses on the New Criticism" in *Rereading the New Criticism*, eds. Miranda Hickman and John D. McIntyre (Columbus: Ohio State UP, 2012), 45.

56. Robert Archambeau, "Aesthetics as Ethics: One and One Half Theses on the New Criticism," 45.

57. William Logan, "Forward into the Past: Reading the New Critics" in *Praising it New: The Best of the New Criticism*, xii.

58. Gerald Graff, *Literature Against Itself*, 5.

59. I. A. Richards, *Principles of Literary Criticism*, viii. For more on how the universities served as the seat of New Criticism, see Davis's editorial notes to "Part 4: Appraising Poets and Periods" (45–46).

60. John Crowe Ransom, "Criticism, Inc," in *Praising it New: The Best of the New Criticism*, 50.

61. T. S. Eliot explains why this value system matters in "The Metaphysical Poets" (1921). He writes, "poets of our civilization, as it exists at present, must be difficult. Our civilization comprehends great variety and complexity, and this variety and complexity, playing upon a refined sensibility, must produce various and complex results. The poet must become more and more comprehensive, more allusive, more indirect, in order to force, to dislocate if necessary" (reprinted in *Praising it New: The Best of the New Criticism*, 149).

62. John Guillory, *Cultural Capital: The Problem of Literary Canon Formation* (Chicago: University of Chicago Press, 1993), 56.

63. For more on the importance of the New Critical textbooks, primarily those by Brooks and Warren, see Tara Lockhart's "Teaching with Style: Brooks and Warren's Literary Pedagogy" in *Rereading the New Criticism*, 195–217. Lockhart quotes Mark Jancovich's statement, "More than any other New Critical activity, these text-books were responsible for redefining the object of literary study. They directed attention to the linguistic forms of

the text, and defined the terms of reference within which literary studies largely continues to operate" (214).

64. The field of textual studies and work by scholars such as Jerome McGann, George Bornstein, and Lawrence Rainey, in particular, seeks to rectify this myopic view by showing how medium, material context (including the format and the venue in which a poem was first published), and bibliographic history crucially inform the text and its interpretation. My own thinking is deeply shaped by this line of scholarship.

65. I am thinking here of Katherine Hayles's claim for a generational distinction between hyper and deep attention, which map onto multi-talking and close reading, in "Hyper and Deep Attention: The Generational Divide in Cognitive Modes," *Profession* (2007), 187–199.

66. Frank Lentricchia, "Preface," *Close Reading: The Reader*, ix.

67. Miranda Hickman and John D. McIntyre, "Acknowledgements," *Rereading the New Criticism*, vii.

68. Miranda Hickman, "Introduction: Rereading the New Criticism" in *Rereading the New Criticism*, 4.

69. Jane Gallop, "The Historicization of Literary Studies and the Fate of Close Reading," *Profession* (2007), 182.

70. Jane Gallop, "The Historicization of Literary Studies and the Fate of Close Reading," 182.

71. Jane Gallop, "The Historicization of Literary Studies and the Fate of Close Reading," 183. Gallop identifies the current state of literary studies thus, "We have become amateur, or rather wannabe, cultural historians" (183).

72. Jonathan Culler, "The Closeness of Close Reading," 21 and 24, respectively. Culler colorfully describes the indefinable role of close reading, "Close reading, like motherhood and apple pie is something we are all in favor of, even if what we do when we think we are doing close reading is very different" (21).

73. N. Katherine Hayles has been forcefully and persuasively making this claim for some time now. In *My Mother Was a Computer: Digital Subjects and Literary Texts* (Chicago: University of Chicago Press, 2005), she writes, "literary and cultural critics steeped in the print tradition cannot simply continue with business as usual. Needed are new theoretical frameworks for understanding the relation of language and code; new strategies for making, reading, and interpreting texts; new modes of thinking about the material instantiation of texts" (11).

74. Astrid Ensslin and Alice Bell, "New Perspectives on Digital Literature: Criticism and Analysis," in *Dichtung-Digital*, no. 37 (2007), accessed October 17, 2012, http://dichtung-digital.de/editorial/2007.htm.

75. David Ciccoricco, "The Materialities of Close Reading: 1942, 1959, 2009," *Digital Humanities Quarterly*, 6.1 (2012), para. 1.

76. On flickering signifiers, see chapter 2 of Hayles's *How We Became Posthuman: Virtual Bodies in Cybernetics, Literature, and Informatics* (Chicago: Chicago UP, 1999), titled "Virtual Bodies and Flickering Signifiers."

77. Mark C. Marino, "Critical Code Studies," *Electronic book review* (December 4, 2006), accessed October 17, 2012, http://www.electronicbookreview.com/thread/electropoetics/codology.

78. In "Digital Code and Literary Text," Florian Cramer explains that code "is solely dependent on how another piece of code—a compiler, a runtime interpreter or the embedded logic of a microprocessor—processes it" (*Beehive*, [2002], http://beehive.temporalimage. com/content_apps43/cramer/0000.html).

79. In "The Code Is not the Text (Unless It Is the Text)," John Cayley highlights the fact that "composed code is addressed to a processor" and "complexities of [this] address should not be bracketed" (*Electronic book review*, 2002), http://www.electronicbookreview.com/ thread/electropoetics/literal.

80. "Platform Studies" book series description, MIT UP website, accessed October 17, 2012, http://platformstudies.com/ and "Software Studies Book Series" description, accessed March 8, 2011, http://mitpress.mit.edu/catalog/browse/browse.asp?btype=6&serid=179.

81. Matthew Kirschenbaum uses the term "screen essentialism" to describe critical analysis focused solely on the screen rather than in the modes of storage and processing involved in producing the onscreen aesthetic; see *Mechanisms: New Media and the Forensic Imagination* (MIT Press, 2008), see chapter 1. Nick Montfort used the term earlier in a presentation titled "Continuous Paper: The Early Materiality and Workings of Electronic Literature," MLA conference, Philadelphia (December 28, 2004).

82. Tara Lockhart writes, "The New Critical method of textual analysis, though often perceived in retrospect as isolationalist, was intended to result in precisely the opposite phenomenon: it sought to restore to literature a central place in the culture at large" ("Teaching with Style," 201).

83. From this we can extrapolate that literary analysis is vital to explaining *how* meaning is produced through our digital interfaces and devices, operating systems, search engines, and communication platforms. Steven Johnson, *Interface Culture: How New Technology Transforms the Way We Create and Communicate* (Basic Books, 1997), 213; italics in original. Media critic Steven Johnson identifies "interface design" as "a kind of art form—perhaps *the* art form of the next century" (from his vantage point at the end of the twentieth century) and explains that metaphors are central to interface design.

84. Hayles writes, "Language alone is no longer the distinctive characteristic of technologically developed societies; rather, it is language plus code" (*My Mother Was a Computer*, 16).

85. Bob Brown, *The Readies* (Roving Eye Press, Bad Ems, 1930), 1. In 2009 Rice University Press (Literature by Design Series) reprinted a new edition of *The Readies*, which contains a substantial afterword by Craig Saper. This edition is an important step toward procuring renewed appreciation of Brown.

Chapter 1

1. Marshall McLuhan, *Understanding Media: The Extensions of Man* (MIT Press, 2001 [1964]), 219.

2. The youth of the hippie counter-culture movement embraced McLuhan. This is understandable because, as we will see, McLuhan identified and supported their sense of a massive historical shift underway. "We now live in a global village," he claimed in *The Medium is the Massage: An Inventory of Effects* (with Quentin Fiore, Bantam Books, 1967), 63. McLuhan considered this communal and even tribal situation to be revolutionary, as did

the hippie culture developing around him and experimenting in communal living. He also defended and took seriously that generation's newest media—television.

3. For example, McLuhan graced the cover of *Newsweek* in 1967, did a lengthy interview for *Playboy* in 1968, and did numerous interviews on various television programs (See *The Video McLuhan* produced by Stephanie McLuhan-Ortved and narrated by Tom Wolfe, 1996). McLuhan was, in short, an international celebrity, although his only work to achieve "bestseller" status was *The Medium Is the Massage*, for which he shares authorial status with designer Quentin Fiore. That book was "produced by" Jerome Agel, who was in part responsible for selecting and excerpting the text (See Philip Marchand, *Marshall McLuhan: The Medium and the Messenger* [New York: Ticknor & Fields, 1989], 192). For more on Agel's behind-the-scenes influence, see Jeffrey T. Schnapp and Adam Michaels, *The Electric Information Age Book: McLuhan/Agel/Fiore and the Experimental Paperback* (Princeton, NJ: Princeton UP, 2012).

4. See *McLuhan Galaxy* http://mcluhangalaxy.wordpress.com/ for a blog devoted to "track[ing the increasing recognition of McLuhan's ideas and relevance" ("About"), accessed October 17, 2012.

5. Hans Enzensberger articulates the latter viewpoint in "Constituents of a Theory of Media" (1970), describing McLuhan as one who "presents a mystique of media which dissolves all political problems in smoke—the same smoke that gets in the eyes of his followers. It promises the salvation of man through the technology of television" (reprinted in *The New Media Reader*, eds. Noah Wardrip-Fruin and Nick Montfort [Cambridge: The MIT Press, 2003] 271, originally published in *New Left Review* [64] 13–36, 1970). For a short history of the critical reception of McLuhan, see Paul Heyer's "Marshalling McLuhan" (in *Marshall McLuhan: Critical Evaluations in Cultural Theory*, ed. Gary Genesko [Routledge, 2005]: 3–10) wherein Heyer describes the critical resuscitation of McLuhan's medial theory in the mid-1980s and 1990s.

6. I will be using the following editions of McLuhan's three seminal texts: *The Mechanical Bride: Folklore of Industrial Man* (Berkeley, CA: Gingko Press, 2002 [1951]), *The Gutenberg Galaxy: The Making of Typographic Man* (Toronto: University of Toronto Press, 1962), and *Understanding Media: The Extensions of Man* (Cambridge, MA: The MIT Press, 2001 [1964]).

7. N. Katherine Hayles describes media-specific analysis in *Writing Machines* (Cambridge, MA: MIT Press, 2002): "Complementing the foundational concepts of material metaphors, inscription technologies and technotexts is a kind of criticism that pays attention to the material apparatus producing the literary work as physical artifact" (29).

8. The term "media ecology" is often attributed to McLuhan but most likely originated with Neil Postman. For an explanation of this and many other misconceptions about McLuhan, see Robert K. Logan's "McLuhan Misunderstood: Setting the Record Straight," a lecture from March 2, 2011, posted to *McLuhan Galaxy* (June 17, 2011), accessed October 17, 2012, http://mcluhangalaxy.wordpress.com/2011/06/17/mcluhan-misunderstood-setting-the-record-straight-by-robert-k-logan/.

9. Qtd. in "Poetry and Play vs. Clarity and Precision," *Lance Strate's Blog Time Passing* (September 5, 2011), accessed October 17, 2012, http://lancestrate.blogspot.com/2011/09/poetry-and-play-vs-clarity-and.html.

10. Marshall McLuhan, *Understanding Media*, 207.

11. Marshall McLuhan, *COUNTERBLAST* (New York: Harcourt, Brace & World, Inc., 1969), 52.

12. Umberto Eco, "Cogito Interruptus," in *Marshall McLuhan: Critical Evaluations in Cultural Theory*, ed. Gary Genesko (Routledge, 2005), 129.

13. At Cambridge, McLuhan took an additional BA in 1936 and a doctorate in 1942. For more on McLuhan's biography, see Philip Marchand, *Marshall McLuhan: The Medium and the Messenger* (New York: Ticknor & Fields, 1989) and W. Terrence Gordon, *Marshall McLuhan: Escape into Understanding, A Biography* (New York: BasicBooks, 1997).

14. Marshall McLuhan, "Foreword" to *The Interior Landscape: The Literary Criticism of Marshall McLuhan, 1943–1962*, ed. Eugene McNamara (New York: McGraw-Hill Book Company, 1969), xiv.

15. Marshall McLuhan, *Letters of Marshall McLuhan*, eds. Matie Molinaro, Corinne McLuhan, and William Toye (Oxford: Oxford University Press, 1987), 79. The letter was addressed to E. K. Brown, chairman of department of English at the University of Manitoba.

16. Glenn Willmott, *McLuhan, or Modernism in Reverse* (Toronto: University of Toronto Press, 1996), 24. Philip Marchand explains that McLuhan "believed that he, virtually single-handedly, was pioneering the techniques of Richards, Empson, and Leavis in the United States" (*Marshall McLuhan*, 59). McLuhan even taught a course on Practical Criticism in which he passed out poems and had students evaluate them, in the style of Richard's famous experiment (Marchand 59).

17. Ezra Pound, *ABC of Reading* (New York: New Directions, 1934), 73.

18. Marshall McLuhan, "A McLuhan Mosaic" in *Marshall McLuhan: The Man and His Message*, eds. George Sanderson and Frank Macdonald (Fulcrum, Inc., 1989), 4. Similarly, in *Understanding Media*, McLuhan writes, "The artist picks up the message of cultural and technological challenge decades before its transforming impact occurs" (65).

19. Marshall McLuhan, "Foreword" to *The Interior Landscape*, xiii–xiv.

20. Marshall McLuhan, *The Gutenberg Galaxy: The Making of Typographic Man* (U Toronto Press, 1962), 75.

21. Marshall McLuhan, *The Gutenberg Galaxy*, 56. He writes, "Literacy gives people the power to focus a little way in front of an image so that we take in the whole image or picture at a glance. Non-literate people have no such acquired habit . . . they scan objects and images as we do the printed page, segment by segment. Thus they have no detached point of view" (50).

22. McLuhan articulates his theory clearly in an interview with *Playboy* magazine in 1969: "Before the invention of the phonetic alphabet, man lived in a world where all the sense were balanced and simultaneous, a closed world of tribal depth and resonance, an oral culture structured by a dominant auditory sense of life" ("The *Playboy* Interview" in *Essential McLuhan*, eds. Eric McLuhan and Frank Zingrone [Basic Books, 1995], 239).

23. Marshall McLuhan, *The Gutenberg Galaxy*, 47.

24. Marshall McLuhan, *The Gutenberg Galaxy*, 153.

25. Marshall McLuhan, *Understanding Media*, 57.

26. Marshall McLuhan, *Medium is the Massage*, 8. The meaning behind the title's pun on McLuhan's own aphorism ("the medium is the message") is clearly explained in the following text: "All media work us over completely. They are so pervasive in their personal,

political, economic, aesthetic, psychological . . . consequences that they leave no part of us untouched, unaffected, unaltered" (10).

27. Marshall McLuhan, *The Gutenberg Galaxy*, 91.

28. Marshall McLuhan, *The Gutenberg Galaxy*, 12.

29. Marshall McLuhan, *Understanding Media*, 13.

30. On the subject of film, McLuhan writes, "The movie, by sheer speeding up of the mechanical, carried us from the world of sequence and connections into the world of creative configuration and structure. The message of the movie medium is that of transition from lineal connections to configurations" (*Understanding Media*, 12).

31. Marshall McLuhan, *Understanding Media*, 54.

32. I. A. Richards, *Practical Criticism*, 3.

33. I. A. Richards, *Practical Criticism*, 6. For a history of the profession of literary criticism, including the emergence and refutation of the New Criticism, see Graff's *Professing Literature: An Institutional History*.

34. I. A. Richards, *Practical Criticism*, 4.

35. I. A. Richards, *Practical Criticism*, 11.

36. I. A. Richards, *Practical Criticism*, 6 and 3, respectively.

37. Marshall McLuhan, *Letters of Marshall McLuhan*, 50.

38. Marshall McLuhan, *Letters of Marshall McLuhan*, 50.

39. I. A. Richards, *Principles of Literary Criticism*, vii.

40. I. A. Richards, *Principles of Literary Criticism*, vii.

41. I. A. Richards, *Principles of Literary Criticism*, 3.

42. I. A. Richards, *Principles of Literary Criticism*, 3.

43. I. A. Richards, *Principles of Literary Criticism*, 190.

44. F. R. Leavis, *How to Teach Reading: A Primer for Ezra Pound* (Cambridge: Gordon Fraser, The Minority Press, 1932), 1.

45. F. R. Leavis, *How to Teach Reading*, 40.

46. F. R. Leavis, *How to Teach Reading*, 48.

47. F. R. Leavis, *How to Teach Reading*, 40. Leavis continues, and his explanation makes clear that such focus would not serve "to discourage further attention to those authors, or attention to other authors. On the contrary, it is impossible that anyone who had done such close work locally would not in any case go on to further exploration . . . ." (40).

48. F. R. Leavis, *How to Teach Reading*, 48–49. Leavis's footnote to this sentence states, "How this may be done is suggested in *Culture and Environment*" (footnote 1, 49).

49. F. R. Leavis and Denys Thompson, *Culture and Environment: The Training of Critical Awareness* (Westport, CT: Greenwood Press, Publishers, 1977 [1933]), 1.

50. Marshall McLuhan, *Letters of Marshall McLuhan*, 166. The letter is addressed to Walter J. Ong and Clement NcNaspy.

51. Marshall McLuhan, *Understanding Media*, xiii–xiv.

52. H. M. McLuhan, "Poetic vs. Rhetorical Exegesis: The Case for Leavis against Richards and Empson," *The Sewanee Review*, vol. 52, no. 2 (Spring, 1944): 266–276. In this essay, McLuhan writes, "Where Mr. Leavis sees the function of poetry as the education or nourishment of the affections, Richards and Empson tend to regard it pragmatically and rhetorically as a means of impinging on a particular situation" (276). Following this distinction, McLuhan can be read as supporting John Guillory's claim, in

"The Genesis of the Media Concept," that media studies originates in studies of rhetoric. See Guillory, "The Genesis of the Media Concept," *Critical Inquiry*, Winter 2010, vol. 36, no. 2.

53. Marshall McLuhan, *Letters of Marshall McLuhan*, 50.

54. H. M. McLuhan, "Poetic vs. Rhetorical Exegesis: The Case for Leavis against Richards and Empson," 272.

55. H. M. McLuhan, "Poetic vs. Rhetorical Exegesis," 276.

56. H. M. McLuhan, "Poetic vs. Rhetorical Exegesis," 271.

57. McLuhan converted in 1937 to Catholicism while at school in London and became catholic in his personal and cultural politics. He was steadfast throughout his life, regularly taking the Eucharist and teaching only at Catholic universities. See Marchand and also Grant Havers's "The Right-Wing Postmodernism of Marshall McLuhan," *Media, Culture & Society*, vol. 25 (2003): 511–525. *The Video McLuhan* is an invaluable resource for getting a sense of McLuhan's performative persona. This rich archive contains recorded segments from McLuhan's numerous appearances on television and his public lectures, astutely contextualized and introduced by Wolfe.

58. For one such recent and astute reconsideration, see Alan Jacobs, "Why Bother with Marshall McLuhan?," *The New Atlantis*, no. 31 (Spring 2011): 123–135, accessed October 17, 2012, http://www.thenewatlantis.com/publications/why-bother-with-marshall-mcluhan.

59. See *Media Archaeology: Approaches, Applications, and Implications*, eds. Erkki Huhtamo and Jussi Parikka (Berkeley: University of California Press, 2011).

60. For more on McLuhan's critique of this aspect of the New Criticism, see Glenn Willmott, *McLuhan, or Modernism in Reverse*, 25.

61. Marshall McLuhan, *Mechanical Bride: Folklore of Industrial Man* (Berkeley, CA: Gingko Press, 1951), v.

62. Marshall McLuhan, *Mechanical Bride*, vii.

63. Qtd. in Stearn, G. E., ed. McLuhan: *Hot and Cool: a primer for the understanding of and a critical symposium with responses by McLuhan* (New York: Dial, 1967), xii.

64. Ezra Pound, "A Retrospect" in *The Literary Essays of Ezra Pound*, ed. T. S. Eliot (London: Faber and Faber, 1954), 4.

65. Marshall McLuhan, *The Mechanical Bride*, vii.

66. Marshall McLuhan, *The Mechanical Bride*, v.

67. Marshall McLuhan, *The Mechanical Bride*, v.

68. F. R. Leavis and Denys Thompson, *Culture and Environment*, 9.

69. Marshall McLuhan, *The Mechanical Bride*, 80.

70. Marshall McLuhan, *The Mechanical Bride*, 80.

71. Marshall McLuhan, *The Mechanical Bride*, 80 and 82.

72. Marshall McLuhan, *The Mechanical Bride*, 82.

73. Marshall McLuhan, *The Mechanical Bride*, 80.

74. Marshall McLuhan, *The Mechanical Bride*, 82.

75. Marshall McLuhan, *The Mechanical Bride*, 82.

76. F. R. Leavis and Denys Thompson, *Culture and Environment*, 9.

77. Steven Johnson defends this mode of reading or "skimming [as] an immensely valuable skill" in his introduction to *The Best Technology Writing of 2009* (New Haven: Yale University Press, 2009), 5.

78. On the distinction between hyper- and deep attention, see Hayles, "Hyper and Deep Attention: The Generational Divide in Cognitive Modes."

79. Marshall McLuhan, *The Gutenberg Galaxy*, 8.

80. Bonnie Mak, *How the Page Matters* (Toronto: University of Toronto Press, 2011), 3.

81. Elena Lamberti, *Marshall McLuhan's Mosaic: Probing the Literary Origins of Media Studies* (Toronto: University of Toronto Press, 2012), 43–44.

82. McLuhan, *The Gutenberg Galaxy*, 19. McLuhan reads *King Lear* as a play about the stripping away and apart of the human senses and, in essence, the separation of sight from the other senses (21). This focus (pardon the pun) supports his argument about print technology—that it divides the senses and separates man from one another.

83. Elena Lamberti, *Marshall McLuhan's Mosaic*, 32.

84. Lewis H. Lapham, "Introduction to the MIT Press Edition: The Eternal Now" reprinted in the 2001 edition of McLuhan's *Understanding Media* (MIT Press, 2001), xi. In this introduction, Lapham writes that McLuhan "repeatedly reminds his readers that his proposition is best understood as a literary trope, not as a scientific theory" (xiii) and rightly explains that "[d]espite its title, the book was never easy to understand" (xi). Donald Theall explains that *The Mechanical Bride* was not a success, but it did introduce a central aspect of McLuhan's critical method of "using poetic methods of analysis in a quasi-poetic style to analyse popular cultural phenomena" (*The Virtual Marshall McLuhan* [Montreal: McGill-Queen's University Press, 2001], 5).

85. Donald Theall aptly describes McLuhan as "an allusive poet and his probes, like the work of poetics from Dante to Pound, are embedded in allusion to poets, philosophers, artists, other cultural producers, and theologians" (*The Virtual Marshall McLuhan*, 28). Harold Rosenberg writes, "McLuhan, then, is a kind of artist, and his quick leaps from datum to axiom . . . are often aesthetically pleasurable. In his communications-constructed world, the artist is the master figure—in fact, the only personage whom he differentiates from the media-absorbing mass" ("Philosophy in a Pop Key" in *Marshall McLuhan: Critical Evaluations in Cultural Theory*, ed. Gary Genesko [Routledge, 2005], 117).

86. Marshall McLuhan, *Letters of Marshall McLuhan*, 246. The letter was dated December 18, 1954.

87. McLuhan began a friendship with Lewis in St. Louis in 1943. When Lewis was suffering financial troubles, McLuhan helped him secure portrait commissions. For more on their relationship, see Theall's *The Virtual Marshall McLuhan*.

88. Marshall McLuhan, *Letters of Marshall McLuhan*, 205.

89. Kenner received his MA at University of Toronto and met McLuhan there. Kenner's first book, *Paradox in Chesterton* (1947), contained an introduction by McLuhan, and his second book, *The Poetry of Ezra Pound* (1951), was dedicated to McLuhan. For more on the complicated relationship between McLuhan and Kenner, see Philip Marchand's *Marshall McLuhan: The Medium and the Messenger*. Or, see Harvey Blume's interview with Hugh Kenner, "Hugh Kenner: The Grand Tour," *Bookwire* (March 2001), accessed October 17, 2012, http://web.archive.org/web/20100103161939/http://bookwire.com/bookwire/bbr/reviews/March2001/hugh_kenner_thegrandtour.htm.

90. For his pro-Fascist radio broadcasts during World War II, Pound was arrested and held in a US Army prison camp in Pisa for three weeks before he was transferred to Washington, where he was found mentally unfit to stand trial. He was subsequently sent to a federal asylum, St. Elizabeths, for twelve years.

91. Leon Surette writes, "McLuhan's principal exemplars of the new culture were the works of James Joyce and Ezra Pound, in which linearity, sequentiality, and external point of view were suppressed, and the intellectual and moral principles of the counterculture, according to which participation, simultaneity, and sphericality were practiced in a perception of the world as a 'global village'" ("McLuhan, Marshall," *The Johns Hopkins Guide to Literary Theory & Criticism*, eds. Michael Groden and Martin Kreiswirth [Baltimore: The Johns Hopkins University Press] 1994: 482). Donald Theall emphasizes the importance of Joyce's influence on McLuhan: "It has been widely accepted that McLuhan's writings anticipated the emergence of our contemporary perception of a digital cyberculture of artificial realities and cyberspace. But the primary source of McLuhan's insights in this area were first, modernist art and literature including Joyce and Lewis" (*Virtual McLuhan*, 177). For more about Pound's influence on McLuhan, see A. Anthony Tremblay, "Ezra Pound and Marshall McLuhan: A Meditation on the Nature of Influence" (Diss., University of New Brunswick, 1995) or Glenn Willmott's *McLuhan, or Modernism in Reverse*.

92. For more on the influence of Joyce on McLuhan, see especially Donald Theall and Joan Theall, "Marshall McLuhan and James Joyce: Beyond Media" in *Canadian Journal of Communication* (vol. 14, no. 4, 1989]): 46–66). See also Donald Theall's *Virtual McLuhan*, and Louis Armand's volume *JoyceMedia: James Joyce, Hypermedia & Textual Genetics*. (Prague: Litteraria Pragensia, 2004). Elena Lambert helpfully distinguishes the influence of Joyce on McLuhan as such, "Joyce was not so important for the development of McLuhan's ideas on media; instead, he was fundamental for the elaboration of McLuhan's own poetics, and especially for the elaboration of his own form of writing" (*Marshall McLuhan's Mosaic*, 181).

93. Marshall McLuhan, *The Mechanical Bride*, 3.

94. Marshall McLuhan, *The Mechanical Bride*, 4.

95. Marshall McLuhan, *The Mechanical Bride*, 59.

96. Marshall McLuhan, *The Mechanical Bride*, 107.

97. Eric McLuhan, *The Role of Thunder in Finnegans Wake* (Toronto: University of Toronto Press, 1997), xiii–xiv.

98. Marshall McLuhan, *The Gutenberg Galaxy*, 260. McLuhan writes, "For the electric puts the mythic or collective dimension of human experience fully into the conscious wake-a-day world. Such is the meaning of the title Finnegans Wake" (19).

99. Marshall McLuhan, *The Gutenberg Galaxy*, 95.

100. Donald Theall and Joan Theall, "Marshall McLuhan and James Joyce: Beyond Media," *Canadian Journal of Communication*, vol. 14, no. 4 (1989), 46.

101. Donald Theall and Joan Theall, "Marshall McLuhan and James Joyce: Beyond Media," 46.

102. Eric McLuhan, *The Role of Thunder in Finnegans Wake*, xii.

103. Eric McLuhan, *The Role of Thunder in Finnegans Wake*, xii.

104. Marshall McLuhan, *Letters of Marshall McLuhan*, 201.

105. Marshall McLuhan, *Letters of Marshall McLuhan*, 210–211.

106. Donald Theall claims, "the major direction of most of McLuhan's work was well developed before the end of the 1950s and prior to the publication of his seminal books on *Gutenberg Galaxy* and *Understanding Media*" (*Virtual McLuhan*), 15.

107. Marshall McLuhan, *Letters of Marshall McLuhan*, 232.

108. Ezra Pound, *ABC of Reading*, 76.

109. Ezra Pound to Harriett Monroe, [18] August, 1912, in *The Selected Letters of Ezra Pound, 1907–1941*, ed. D. D. Paige. (London: Faber and Faber, 1971), 9.

110. Ezra Pound, "A Retrospect" in *Literary Essays*, 256.

111. Ezra Pound, "How to Read" in *Literary Essays*, 20.

112. Marshall McLuhan *COUNTERBLAST*, 93.

113. Marshall McLuhan *COUNTERBLAST*, 93.

114. Hugh Kenner, *The Pound Era* (Berkeley: University of California Press, 1971), 90.

115. McLuhan, *Letters of Marshall McLuhan*, 250. For more on Pound and his technologically driven, typewriter-based aesthetic, see Kenner's *The Mechanic Muse* (Oxford: Oxford University Press, 1987) and Jerome McGann's *The Black Riders: The Visible Language of Modernism* (Princeton, Princeton University Press, 1993).

116. Marshall McLuhan, *Letters of Marshall McLuhan*, 250.

117. Marshall McLuhan, *Letters of Marshall McLuhan*, 250.

118. Letters to Marshall McLuhan. Canada's National Public Archives, Ottawa. Qtd. in Edwin Barton, "On the Ezra Pound/Marshall McLuhan Correspondence," *McLuhan Studies*, no. 1 (1998), accessed October 17, 2012, http://projects.chass.utoronto.ca/mcluhan-studies/v1_iss1/1_1art11.htm.

119. Glenn Willmott explains that McLuhan saw *The Cantos* as "a kind of trans-mythic 'landscape'—an unfolding terrain of structural principles, a *techne*, a medium" (49). McLuhan was personally interested in seeing Pound's *Cantos* represented in different media forms. In a letter dated June 16, 1948, McLuhan writes to the poet, "It would be of the utmost interest and value if you would make some recordings of your poems" (*Letters of Marshall McLuhan*), 193.

120. Marshall McLuhan, *Letters of Marshall McLuhan*, 193.

121. Marshall McLuhan, *Letters of Marshall McLuhan*, 194.

122. Marshall McLuhan, *Letters of Marshall McLuhan*. From an undated letter to Felix Giovelli, 201.

123. Marshall McLuhan, *Letters of Marshall McLuhan*. From an undated letter to Felix Giovelli, 201.

124. McLuhan explains that hot media are high definition, densely filled with data to the point that they saturate attention and leave little participation to the viewer. Radio, film, and books are hot media. For McLuhan these media incite revolution rather than unification because they destroy tribal cultures and instead inspire isolated, specialist pursuits and knowledge (*Understanding Media* 24). In contrast, cool media are defined by low definition and high participation on the part of the audience to fill in gaps of data, which means intensified involvement and participation (*Understanding Media* 319). He lists the telephone, cartoons, and speech in this category (*Understanding Media* 23). Thirty-five years later, in *Cybertext: Perspectives on Ergodic Literature* (Baltimore: Johns Hopkins University Press, 1997), Espen Aarseth argues for a function-oriented perspective for reading media and new media objects that shares McLuhan's ambition to distinguish between mean forms based on user interaction. This book would become the cornerstone of games studies and a key text in digital scholarship.

125. Marshall McLuhan, *The Gutenberg Galaxy*, 104. The inclusion of Stein here is rather anomalous because McLuhan, like Pound, generally avoided writing about (and certainly praising) Stein, Virginia Woolf, or other female modernist writers. This narrow conservative

perspective is one of the reasons for general condemnation and rejection of McLuhan (and Pound) by later critics. In his biography of McLuhan, Marchand describes an apocryphal scene in McLuhan's maturation at Cambridge whereby he grew into the role of the "great men" he admired by publicly humiliating Stein. McLuhan "enjoyed the distinction of being threatened by Gertrude Stein when that formidable lady spoke on the topic 'I am I because my little dog knows me.' McLuhan, from the back of the room, interrupted her talk with a rude comment to the effect that her prose style was rather childlike, if not infantile. Stein, who realized this student has been reading her mortal enemy Wyndham Lewis, expressed her annoyance in a direct fashion. She grabbed her umbrella and made her way through the audience to McLuhan" (46).

126. Marshall McLuhan, *Understanding Media*, 4.

127. Marshall McLuhan, *Understanding Media*, 4.

128. Marshall McLuhan, *Understanding Media*, 3–4.

129. Marshall McLuhan, *Understanding Media*, 5.

130. It makes sense that McLuhan would chose *Blast* as a point of origin not only because of his admiration for Pound and personal relationship with Wyndham Lewis but because Vorticism centers around metaphors of energy and electricity. Rather than the static nature implied by Imagism, Vorticism employs the analogy of the electric currents. Pound describes the vortex in language that resonates with that which McLuhan later uses to present his probes: "'The image is not an idea. It is a radiant node or cluster; it is what I can, and must perforce, call a VORTEX, from which, and through which, and into which, ideas are constantly rushing'" (*Gaudier-Brzeska: A Memoir Including the Published Writings of the Sculptor and a Selection from His Letters* [John Lane, 1916. Rpt. New Directions, 1961], 92).

131. The special edition is published by *transmediale* and Gingko Press (2011), and the quote is taken from its inside cover, as is the following statement about the book's publication: it "launches the centennial 'McLuhan in Europe wu' network of events celebrating McLuhan's vision and impact on European art and culture," *COUNTERBLAST 1954 edition* (Berlin: transmediale, 2011).

132. Marshall McLuhan, *COUNTERBLAST*, 5.

133. Marshall McLuhan, *The Medium Is the Massage*, 74–75.

134. I would suggest that, in these ways, McLuhan's *COUNTERBLAST* and *The Medium is the Massage* has a contemporary parallel to the millennial phenomenon of fetishizing the book and expressing nostalgia for book-bound reading practices in an age of ereaders and digital literacy. I discuss this phenomenon, which I call "bookishness," in "The Aesthetic of Bookishness in 21st-Century Literature," *The Michigan Quarterly Review* (Fall 2009): 465–482.

135. Donald Theall, *The Virtual McLuhan*, 22–23.

136. Marshall McLuhan, *The Gutenberg Galaxy*, 97.

Chapter 2

1. Jennifer Schuessler, "The Godfather of the E-Reader," *The New York Times Sunday Book Review* (April 8, 2010), 27.

2. Bob Brown, *The Readies* (Cagnes-sur-Mer: Roving Eye Press, 1930), 35. An essay version of "The Readies" was also published in the journal *transition*, no. 19 (1930).

3. Craig Saper writes, "Although some scholars now frame Brown as a dilettante of the European avant-garde, the modernists saw him as a precursor, and central innovator, to their revolution" ("Afterword: The Adventures of Bob Brown and His Reading Machine: Abbreviated Writing and Browsers Fifty Years Before Txt, Tweets, and WWW," in *The Readies by Bob Brown*, ed. Craig Saper [Houston, TX: Rice University Press, 2009]: 67). Saper's afterword in *The Readies* contains biographical information on Brown's fascinating life, but a full biography of this larger-than-life figure has not yet been written. This is despite the fact that McGann calls Brown, "that strange and arresting American, now academically forgotten, whose work culminates the extraordinary tradition of modern experimentalist writing" (*Black Riders: The Visible Language of Modernism* [Princeton: Princeton University Press, 1993], 84). Similarly, Augusto de Campos claims that Brown has been "strangely marginalized even by the marginal vanguard" (*A Margem da Margem* [São Paulo, Brazil: Companhia das Letras, 1989], 127, translation by Edgar Garcia). The reasons *why* Brown has been forgotten by literary history are beyond the scope of this essay, but Saper does offer a few suggestions. First, the Readies manifesto was published (by Brown) in a limited run of 150 copies that "assured that it would pass into obscurity" (Saper, "Afterword," 78); second, Brown's "huge success in popular genres of writing and the great variability in the types of his writing—have made it challenging for literary scholars to find a place for him" (Saper, "Afterword," 78–79). These challenges are, I think, precisely what makes him so intriguing.

4. My critical approach builds upon the work of scholars such as Jerome McGann, whose textual criticism, particularly in *The Textual Condition* (New Jersey: Princeton University Press, 1991), reminds us that literature is always created, distributed, accessed, and archived in material contexts and media-specific conditions that inform (whether we realize it or not) the ways in which we read and study literature.

5. William Poundstone's *Project for the Tachistoscope {Bottomless Pit}* (2005) is accessible on the author's webpage at http://www.williampoundstone.net/ or in the Electronic Literature Organization's *Electronic Literature Collection, Volume 2* at http://collection.eliterature. org/1/works/poundstone__project_for_tachistoscope_bottomless_pit.html. For the sake of brevity, I will henceforth refer to *Project for the Tachistoscope {Bottomless Pit}* as *Project*.

6. Thus a book, scroll, or computer is a reading machine but eyeglasses or libraries are not.

7. Poundstone is the author of twelve books of nonfiction and has been twice nominated for the Pulitzer Prize. His titles include *The Recursive Universe: Cosmic Complexity and the Limits of Scientific Knowledge* (New York: William Morrow and Company, 1984); *Labyrinths of Reason: Paradox, Puzzles, and the Fragility of Knowledge* (New York: Doubleday, 1988); and *Prisoner's Dilemma: John Von Neumann, Game Theory, and the Puzzle of the Bomb* (New York: Doubleday, 1992).

8. Jay David Bolter and Richard Grusin, *Remediation: Understanding New Media* (Cambridge, MA: MIT Press, 1999), 45, 47.

9. N. Katherine Hayles, *My Mother Was a Computer* (Chicago: University of Chicago Press, 2005), 33.

10. In her seminal article on the tachistoscope, "What Is a Tachistoscope?: Historical Explorations of an Instrument," Ruth Benschop explains, "it has become apparent that the answer to the question as to what the tachistoscope is, is not to be found only in the single

and clear function an instrument has, the function that can be depended upon, the function that resides within the working instrument. Rather the establishment of that function takes different forms and unfolds in a diversity of places" (in *Science in Context* vol. 11. no. 1 [1998]: 44). Benschop writes, "All the varieties and forms of the taschistoscope can be organized by reference to what it is used *for*" (26).

11. In *Manual of Mental and Physical Tests* (1910), Guy Montrose Whipple explains that the tachistoscope's primary use is as a reading machine: "In the main, the tachistoscope has been most used for the experimental investigation of the *process of reading*, and, accordingly, with an exposure field containing printed texts, isolated words, nonsense syllables, single letters, etc., but it has also been used for determining the range of attention of the visual apprehension of groups of lines, geometrical drawings, objects, colors, etc." (*Manual of Mental and Physical Tests: A Book of Directions Compiled with Special Reference to the Experimental Study of School Children in the Laboratory or Classroom* [Baltimore: Warwick & York, 1910]), 222. During World War II, the tachistoscope was used to train pilots to quickly, even subliminally, discern signs identifying approaching planes as friend or foe. Psychologist Samuel Renshaw lent his name to the Renshaw Recognition System used by the United States Army and Navy for this purpose. In the civil sector, the tachistoscope was used to teach speed-reading. This use is evident in an advertisement from 1960 for "FLASH-X," a tachistoscopic device developed by Educational Developmental Laboratories, Inc., a division of McGraw-Hill Book Co., which, when used daily, "for five or ten minutes can produce a marked improvement in attention and concentration, speed and accuracy of perception, and visual memory" ("Front Matter," *Journal of Developmental Reading*, vol. 3, no. 4 [Summer 1960]). For more on speed reading, see Sue Currell, "Streamlining the Eye: Speed Reading and the Revolution of Words, 1870–1940," in *Residual Media*, ed. Charles Acland (Minneapolis: University of Minnesota Press, 2007), 344–60.

12. Jonathan Crary, *Suspensions of Perception: Attention, Spectacle, and Modern Culture* (Cambridge, MA: MIT Press, 1999), 306. Charles R. Acland agrees. In his recent book *Swift Viewing: The Popular Life of Subliminal Influence* (Durham: Duke University Press, 2012), Acland provides a much-needed history of the tachistoscope and its cultural usage, and he describes the tachistoscope as "a material manifestation of what we take to be quintessential modern qualities: mechanized sight, Taylorist instruction, and contained and focused attention" (380).

13. Charles Acland, *Swift Viewing*, 68. Acland's illuminating new cultural history does much to address the previously ignored story connecting the tachistoscope and subliminal messaging but his work neglects consideration of the poetic and artistic usages of the machine. Since Acland's book appeared just as my own was going to press, I see this elision as an opportunity to restate my argument in this book—that media studies must consider the implications of poetic aesthetics and effects.

14. N. Katherine Hayles, "Hyper and Deep Attention: The Generational Divide in Cognitive Modes," 187.

15. For these reasons, *Project* inspired a collaborative effort to close read (with Mark C. Marino and Jeremy Douglass) it from diverse methodological perspectives: onscreen analysis (me), Critical Code Studies (Marino), and data visualizations (Douglass). See our *Reading Project: A Collaborative Interpretation of William Poundstone's Bottomless Pit* (under contract from University of Iowa Press).

16. Erkki Huhtamo, "Resurrecting the Technological Past: An Introduction to the Archaeology of Media Art," *Intercommunication* 14 (1995), accessed August 23, 2011, http://www.ntticc.or.jp/pub/ic_mag/ico14/huhtamo/huhtamo_e.html. Also see *Media Archaeology: Approaches, Applications, and Implications,* eds. Erkki Huhtamo and Jussi Parikka. In her introduction to *New Media, Old Media,* Wendy Hui Kyong Chun identifies media archeology as offering the opportunity for "seemingly forgotten moments in the history of the media we glibly call 'old' [to] be rediscovered and transformed" ("Introduction: Did Somebody Say New Media?" *New Media, Old Media: A History and Theory Reader* [2nd ed.], eds. Wendy Hui Kyong Chun and and Thomas Keenan [New York: Routledge, 2006: 9]). I maintain that media archaeology also supports the excavation of literary works like (as I discuss later in this chapter) *Readies for Bob Brown's Machine* and promotes seeing anew through the lens of new media older, well-known works. For exemplary work in media archeology of the literary bent, see Matt Kirschenbaum's *Mechanisms: New Media and the Forensic Imagination* (Cambridge, MIT University Press, 2008); Cornelia Vismann's *Files: Law and Media Technology* (trans. Geoffrey Winthrop-Young [Palo Alto: Stanford University Press, 2008]); and Terry Harpold's *Ex-foliations: Reading Machines and the Upgrade Path* (Minneapolis: University of Minnesota Press, 2009).

17. Friedrich Kittler, *Discourse Networks,* 369.

18. Terry Harpold, *Ex-foliations: Reading Machines and the Upgrade Path* (Minneapolis: University of Minnesota Press, 2009), 11.

19. Terry Harpold, *Ex-foliations,* 137.

20. For a survey of the many uses of the tachistoscope in cognitive research on optics and perception, see Edward C. Godnig, "The Tachistoscope: Its History & Usages," *Journal of Behavioral Optometry,* vol. 14, no. 2 (2003): 39–42.

21. "Imagetext" is W. J. T. Mitchell's term. See *Picture Theory: Essays on Verbal and Visual Representation* (Chicago: University of Chicago Press, 1994), 89 in particular. For a more detailed discussion of the visual contents of *Project*'s design and aesthetics, see Pressman, Marino, and Douglass's *Reading Project.*

22. In the following chapter, I discuss a similar aesthetic at work in Young-hae Chang Heavy Industries's *Dakota* (2002), another web-based Flash animation. However, whereas Young-hae Chang Heavy Industries, I argue, promotes close reading for the sake of compelling the reader to situate the digital work in within a canonical literary history, Poundstone promotes close reading for a different purpose—to promote media archaeology.

23. Here I am thinking of such new critical methodologies such as those mentioned in the Introduction, including Critical Code Studies, Platform Studies, and Software Studies. See my discussion of these recent scholarly trends in this book's Introduction.

24. William Poundstone, "Author Description" for *Project for the Tachistoscope {Bottomless Pit}, Electronic Literature Collection. Vol. 1* home page, accessed August 23, 2011, http://collection.eliterature.org/1/works/poundstone__project_for_tachistoscope_bottomless_pit.html.

25. Marshall McLuhan, *Mechanical Bride,* v.

26. For more on the cultural history of subliminal messaging, see Charles Acland's *Swift Viewing.*

27. Vance Packard, *Hidden Persuaders* (New York: Ig Publishing, 2007 [1957]), 31.

28. In *Adcult USA: The Triumph of Advertising in American Culture* (New York: Columbia University Press, 1996), James B. Twitchell argues that advertising and art have become inseparable and therefore, à la McLuhan, advertising deserves to be read with as much critical diligence as art. In his most recent book, *Priceless: The Myth of Fair Value (and How to Take Advantage of It)* (2010), Poundstone explores the power of suggestion and persuasion in advertising and price fixing.

29. Opening screen titled "Concrete Poetry and Subliminal Advertising."

30. Opening screen titled "The Subliminal Con."

31. For more on Vicary and his role in subliminal messaging, real and imagined, see Acland's *Swift Viewing.*

32. Drucker, "Experimental/Visual/Concrete" in *Figuring the Word: Essays on Books, Writing and Visual Poetics* (New York: Granary Books, 1998), 111.

33. Foundational accounts of the avant-garde, such as Peter Bürger's *Theory of the Avant-Garde* (Minneapolis: University of Minnesota Press, 1984), identify the avant-garde as constituted by its opposition to bourgeois culture, politics, and consumer ideology. Exemplary is Theodor Adorno's claim that all art, not only that of the avant-garde variety, operates through an antagonistic and external position to the dominant cultural ideology (which would certainly include advertising). See Adorno's *Aesthetic Theory*, trans. and eds. Gretel Adorno and Rolf Tiedemann (Minneapolis: University of Minnesota Press, 1970).

34. Visit UbuWeb for examples of digital concrete poetry. UbuWeb (http://www.ubuweb.com) is an online collection of avant-garde visual and aural poetry. The website describes itself thus, "UbuWeb is a completely independent resource dedicated to all strains of the avant-garde, ethnopoetics, and outsider arts" (http://ubuweb.com). Poundstone's interest in concrete poetry extends into other works of digital poetry including his "Four Poems," which also explores the relationship between advertising and avant-garde poetics. "Four Poems" is a series of short, Flash-based concrete poems animates the colors and iconography of different brand-name products (Nabisco, Mr. Goodbar, Nilla Wafers, and Tide) in ways that draw upon the reader's familiarity with the signs to subvert expected messages. See William Poundstone's "Four Poems" (2000), accessed October 17, 2012, http://www.williampoundstone.net/Poems.html.

35. The first reporting on Vicary's experiment (at a press conference that he called in order to announce his experiment) implies that the danger of "advertising's new weapon" is that it evades reading: "Advertising has simply gone underground . . . the company can get the word into your thoughts without causing you the awful inconvenience of having to see and read it" (E. Adler and John McCarter, "The Talk of the Town," *The New Yorker* September 21, 1957: 33). The description of advertising going underground means that to read it one must first excavate it.

36. For more on the influence of such poetic practices on digital literature, see C. T. Funkhouser, *Prehistoric Digital Poetry: An Archaeology of Forms, 1959–1995* (Tuscaloosa: University of Alabama Press, 2007) and Roberto Simanowski, *Digital Art and Meaning: Reading Kinetic Poetry, Text Machines, Mapping Art, and Interactive Installations* (Minneapolis: University of Minnesota Press, 2011).

37. Stuart Rogers, "How a Publicity Blitz Created the Myth of Subliminal Advertising," *Public Relation Quarterly* 37 (Winter 1992–1993), 15.

38. Pressman, Marino, and Douglass, *Reading Project: A Collaborative Interpretation of William Poundstone's Bottomless Pit.*

39. William Poundstone, "Author Description."

40. Flash, formerly owned by Macromedia, is distributed by Adobe Systems.

41. I am grateful to Mark C. Marino for helping shape my thinking here. The similitude between tweens and subliminal messages in the Flash authorware also operates at the level of creation, as Julian Sefton-Green explains: "working in Flash can be a liminal experience" because "At the same time as users appear to be working intuitively, making marks on the screen and applying menus, some actions will expose the complete mathematical 'encoded' nature of all these actions" ("Timelines, Timeframes and Special Effects: Software and Creative Media Production," *Education, Communication & Information* 5.1 [March 2005]: 107).

42. Bob Brown, *The Readies*, 1.

43. Bob Brown, *The Readies*, 1.

44. Jerome McGann, *Black Riders*, 84.

45. See Craig Dworkin, " 'Seeing Words Machinewise': Technology and Visual Prosody," *Sagetrieb*, vol. 18, no. 1 (Spring 1999): 59–86.

46. Michael North, "Words in Motion: The Movies, the Readies, and 'the Revolution of the Word,'" *Modernism/Modernity*, vol. 9, no. 2 (2002), 76.

47. Augusto de Campos, *A Margem da Margem*, 127.

48. Bob Brown (Robert Carlton Brown), "Eyes on the Half Shell" published in *1450–1950* (Paris: Black Sun Press, 1929).

49. Bob Brown, *The Readies*, 28.

50. Bob Brown, *Readies for Bob Brown's Machine* (Cagnes-sur-Mer: Roving Eye Press, 1931), Yale Collection of American Literature, Beinecke Rare Book and Manuscript Library, 161.

51. Bob Brown, *Readies for Bob Brown's Machine*, 168.

52. Bob Brown, *Readies for Bob Brown's Machine*, 153. Stymied by patent and engineering issues, the Readies remained a conceptual rather than actual machine. Brown was certainly more interested in imagining the literary potential of the machine than in building it, but his correspondence (contained in Special Collections at UCLA) shows serious efforts to have the machine built. His correspondence with engineer Albert Stoll (of National Machine Products Company) implies that the Readies might depict words scrolling rather than flashing; but it is also evident from these letters that Brown sought to use speed to elicit a flashing effect. Craig Saper has created a web-based interpretation of the Readies which depicts text scrolling horizontally, which can be viewed at http://www.readies. org or in the context of his recent essay, "Readies Online" in *Digital Humanities Quarterly*, vol. 5, no. 3 (2011), accessed October 17, 2012, http://www.digitalhumanities.org/dhq/vol/5/3/000108/000108.html.

53. Bob Brown, *The Readies*, 13.

54. Qtd. in Benschop, 27.

55. Jerome Rothenberg, "Bob Brown" in *Revolution of the Word: A New Gathering of American Avant-Garde Poetry*, 1914–1945, ed. Jerome Rothenberg (Boston: Exact Change, 1974), 9.

56. Qtd. in Jerome Rothenberg, "Bob Brown," 9.

57. Bob Brown, *The Readies,* 12 and 13, respectively.

58. Bob Brown, *The Readies,* 12.

59. Bob Brown, *The Readies,* 28.

60. Bob Brown, *The Readies,* 28.

61. Bob Brown, *The Readies,* 12.

62. Bob Brown, *Readies for Bob Brown's Machine,* 185.

63. Ezra Pound, "A Retrospect," 3.

64. Bob Brown, *The Readies,* 26.

65. Bob Brown, *The Readies,* 36.

66. The final table in *The Readies* listing the non-"meaty" words is preceded by the following explanation: "Statisticians have found that in a novel of 80,000 printed words the following twenty-five are used the number of times indicated: The . . . . . 5,848/Of . . . . 3,198," etc. (52).

67. Bob Brown, *Readies for Bob Brown's Machine,* 166.

68. Bob Brown, *Readies for Bob Brown's Machine,* 166.

69. Bob Brown, *Readies for Bob Brown's Machine,* 160.

70. Gertrude Stein not only submitted a piece to Brown's collection for the Readies but also wrote a "portrait" of Brown titled *Absolutely Bob Brown; or, Bobbed Brown* (1955). Craig Saper writes, "Gertrude Stein understood that Brown's machine, as well as his processed text for it, suggested a shift toward a different way to comprehend texts. That is, the mechanism of this book, a type of book explicitly built to resemble reading mechanisms like ticker-tape machines rather than a codex, produced—at least for Stein—specific changes in reading practices" ("Afterword," 64).

71. Bob Brown, *The Readies,* 41.

72. The newspaper article is preserved as a clipping, presumably selected by Brown himself, at UCLA Special Collections, Bob Brown Collection, 732, Box 32, Folder "Reading Machine."

73. Hilaire Hiler, "Preface," *Readies for Bob Brown's Machine,* 7.

74. Bob Brown, *Readies for Bob Brown's Machine,* 100, 136, 16, respectively.

75. Craig Dworkin, "'Seeing Words Machinewise': Technology and Visual Prosody," 60–61.

76. Williams Carlos Williams, "Author's Introduction" to *The Wedge* (1944) in *Selected Essays of William Carlos Williams* (New York: New Directions, 1969), 256.

77. Williams Carlos Williams, "Author's Introduction," 256.

78. Williams Carlos Williams, "Readie Pome." *Readies for Bob Brown's Machine,* 114.

79. Bob Brown, *The Readies,* 2.

80. Brown's poem supports Jerome McGann's argument, most forcefully articulated in *Radiant Textuality: Literature after the World Wide Web* (Palgrave, 2001), that print texts are—and have always been—marked-up by the technical and technological processes of print publishing.

81. At least, HTML could claim this position until Web 2.0 and XML emerged around 2004. Tim Berners-Lee is credited with inventing HTML and thus with inventing the World Wide Web. For more on Berners-Lee and the development of HTML and the Web, see Tim Berners-Lee with Mark Fishcetti, *Weaving the Web: The Original Design and Ultimate Destiny of the World Wide Web* (HarperBusiness, 1999).

Chapter 3

1. John Zuern notices a connection to Ezra Pound even before this cinematic count-down. While the work is loading, the screen flashes through a grey spectrum before becoming white, and Zuern reads this short sequence as a visual reference that "connects intertextually to Pound as Pound's own dawn-image connects to Homer and other classical writers" while also "contain[ing] another allusion—to the 'loading sequences' that introduce any number of Flash productions currently on the Internet" ("Matter of Time: Toward a Materialist Semiotics of Web Animation," *Dichtung-Digital* [February 14, 2003], accessed October 17, 2012, http://www.dichtung-digital.de/2003/issue/1/zuern/index.htm).

2. YHCHI present all O's as zeros, a circle with a strike-through. I maintain their typographical decision in quotations from the text, and I discuss this poetic choice later in this chapter. *Dakota* is accessible at the authors' website, http://www.yhchang.com.

3. Including the Whitney (New York City), the San Francisco Museum of Modern Art, the Getty (Los Angeles), the Tate (London), the Pompidou (Paris) as well as at the Venice, São Paulo, and Istanbul Biennials and numerous online galleries. In 2008 YHCHI presented its first international solo show at the New Museum of Contemporary Art in New York, which was followed by one at the National Museum of Contemporary Art in Athens in 2009. YHCHI also won Honorable Mention at the 2000 *SFMOMA Webby Prize for Excellence in Online Art*. They participated in the Mercosul 2011 Biennial in Porto Alegre Brazil, the first Kiev Biennial in 2012, and they are Rockefeller Foundation Bellagio Creative Arts Fellows (2012).

4. For more on comparative media studies of the literary, see the volume I coedited with N. Katherine Hayles, *Comparative Textual Media: Transforming the Humanities in the Postprint Era* (forthcoming from Minnesota University Press, 2013).

5. Qtd. in Thom Swiss, "'Distance, Homelessness, Anonymity, and Insignificance': An Interview with Young-Hae Chang Heavy Industries." *The Iowa Review Web* (December 15, 2002), accessed July 24, 2013, http://iowareview.uiowa.edu/TIRW/TIRW_Archive/tirweb/feature/younghae/interview.html.

6. Qtd. in Thom Swiss, "'Distance, Homelessness, Anonymity, and Insignificance': An Interview with Young-Hae Chang Heavy Industries."

7. Young-hae Chang Heavy Industries, "Artists' Statement" for "Threads of the Woven Maze" Virtual Exhibition. Pat Binder, Curator (2000), accessed March 2006, http://www.universes-in-universe.de/woven-maze/chang.

8. Young-hae Chang Heavy Industries, "Artists' Statement" for "Threads of the Woven Maze" Virtual Exhibition.

9. See George Landow and Robert Coover.

10. Qtd. in Thom Swiss, "'Distance, Homelessness, Anonymity, and Insignificance': An Interview with Young-Hae Chang Heavy Industries." Recall that, as I discussed in this book's introduction, that the tagline for Eastgate Systems, the first and primary publisher of electronic hypertexts, is "*serious* hypertext" (my emphasis).

11. *The Cantos* is one of the least read and least taught of modernist works, but this fact does not diminish its status as a central modernist text of high cultural capital. Indeed, the authority it evinces without even being read might paradoxically support and testify to its canonical status. To see this counterintuitive argument at work as it is applied to Joyce's *Ulysses*, see Lawrence Rainey's "Consuming Investments: Joyce's *Ulysses*," chapter 2

in *Institutions of Modernism: Literary Elites and Public Culture* (New Haven: Yale University Press, 1998). Moreover, YHCHI's close reading might even reintroduce *The Cantos* to a new generation of readers. I certainly hope that my own close reading of *Dakota* has this effect.

12. T. S. Eliot, "Introduction," *The Literary Essays of Ezra Pound*, ed. T. S. Eliot (London: Faber and Faber Limited, 1954), xi., The title of Hugh Kenner's classic work, *The Pound Era* (Berkeley: University of California Press, 1971), also identifies Pound as the center of the modernist era. In *The Dance of the Intellect: Studies in the Poetry of the Pound Tradition* (Cambridge, MA: Cambridge University Press, 1985), Marjorie Perloff identifies and traces a schism in modernist scholarship based on the identification of either Ezra Pound or Wallace Stevens as the central figure of literary modernism.

13. Jerome McGann, *Black Riders,* 80. McGann also writes, "This bibliographic contrast also helps to define the historical meaning, or argument, which these two installments of the Cantos are making" (80).

14. Jerome McGann, *Black Riders,* 80.

15. Ezra Pound, *The Cantos of Ezra Pound* (New York: New Directions. Reprint edition, 1996 [1934]), 3.

16. It is impossible to transcribe *Dakota* into print. For the sake of differentiating between consecutively flashing screens and line-breaks contained on a single screen, I use the conventional backslash (/) to denote a line-break and thick dashes (—) to designate the flashing replacement of text between screens.

17. Ezra Pound, *The Cantos,* 3.

18. In his reading of Burma Shave billboards erected along US highways from 1926 to 1963, Mike Chasar describes of the practice of reading poetic fragments across billboards from inside a moving car as a kind of textual montage: "readers regularly encountered gaps in the poems that needed to be—and were—mentally bridged" ("The Business of Rhyming: Burma-Shave Poetry and Popular Culture," *PMLA*, 125.1 [Jan. 2010], 36). His study adds another precedent and dimension to my analysis of speeding textual montage in modernism and especially connects to *Dakota*'s road-trip narrative.

19. See Alfred Appel, Jr.'s *Jazz Modernism: From Ellington and Armstrong to Matisse and Joyce* (New York: Alfred. A Knopf, 2002).

20. Ezra Pound, "The Tradition" (1913) in *Literary Essays of Ezra Pound*, ed. T. S. Eliot (New York: New Directions, 1954), 91. In "How to Read," Pound identifies the first of the three kinds of poetry Pound identifies is "melopoeia" "wherein words are charged, over and above their plain meaning, with some musical property, which directs the bearing or trend of that meaning" ("How to Read" in *Literary Essays of Ezra Pound,* 172). In "A Retrospect," Pound provides the following advice to poets: "behave as a musician, a good musician, when dealing with that phase of your art which has exact parallels in music" (6).

21. See Murray R. Schafer's *Ezra Pound and Music* (New York: A New Directions Book, 1977).

22. In *The Language of New Media*, Lev Manovich identifies digital art and the culture it reflects as operating through the metaphor and practice of "the remix." He sees that "electronic art from its very beginning was based on a new principle: *modification of an already existing signal*" (126), so that "authentic creation has been replaced by selection from a menu" (124). He thus identifies the DJ as the paradigmatic figure of the contemporary artist (135). The concept of remixing is certainly related to YHCHI's relationship to

modernism, but, whereas Manovich reads (and celebrates) the remix as constitutive of the digital medium (and of its postmodern culture), I see YHCHI using their remixes and remediations to counter such media-based assumptions. This distinction typifies the greater difference between how Manovich and I read the relationship between modernism and digital art, which I discuss in this book's introduction.

23. Ezra Pound, *The Cantos*, 4.

24. Ezra Pound, *The Cantos*, 4.

25. Ezra Pound, *The Cantos*, 4.

26. Ezra Pound, *The Cantos*, 4.

27. In *Postmodernism: Or, The Cultural Logic of Late Capitalism*, Fredric Jameson identifies pastiche—"the imitation of a peculiar or unique, idiosyncratic style" as "blank parody" (17) and the "cannibalization of all styles of the past" (18)—as a constitutive characteristic of postmodernism.

28. Young-hae Chang Heavy Industries, email to author, May 4, 2004.

29. *Dakota* was shown at "The American Effect" (2003) exhibit at the Whitney Museum and "Video and Media Art by Contemporary Artists" (2004) at the Getty Museum.

30. "Artist Statement" for "On the Web" (2001–2002) Anthony Huberman, Curator, P. S. 1 Contemporary Art Center, an affiliate of The Museum of Modern Art in New York, accessed July 5, 2007, http://www.ps1.org/cut/animations/web/chang.html.

31. Ezra Pound, "How to Read," 16. Pound shows that the difference between prose and poetry is one of degree: "The language of prose is much less highly charged, that is perhaps the only availing distinction between prose and poesy" ("How to Read," 26). He writes, "verse-writing can or could no longer be clearly understood without the study of prose-writing" ("How to Read," 30).

32. Sergei Eisenstein, "A Dialectic Approach to Film Form," *The Film Form: Essays in Film Theory*. trans. and ed. Jay Leyda (New York: Harcourt Brace Jovanovich, 1949), 49.

33. Sergei Eisenstein, "Synchronization of the Senses," *The Film Sense*, trans. and ed., Jay Leyda (New York: Harcourt Brace Jovanovich, 1975), 79.

34. Eisenstein, "Word and Image" (1938), *The Film Sense*. trans. and ed., Jay Leyda (New York: Harcourt Brace Jovanovich, 1975), 4.

35. Ezra Pound, "A Retrospect," 4. Pound writes, "It is the presentation of such a 'complex' *instantaneously* which gives that sense of sudden liberation . . . which we experience in the presence of the greatest works of art" (4, emphasis added).

36. In *The Pound Era* Hugh Kenner explains that Pound's vocabulary for describing "the image" shifts at this time from a static "thing" in Imagism (the "Direct treatment of the 'thing'" [1913]), to a dynamic vortex. Pound writes, "The image is not an idea. It is a radiant node or cluster; it is what I can, and must perforce, call a VORTEX, from which, and through which, and into which, ideas are constantly rushing" (*Gaudier-Brzeska: A Memoir Including the Published Writings of the Sculptor and a Selection from His Letters* [John Lane, 1916. Rpt. New Directions, 1961]), 106. The image is no longer described in static terms as the "the poet's pigment" or "the word beyond formulated language" (*Gaudier-Brzeska*, 99 and 102), but becomes itself a source of energy and speed. For the transition from Imagism to Vorticism, see Levenson's *Genealogy of Modernism*, particularly chapter 8, and Kenner's *The Pound Era*, particularly the chapter titled "Knot and Vortex." For more on Vorticism, see Reed Way Dasenbrock's *The Literary Vorticism of Ezra Pound & Wyndham*

Lewis: Towards the Condition of Painting (Baltimore: Johns Hopkins University Press, 1985). YHCHI adapt Pound's "image" into a programmable category and literary tool that appears not only in "an instant of time" but in real-time. They remediate the vortex, which Wyndham Lewis describes as the place "at the heart of the whirlpool [where there] is a great silent place where all the energy is concentrated, and there at the point of concentration is the Vorticist" (Qtd. in Dasenbrock, 17), creating a digital vortex at the center of the computer screen through whose center words rush.

37. Ezra Pound, *Gaudier-Bzeska*, 103. Some critics take Pound's narrative of his poetic epiphany with a grain of salt, but Pound's claim has a contemporary parallel in Young-hae Chang Heavy Industries claim that *The Cantos* was their inspiration for *Dakota*.

38. Pound uses "ply over ply" in numerous places in *The Cantos*, but in "Canto IV" the phrase appears twice in a condensed, imagistic section: "Ply over ply, thin glitter of water;/Brook film bearing white petals." and a few lines later, "Forked branch-tips, flaming as if with lotus./Ply over ply/The shallow eddying fluid,/beneath the knees of the gods" (15).

39. Lazlo Gefin, *Ideogram: History of a Poetic Method* (Austin: University of Texas Press, 1982), xi. Gefin also claims that Pound's early definition of "super-position" is "inexact" because "'superposition' is physically impossible in writing; only juxtaposition is available to the poet" (11). But the fact that "super-position" is "impossible" in print does not make the definition "inaccurate"; it shows Pound aspiring towards a literary aesthetic in need of a new medium.

40. Around the time Pound writes about "super-position," he denigrates cinema in an article for *The New Age* (written under the pseudonym B. H. Dias). In "Art Notes: Kinema, Kinesis, Hepworth, Etc." (September 26, 1918), Pound writes, "cinema is not Art" because "Art is a stasis" (in *Ezra Pound and the Visual Arts*, ed. Harriet Zines [New York: New Directions, 1980], 78). Pound's article proceeds the modernist period in cinema and Eisenstein's work on montage (his masterpiece, *Battleship Potemkin*, is dated 1925). Pound's disparagement of cinema's current form stems primarily from its current content. He writes, "[cinema] plays to the same type of slushy and sentimental mediocrity" as "contemporary theatricals" (79). As attested by Pound's own experimentations into photography (the "vortoscope" experiments), his critique of film is based on its current state, which would change quickly, particularly through innovations in montage.

41. Marshall McLuhan, *Letters of Marshall McLuhan*, 193. The letter is date June 16, 1948. For more on the correspondence between Pound and McLuhan, see Edwin J. Barton, "On the Ezra Pound/Marshall McLuhan Correspondence." For the influence of Pound on McLuhan, see A. Anthony Tremblay, "Ezra Pound and Marshall McLuhan: A Meditation on the Nature of Influence," Glenn Willmott's *McLuhan, or Modernism in Reverse*, and Donald F. Theall's *The Virtual Marshall McLuhan*.

42. On suture, see Kaja Silverman, *The Subject of Semiotics* (New York: Oxford University Press, 1983), chapter 5 in particular.

43. "Flash Professional" Product Description. Adobe, accessed July 23, 2013, http://www.adobe.com/products/studio/productinfo/products/.

44. For a discussion of the technologized mediation of "liveness," see Philip Auslander, *Liveness: Performance in a Mediatized Culture* (New York: Routledge, 1999).

45. Ezra Pound, *The Cantos*, 6.

46. A parallel between Art Blakey and Ezra Pound might also be pursued in light of the fact that both served as not only as innovators in their respective arts but also as mentor figures to younger artists. "By the time of Blakey's death in 1990, a tour with the peripatetic Messengers was viewed as a sort of pre-requisite for up-and-coming jazz musicians. A quick way to be taken seriously by critics, record producers and audiences was to pass through Blakey's free-form university" (Bruce H. Klauber "Art Blakey" entry, accessed July 30, 2013, *Drummerworld*, website http://www.drummerworld.com/drummers/Art_Blakey. html).

47. See *How We Become Posthuman*, wherein Katherine Hayles shows how "a historically specific construction called *the human is giving way to a different construction called the posthuman*" (2, original emphasis). The "posthuman view configures human being so that it can be seamlessly articulated with intelligent machines," Hayles writes, and this concept "implies a distributed cognition located in disparate parts" (3). I discuss this idea in more detail in Chapter 4.

48. John Zuern, "Matter of Time: Toward a Materialist Semiotics of Web Animation," 3.

49. Mark B. N. Hansen, *New Philosophy for New Media* (Cambridge, MA: The MIT Press, 2004), 10.

50. John Clellon Holmes, "This Is The Beat Generation," *The New York Times Magazine* (November 16, 1952). Holmes explains that being "beat" expresses a connection to the wasted spirit of the Lost Generation, the flipside of modernism that the Beats consciously adapted in a similar way to YHCHI's own adaptation. Indeed, in that modernist form of literary assertion, the manifesto, the Beat poets solidify their connection to and difference from literary modernism. As Holmes writes, "unlike the Lost Generation, which was occupied with the loss of faith, the Beat Generation is becoming more and more occupied with the need for it."

51. Carroll. T. Terrell, *A Companion to The Cantos of Ezra Pound* (Berkeley: University of California Press, 1980), 2.

52. In *ABC of Reading*, Pound writes of the *Odyssey*: "The news in the Odyssey is still news. Odysseus is still 'very human'" (44).

53. Donald Davie, *Ezra Pound* (Chicago: University of Chicago Press, 1982 [1975]), 229.

54. Ezra Pound, *Gaudier-Brzeska*, 84; Young-hae Chang Heavy Industries, email to the author, February 28, 2004.

55. John Guillory, *Cultural Capital*, 168.

56. Leonard Diepeveen, *The Difficulties of Modernism* (New York, Routledge, 2003), xi.

57. For more on the creation of professional readers via modernist literature, see Thomas Strychacz, *Modernism, Mass Culture, and Professionalism*. (Cambridge, MA: Cambridge University Press, 1993).

58. For examples of YHCHI's decidedly more political works, see "Operation Nukorea," "Cunnilingus in North Korea," or "Samsung," all of which can be accessed at yhchang.com

59. Young-hae Chang Heavy Industries, "Artists' Statement" for "Threads of the Woven Maze."

60. Ezra Pound, *The Cantos*, 5.

61. Ellmann actually shares editorial duties with Robert O'Clair, but YHCHI cast Ellmann as the editor-translator figure, a contemporary renovation of Divus. An anonymous reader at *Modern Fiction Studies* suggested an interesting interpretation of YHCHI's

outburst against Ellmann, "FUCK—YOU,—ELLMANN": the line might be read as an al-lusion to Pound's anti-Semitism. Read in this manner, the line lashing out at Ellmann is an adaptation of Pound's own verbal attacks against Jews in his later cantos. This reading adds another layer to YHCHI's adaptation and the depth of their knowledge about Pound, but it does not discount my reading of Ellmann as a subject of critique due to his New Critical approach to explaining *The Cantos*. The line from *Dakota*, when read in its entirety, specif-ically identifies Ellmann not only as an individual (or a Jewish individual), but as a critic writing "ØN—PØUND" in the "NØRTØN,—NEW YØRK—1973."

62. Richard Ellmann, *The Norton Anthology of Modern and Contemporary Poetry*, vol. 1, 3rd ed., eds. Jahah Ramazani, Richard Ellmann, and Robert O'Claire (New York: Norton, 2003 [1973]), 357.

63. Ezra Pound, *The Cantos*, 5.

64. Ezra Pound, *The Cantos*, 10.

65. See Theodor Adorno's *Aesthetic Theory*, especially the sections titled "Situation" and "Society."

66. Michael Fried, "Art and Objecthood" in *Art and Objecthood: Essays and Reviews* (Chicago: University of Chicago Press, 1998 [1967]), 153.

67. See "Creating Your First Flash Professional CS5 Document," Adobe Flash Devel-oper Center blog, accessed October 18, 2012, http://www.adobe.com/devnet/flash/articles/flash_cs5_createfla.html.

68. Lev Manovich, *The Language of New Media*, xxxiii.

Chapter 4

1. For a taste of this conversation, see the collection *Debates in the Digital Humanities*, ed. Matthew K. Gold (Minneapolis: University of Minnesota Press, 2012), in particular Mat-thew K. Kirschenbaum's essay in that volume, "What Is the Digital Humanities and What's It Doing in English Departments?" 3–11.

2. Lev Manovich, *The Language of New Media*, 218.

3. Lev Manovich, *The Language of New Media*. Manovich continues: "it is also appropri-ate that we would want to develop a poetics, aesthetics, and ethics of this database" (219). For Manovich, the larger point is not about narrative or literature—indeed, narrative is the strawman of sorts here—but about the fact that "[t]he database becomes the center of the creative process in the computer age" (227).

4. Lev Manovich, *The Language of New Media*, 225.

5. Lev Manovich, *The Language of New Media*, 225.

6. In "The Changing Profession" section of *PMLA* (October 2007), Folsom's essay, "Da-tabase as Genre: The Epic Transformation of Archives" (1571–1579) prompted responses from an array of scholars including Peter Stallybrass, Jerome McGann, Meredith L. McGill, Jonathan Freedman, and Katherine Hayles; this was, in turn, followed by a short response to these ripostes by Folsom, that appears at the end of the section.

7. N. Katherine Hayles, "Narrating Bits," *Vectors*, issue 1 (Winter 2005), lexia and par-agraph 1, accessed October 18, 2012, http://www.vectorsjournal.org/projects/index.php?project=6.

8. N. Katherine Hayles, "Narrating Bits," lexia and paragraph 1.

9. T. S. Eliot, "*Ulysses*, Order, and Myth," 92.

10. Ian Bogost and Ian McCarthy's "Wandering Rocks" is accessible on Ian Bogost's website at http://www.bogost.com/blog/bloomsday_on_twitter.shtml.

11. Ian Bogost, Blogpost, "Bloomsday on Twitter: A performance of Wandering Rocks on Twitter, and a commentary on both. Created with Ian McCarthy" (June 16, 2007), accessed October 18, 2012, http://www.bogost.com/blog/bloomsday_on_twitter.shtml.

12. Ian Bogost, Blogpost, "Bloomsday on Twitter."

13. Ian Bogost, Blogpost, "Bloomsday on Twitter."

14. Ian Bogost, Blogpost, "Bloomsday on Twitter."

15. When I first starting thinking about this topic (in February 2009), the writing prompt on Twitter was "What are you doing?"

16. The title screen distributes authorship between Morrissey and Talley thusly, "Programmed and crafted by the author, Judd Morrissey" with "Mechanics of reconfiguration designed in collaboration with Lori Talley," accessed November 10, 2010, http://www.thejewsdaughter.com/. *The Jew's Daughter* is archived and accessible in the Electronic Literature Organization's *Electronic Literature Collection, Volume 1*, where it is identified as being authored by Morrissey, http://collection.eliterature.org/1/works/morrissey__the_jews_daughter.html. Since I rely on that edition, I will maintain the latter authorial designation throughout.

17. Matthew Mirapaul, "Pushing Hypertext in New Directions," *New York Times* (July 27, 2000), accessed October 22, 2012, http://partners.nytimes.com/library/tech/00/07/cyber/artsatlarge/27artsatlarge.html.

18. David Ciccoricco, *Reading Network Fiction* (Tuscaloosa: University of Alabama Press, 2007), 162.

19. In particular, see Landow and Coover.

20. Espen Aarseth threw the arrow that wounded the hypertext myth. See Aarseth's *Cybertext: Perspectives on Ergodic Literature*.

21. Judd Morrissey, *The Jew's Daughter*, Screen 227. The novel is *Venus in Furs*, a nineteenth century romp by Leopold von Sacher-Masoch, whose name became tied to the sexual practice of masochism, a detail made known through an allusion on screen 280. For the influence of Sacher-Masoch and masochism on *Ulysses*, see Frances L. Restuccia, "Molly in Furs," *Novel*, vol. 18, no. 2, (Winter 1985), and also Richard Ellmann's *James Joyce* (New York: Oxford UP, 1959), 381–382.

22. Judd Morrissey, *The Jew's Daughter*, Screen 6.

23. Louie Edmundson reads this section of *Ulysses* as grounded upon the etymological duality of the word "host," which means a guest, ally, or provider of shelter ("hoste") but also a stranger or enemy ("hostis") and, finally, a victim of sacrifice, in particular, the religious ritual of taking the "host" ("hoistie") (233). The aspect of sacrifice is evident in Stephen's commentary on the ballad he sings, in which he perceives the ballad as a tale of a "the victim predestined" who is led "to a strange habitation, to a secret infidel apartment, and there, implacable, immolates him, consenting" (692). For a detailed analysis of the role of the Child Ballad 155, "Sir Hugh, or the Jew's Daughter" in *Ulysses*, see Edmundson's *Theme and Countertheme: The Function of Child Ballad 155, "Sir Hugh, or the Jew's Daughter" in James Joyce's* Ulysses (PhD diss., Middle Tennessee State University, 1975).

24. In his textual history of the "Harry Hughes" ballad, David Ciccorrico states that the act of decapitating the boy with a penknife is a detail that "does not appear in any of the

eighteen versions originally collected by Child [Francis J. in 1888], nor does it appear in any of the twenty-one versions in Sargent and Kittredge's volume" (179).

25. Various scholars, for various reasons, identify "Ithaca" as the center of Joyce's novel, the home of the wandering narrative. Joyce himself identified it as "'the ugly duckling of [*Ulysses*] and therefore, I suppose, my favourite'" (qtd. in Andrew Gibson, "Introduction," *Joyce's "Ithaca,"* ed. Andrew Gibson [Atlanta: Rodopi, 1996], 3). Walton A. Litz writes, "both the action and the stylistic development of *Ulysses* reach a climax in 'Ithaca'" ("Ithaca" in *James Joyce's* Ulysses: *Critical Essays*, eds. Clive Hart and David Hayman [Berkeley: University of California Press, 1974] 386). Donald Theall identifies "Ithaca" as a central hub for traffic around the topic of simultaneity: "Joyce only uses the terms 'simultaneous' and 'simultaneously' (with one exception) from the fourteenth episode ('Oxen of the Sun') through the seventeenth ('Ithaca'), with more than half (60 per cent) of those references occurring in the mathematical catechism of 'Ithaca'" (*James Joyce's Techno-Poetics* [Buffalo: University of Toronto Press, 1997] 37). In *James Joyce, Authorized Reader* (Baltimore: Johns Hopkins University Press, 1991), Jean-Michel Rabate sees Ithaca as "the moment when Bloom's unconscious is scarcely distinguishable anymore from Stephen's, shortly before the separation" (114), when Stephen "seems to exchange places with Bloom and to leave the scene of 'Ithaca' with the added weight of a double exile" so that "Stephen takes charge of a wandering given up too soon by Bloom" (174). Tracing a different thematic strain, Louie Edmundson argues that, with eighty occurrences of the word "Hugh" (248) in *Ulysses* and four characters called Hugh or Hughes (269), the section of "Ithaca" that contains the ballad of "Harry Hughes" (also known as "The Jew's Daughter") "may be regarded in many ways as the thematic center of the book" (222).

26. James Joyce, *Ulysses* (Vintage International, 1990 [Modern Library 1934]), 690.

27. As the *Oxford English Dictionary* defines it, a database is "a collection of entries containing item information that can vary in its storage media and in the characteristics of its entries and items" (1962), a collection whose "Search area provides a means of querying the data base" (1967), and thus, "a generalised collection of data not linked to one set of functional questions" (1972).

28. James Joyce, *Ulysses*, 692.

29. James Joyce, *Ulysses*, 692.

30. Other critics have described the database effect in various ways. Patrick Parrinder reads the chapter as displaying the fact that "Joyce has a vast backlog of information about Bloom in particular which he has still not managed to incorporate" (*James Joyce* [Cambridge: Cambridge University Press, 1984]) 183. Andrew Gibson concurs: "'Ithaca' is the storehouse of facts in *Ulysses*, the repository of missing knowledge" (15). John Rickard similarly describes the whole of *Ulysses* as "a textual repository of words, phrases, objects, and sounds" (*Joyce's Book of Memory: The Mnemotechnic of Ulysses* [Durham, Duke University Press, 1999]), 118. Parrinder comes closest to using the word "database" when he writes, "In 'Ithaca' [Joyce] at last chose a form within which to unloose the *data-bank*" (183, emphasis added). Fritz Senn identifies the chapter as being "as close to a catalogue as anything in literature ever will" (37) because "it puts in a row items that are connected either obviously (books, dates, properties) or at times subliminally or enigmatically" ("'Ithaca': Portrait of the Chapter as a Long List" in *Joyce's "Ithaca,"* ed. Andrew Gibson [Atlanta: Rodopi, 1996:

31–76], 62). A. Walton Litz claims that "the chief effect of the question-and-answer method in 'Ithaca,' [is] a breaking-down of the narrative into discrete aesthetic units" (386, footnote); in other words, "Ithaca" operates through a kind of literary digitization of narrative information.

31. Qtd. in Litz, 392.

32. For more on the catechism in "Ithaca," see Robert Hampsom, "'Allowing for Possible Error': Education and Catechism in 'Ithaca'" in *Joyce's "Ithaca,"* ed. Andrew Gibson (Atlanta: Rodopi, 1996: 229–267).

33. James Joyce, *Ulysses,* 689. Don Gifford's <u>Ulysses</u> *Annotated* (Berkeley: University of California Press, 1989) contains a pertinent note about the presentation of "The Jew's Daughter" ballad in "Ithaca": "Apparently Joyce recalled his version from memory" (579).

34. Bonnie Mak, *How the Page Matters* (University of Toronto Press, 2011), 21.

35. Kenner explains that David Hayman describes the Arranger as "a figure who can be identified neither with the author nor with his narrators, but who exercises an increasing degree of overt control over his increasingly challenging materials" (*Ulysses: The Mechanics of Meaning.* Englewood Cliffs: Prentice-Hall Inc., 1970), 70.

36. Hugh Kenner, *Ulysses,* 65.

37. Jerome McGann, "Database, Interface, and Archival Fever," *PMLA,* vol. 122, no. 5 (October 2007): 1588–1592, 1588.

38. Jerome McGann, "Database, Interface, and Archival Fever," 1588.

39. N. Katherine Hayles, *How We Became Posthuman,* 2. Hayles writes, "No longer is human will seen as the source from which emanates the mastery necessary to dominate and control the environment. Rather, the distributed cognition of the emergent human subject correlates with—in Bateson's phrase, becomes a metaphor for—the distributed cognitive system as a whole, in which 'thinking' is done by both human and nonhuman actors" (290).

40. Judd Morrissey, *The Jew's Daughter,* Screen 243.

41. Judd Morrissey, *The Jew's Daughter,* Screen 17.

42. See David Ciccorrico for a nice reading of this scene's formal presentations embodying the act of decapitation, in which "a macabre play of works reinforces the act of detaching a woman's head. *She,* the word itself, is severed" (165).

43. Flash developed out of FutureSplash Animator, which was built in Java. For a narrative describing the creation of Flash, see John Gay's "The History of Flash: The Dawn of Web Animation," accessed October 22, 2012, http://www.adobe.com/macromedia/events/john_gay/page04.html.

44. I want to thank Caleb Smith for helping me see this point.

45. In *Stream of Consciousness in the Modern Novel* (Berkeley: University of California Press, 1954), Robert Humphrey claims, "there is no stream-of-consciousness technique. Instead, there are several quite different techniques which are used to present stream of consciousness" (4).

46. William James, *The Principles of Psychology* (New York: Henry Holt [Reprinted Bristol: Thoemmes Press, 1999] [1890]), 239. James first presented the idea of "stream of thought" in an essay from 1884.

47. William James, *The Principles of Psychology,* 239.

48. William James, *The Principles of Psychology,* 239.

49. Judith Ryan, *The Vanishing Subject: Early Psychology and Literary Modernism*. (Chicago: University of Chicago Press, 1991), 14.

50. Edouard Dujardin's *The Bays are Sere* and *Interior Monologue*, trans. Anthony Suter (London: Libris, 1991), 100. In *Le Monologue Intérieur* (1931), Dujardin states that with Joyce's novel the question arose: "what are the origins of this sensational innovation? ... But who knows when the question would have been elucidated, if James Joyce, with a generosity unparalleled in the history of letters, had not revealed that thirty-five years before the publication of *Ulysses*, interior monologue had in fact been used in my novel, *Les Lauriers sont coupés*" (87).

51. Qtd. in Melvin Freidman, *Stream of Consciousness: A Study in Literary Method* (New Haven: Yale University Press, 1955), 24; qtd. in Erwn R. Steinberg, *The Stream of Consciousness and Beyond in* Ulysses (Pittsburgh: University of Pittsburgh Press, 1958), 3.

52. Qtd. in Edouard Dujardin's *The Bays are Sere* and *Interior Monologue*, trans. Anthony Suter (London: Libris, 1991), 108.

53. In *The Vanishing Subject* Judith Ryan argues that stream of consciousness emerged at a particular cultural moment because of developments in pre-Freudian psychology that would pave the way for modernism's engagement with a fluid subjectivity. "The new problem which empiricism seemed to raise was that subjectivity was not itself a stable entity" (19); and, for, "Many of the most striking formal innovations of early twentieth-century literature can be seen as responses to this challenge" (3). As contemporary conceptions of subjectivity and experience shift in a digital world of real-time, technologically mediated communications, twenty-first century literature is faced with a challenge similar to that which inspired its modernist predecessors. See also Nicolas Dames's "Wave-Theories and Affective Physiologies: The Cognitive Strain in Victorian Novel Theories," *Victorian Studies*, vol. 46 (2004), 206–160, wherein he focuses on literary criticism to argue that pre-Freudian psychology provides an early, important, and "obscured" history for critical methodologies of reading.

54. Melvin Friedman writes, "The key to the emergence of the stream of consciousness novel lies in this new awareness of experience, this marked shift from a conception of personality as built round a hard and changeless core to a realization of it as a dynamic process" (*Stream of Consciousness: A Study in Literary Method* [New Haven: Yale UP, 1955]), 10. Shiv K. Kumar, in *Bergson and the Stream of Consciousness* (London: Blackle & Son Limited, 1962), argues that stream of consciousness is best understood in relation to Bergson's concept of "la durée": "It is this durational aspect of consciousness which defines the basis of the stream of consciousness novel" (15), because the modernist writer employing this device "does not conceive character as a state but as a process of ceaseless becoming **in a medium** which may be termed Bergson's *durée réelle*" (bold added). However, the focus of Kumar's analysis is not the media-specific ways in which material aspects of media mediate.

55. Adelaide Morris, "New Media Poetics: As We May Think/How to Write," in *New Media Poetics: Contexts, Technotexts, and Theories*, eds. Adelaide Morris and Thomas Swiss (Cambridge, MA: MIT Press, 2006), 3.

56. In Proc. 20th Nat. Conf. Assoc. Computing Machinery 96, (1965) Nelson writes, "Let me introduce the word 'hypertext' to mean a body of written or pictorial material interconnected in such a complex way that it could not conveniently be presented or represented on paper."

57. For an account of the publishing history and variations of this essay and its later companion piece, "Memex Revisited," see Terry Harpold's *Ex-foliations*, chapters 1 and 2.

58. The editor for *The Atlantic* expresses the significance of Bush's essay by introducing it through a comparison to Emerson's "The American Scholar" (Qtd. in *The New Media Reader*, eds. Noah Wardrip-Fruin and Nick Montfort, [Cambridge, MA: MIT Press, 2003], 37). Wendy Hui Kyong Chun cautions, "Conflating the memex and the Internet covers over the ephemerality of digital media and, more importantly, turns questions of forgetting and degradation into the problems for media to solve, as one medium becomes the 'memory' of the next" ("The Enduring Ephemeral, or The Future is a Memory" in *Media Archaeology: Approaches, Applications, and Implications*, eds. Erkki Huhtamo and Jussi Parikka [Berkeley: University of California Press]), 189.

59. Vannevar Bush, "As We May Think," (reprinted in *The New Media Reader*, eds. Wardrip-Fruin and Montfort, 35–47), 45; also available online at http://www.theatlantic.com/doc/194507/bush.

60. The connection between human and computer memory remains evident in the language used to describe digital technology and, in particular, their central hardware: computers function through the byte-driven "physical memory" of RAM (Random Access Memory) and ROM (read-only memory) as well as the "virtual memory" of detachable hard discs.

61. Vannevar Bush, "As We May Think," 44.

62. Vannevar Bush, "As We May Think," 46.

63. Theodor Holm Nelson, *Literary Machines* (Mindful Press, 87.1 ed. 1987 [1980]), 1.5.

64. Marshall McLuhan also famously considered media forms to be technological prosthesis. The subtitle of *Understanding Media* is "The Extensions of Man," and, in that book he writes, "our human senses, of which all media are extensions" (21).

65. Theodor Nelson, *Literary Machines*, 2.

66. See *Literary Machines* or visit http://xanadu.com/. Nelson describes his book in the rhetoric of a visionary that resonates with Bush's description of the Memex: "This is a form of storage, a new form of literature, and a network that might just revitalize human life." Nelson describes Xanadu as "a single great universal text and data grid, or, as we call it, the *docuverse*" (*Literary Machines* 2.53). The literary reference to Coleridge's poem imparts the importance of fragments in creative thought and its representation in Nelson's experiment and situates it within a genealogy of literary history that goes back to the Romantics.

67. Douglas Engelbart expresses the influence of Bush in a letter he wrote to Bush in 1962 that is reprinted as "Letter to Vannevar Bush and Program On Human Effectiveness," in *From Memex to Hypertext: Vannevar Bush and the Mind's Machine*, eds. James M. Nyce and Paul Kahn (New York: Academic Press, 1991), 235–236. He writes, "I might add that this article of yours has probably influenced me quite basically . . . . I re-discovered your article about three years ago, and was rather startled to realize how much I had aligned my sights along the vector you had described . . . . For me it is more the public debut of a dream," 235.

68. The idea of an open, accessible "docuverse" (Nelson's term) constituted by associative links was, Berners-Lee claims, "a philosophical change from the approach of previous computer systems" (*Weaving the Web*, 37). But it has its conceptual predecessors in a lineage of experimentations in hypertext that connect Bush, Nelson, Englebart, Berners-Lee,

and also, as I will argue, literary authors like James Joyce and Judd Morrissey. For more on the development of HTML, see Tim Berners-Lee's "Information Management: A Proposal," CERN (March 1989, May 1990), http://www.w3.org/History/1989/proposal.html, and his, with Mark Fischetti, *Weaving the Web: The Original Design and Ultimate Destiny of the World Wide Web* (New York: Harper Collins, 1999).

69. Michael Joyce, qtd. in Karlin Lillington, "Ulysses in Net-town," *Salon* (June 16, 1998), accessed July 3, 2006, http://archive.salon.com/21st/feature/1998/06/16feature.html.

70. Mark Nunes, "Gaps and Convergences in the Joycean Network," *joyceMedia: James Joyce, Hypermedia &Textual Genetics*, ed. Louis Armand (Prague: Litteraria Pragensia, 2004). 44–65, 45; Groden qtd. in Armand, *joyceMedia*, 18; Landow and Delany qtd. in *Hypermedia and Literary Studies*, eds. George P. Landow and Paul Delany (Cambridge, MA: MIT Press, 1995), 18,. For other examples of literary critics who claim Joyce to be a prescient practitioner of hypertext, see the online journal edited by Louis Armand, *Hypermedia Joyce Studies* or his edited collection, *Joycemedia: James Joyce, Hypermedia & Textual Genetics*. In particular, Darren Toft's "Ulysses and the Poetics of Hypertextuality," (vol. 3, 2002) wherein he claims, "Hypertextuality is a term that we have come to associate with digital connectivity, hypertext and the computer revolution. It is also a term that has, in retrospect, been applied to James Joyce's *Ulysses*." Confluences between Joyce's writing style and hypertext have also prompted literary critics to apply digital technologies, and the web in particular, to *Ulysses* in a variety of creative and critical ventures. For example, Michael Groden's "Digital *Ulysses*" (1996–2003) sought to represent the novel as an online hypertext.

71. Jacques Derrida, "Two Words for Joyce," in *Post-Structuralist Joyce: Essays from the French*, eds. Derek Attridge and Daniel Ferrer (Cambridge University Press, 1984), 147.

72. Jacques Derrida, "Two Words for Joyce," 147.

73. Jacques Derrida, "Two Words for Joyce," 148.

74. Jacques Derrida, "Two Words for Joyce," 148.

75. *My Molly (Departed)*, formerly *Twittering: A Procedural Novel* can be accessed at http://talanmemmott.com/elit.html.

76. Author's website, http://talanmemmott.com/elit.html, accessed October 15, 2012.

77. For analysis of *Lexia to Perplexia*, see Hayles's *Writing Machines*, chapter 4: "Electronic Literature as Technotext: Lexia to Perplexia" and Lisa Swanstrom's "Terminal Hopscotch: Navigating Networked Space in Talan Memmott's *Lexia to Perplexia*", *Contemporary Literature*, vol. 52, no. 3 (2011): 492–521.

78. For more on codework see Rita Raley's "Interferences: [Net.Writing] and the Practice of Codework," *Electronic Book Review*, 2002, http://www.electronicbookreview.com/thread/electropoetics/net.writing, and Alan Sondheim's "Introduction: Codework" (*American Book Review*, vol. 22, no. 6 [2001]).

79. Email to author, October 20, 2008.

80. Jessica Pressman, "Flying Blind: An Interview with Judd Morrissey and Lori Talley" (*The Iowa Review Web*, vol. 5, no. 2 [2003]), accessed October 22, 2012, http://iowareview.uiowa.edu/TIRW/TIRW_Archive/tirweb/feature/morrissey_talley/interview.html.

Chapter 5

1. Erik Loyer, *Chroma* (2001), "Prologue." *Chroma* can be accessed at http://www.marrowmonkey.com/chroma/menu.html or in the Electronic Literature Organization's

Electronic Literature Collection, Volume 2 at http://collection.eliterature.org/2/works/loyer_chroma.html.

2. See N. Katherine Hayles, *How We Became Posthuman*, chapter 2.

3. Erik Loyer, *Chroma* (2001), Prologue.

4. Erik Loyer, *Chroma* (2001), Prologue.

5. Erik Loyer, *Chroma* (2001), Prologue.

6. Erik Loyer, *Chroma* (2001), Chapter 2.

7. Erik Loyer, *Chroma* (2001), Chapter 3.

8. Erik Loyer, *Chroma* (2001), Chapter 5.

9. Leibniz's discussion of the "windowless monad" is contained in *Monadology* (1714).

10. Erik Loyer, *Chroma* (2001), Chapter 5.

11. Erik Loyer, *Chroma* (2001), Chapter 5.

12. Alan Liu, "Transcendental Data: Toward a Cultural History and Aesthetics of the New Encoded Discourse," *Critical Inquiry*, vol. 31, no. 4 (2004): 7.

13. Alan Liu, "Transcendental Data," 8.

14. Lisa Nakamura, "Race In/For Cyberspace: Identity Tourism on the Internet," *The Cybercultures Reader*, ed. David Bell (New York: Routledge Press, 2000), 713.

15. Erik Loyer, *Chroma* (2001), Chapter 5.

16. Erik Loyer, *Chroma* (2001), Chapter 6.

17. Erik Loyer, *Chroma* (2001), Chapter 6.

18. Erik Loyer, *Chroma* (2001), Chapter 6.

19. Erik Loyer, *Chroma* (2001), Chapter 6. Thomas Foster states, "Cyberspace may mean that we can assume whatever form or identity we wish, regardless of whether it matches our physical embodiment, but we still cannot escape the possibility that some types of preconceptions are likely to be hard-wired into the people we interact with in cyberspace" (160). "The Souls of Cyber-Folk: Performativity, Virtual Embodiment, and Racial Histories" in *Cyberspace Textuality: Computer Technology and Literary Theory*, ed. Marie-Laure Ryan (Indiana University Press, 1998). For more on race in cyberspace, see Lisa Nakamura's *Cybertypes: Race, Ethnicity, and Identity on the Internet* (New or York: Routledge, 2002).

20. Erik Loyer, *Chroma* (2001), Chapter 4.

21. Erik Loyer, *Chroma* (2001), Chapter 6.

22. Erik Loyer, *Chroma* (2001), Chapter 6.

23. *Chroma* remains unfinished and in the same state of incompletion since 2002. Loyer wrote the script for fifteen chapters but only completed six. A static screen appears after the sixth chapter explaining that the six completed chapters were produced through funding by a Rockefeller Media Fellowship which, when it ran out, put an end to the creation of *Chroma*.

24. John Guillory, "The Genesis of the Media Concept," 335.

25. John Guillory, "The Genesis of the Media Concept," 322, footnote 3.

26. John Guillory, "The Genesis of the Media Concept," 322, footnote 3.

27. Ferdinand de Saussure, *Course in General Linguistics*, trans. Wade Baskin, eds. Charles Bally and Albert Sechehaye in collaboration with Albert Reidlinger (London: Peter Owen, 1960, [1916]), 26. Saussure introduced his linguistic theory in a series of lectures delivered between 1906 and 1911, a time when Ezra Pound was searching for his own poetic

theory. In *Course in General Linguistics*, Ferdinand de Saussure explains that there are two types of writing systems, ideographic and phonetic, and that his linguistic theory would "limit discussion to the phonetic system, and especially to the one used today, the system that stems from the Greek alphabet" (26). Saussure does not engage the ideogram because, he claims, it operates in a different way than alphabetic, phonetic language.

28. Terry Winograd, "Computer Software for Working with Language," *Scientific American*, vol. 251, no. 3 (September, 1984), 131.

29. Terry Winograd, "Computer Software for Working with Language," 11.

30. David Golumbia, *The Cultural Logic of Computation* (Cambridge, MA: Harvard University Press, 2009), 1.

31. David Golumbia, *The Cultural Logic of Computation*, 3.

32. David Golumbia, *The Cultural Logic of Computation*, 103.

33. David Golumbia, *The Cultural Logic of Computation*, 94.

34. David Golumbia, *The Cultural Logic of Computation*, 14.

35. N. Katherine Hayles, *My Mother Was a Computer*, 15.

36. Umberto Eco differentiates between universal and perfect language explaining that perfect language is "capable of mirroring the true nature of objects" while universal language is a "language which everyone might, or ought to, speak" (*The Search for the Perfect Language*, trans. James Fentress [Hoboken, NJ: Blackwell, 1995], 73).

37. Wendy Hui Kyong Chun, *Programmed Visions: Software and Memory* (Cambridge, MA: MIT Press, 201), 55.

38. Wendy Hui Kyong Chun, *Programmed Visions*, 56.

39. See *Selected Poems*, edited and with an introduction by T. S. Eliot (Faber & Gwyer, 1928, Laughlin, 1957). Pound's subtitle for *Cathay* presents, albeit long-windedly, his translating debt: *For the Most Part from the Chinese of Rihaku, from the notes of the late Ernest Fenollosa, and the Decipherings of the Professors Mori and Ariga. Cathay* is a collection of translations of Chinese poems that sandwich the Anglo-Saxon poem "The Seafarer," a hybrid selection that Eric Hayot argues serves to show Pound "reminding his readers that the value in Li Po lay not in his Chineseness, but in his universality, in the fact that his poems revealed a shared history of ideas across time and space" (33).

40. Pound's lack of knowledge of Chinese obviously impairs and renders suspect his editorial ability to comment on the linguistic system and should render his engagement with Chinese more Orientalism rather than Sinology. Many critics have debated, attacked, and defended the accuracy, and implications of Pound's Chinese translations, a debate which is not the topic of this chapter. To cite just one example, here is J. Marshall Unger, from *Ideogram: Chinese Characters and the Myth of Disembodied Meaning* (Honolulu: University of Hawai'i Press, 2004): Pound and Fenollosa's translations "can best be described as an exercise in literary narcissism. Just as the mythical Narcissus fell in love with his own reflection, Fenollosa and Pound fell in love with their own aesthetic preconceptions, which they projected onto Chinese poetry by means of naive pictorial etymologies of characters" (59). See Pound's *Cathay* (London: Elkin Mathews, 1915). For more on Pound and Orientalism, see the work of Zhaoming Qian: *Orientalism and Modernism: The Legacy of China in Pound and Williams* (Durham: Duke University Press, 1995), *The Modernist Response to Chinese Art: Pound, Moore, Stevens* (Charlottesville: University of Virginia Press, 2003), and *Ezra Pound and China*, ed. Zhaoming Qian (Ann Arbor: University of Michigan Press, 2003).

Also see Yunte Huang, *Transpacific Displacement: Ethnography, Translation, and Intertextual Travel in Twentieth-Century American Literature* (Berkeley: University of California Press, 2002) and Eric Hayot's *Chinese Dreams: Pound, Brecht, Tel Quel* (Ann Arbor: University of Michigan Press, 2004).

41. For Pound, translation was not the transcription of linguistic signs from one language into another but an artistic act of interpretation. Hugh Kenner relates that Pound once criticized a German translator of his work saying "Don't translate what I wrote, translate what I MEANT to write" (qtd. in Kenner's *The Pound Era*, 150). Pound worked as both a poet and a translator throughout his career and viewed the roles as symbiotic. In "How to Read," he writes, "English literature lives on translation, it is fed by translation" (34). The image of feeding literature, of giving life through the intake of sustenance, is present in the first canto wherein Odysseus brings a drink to Tiresias to inspire his translation from the language of the Dead. Hugh Kenner writes, "Pound came to think of translation as a model for the poetic act: blood brought to ghosts" (*Pound Era*, 150). In his advice to writers in "A Stray Document," Pound admonishes that reading and writing is not enough: "Translation is likewise good training" (*Make it New: Essays by Ezra Pound* [New Haven: Yale University Press, 1935]), 340. For "A great age of literature is perhaps always a great age of translations; or follows it." ("Notes on Elizabethan Classicists," in *Make It New: Essays by Ezra Pound*, 101).

42. Ira Nadel points out that Chinese cultural objects infiltrated Pound's early consciousness through an American environment excited by all things Oriental. Philadelphia was in 1889 when the Pounds moved there, at the center of America's Orientalism. See "Constructing the Orient: Pound's American Vision," wherein Nadel writes, "Prefiguring Pound's obsession with ideograms, minimalist expression, and order, emerging from his study of Fenollosa, Nō, and Confucius, was his response to an earlier American discourse of the Orient that was material as well as exotic, but atmospheric rather than poetic" (in *Ezra Pound and China*, ed., Zhaoming Qian), 26.

43. See Zhaoming Qian's *The Modernist Response to Chinese Art: Pound, Moore, Stevens* (Charlottesville: University of Virginia Press, 2003), 4.

44. Also in 1910 the British Museum's Exhibition of Chinese and Japanese paintings opened, and in 1912 Ernest Fenollosa's *Epochs of Chinese and Japanese Art* was posthumously published in London. See Zhaoming Qian, *The Modernist Response to Chinese Art: Pound, Moore, Stevens.*

45. Hugh Kenner, *The Pound Era*, 161.

46. To cite one example, Herbert Schneidau writes, "the advent of the Fenollosa materials was the single most important event in the development of Pound's poetics" (Qtd. in Lazlo Gefin, *Ideogram: History of a Poetic Method* [Austin: University of Texas Press, 1982]), xii.

47. Ernest Fenollosa and Ezra Pound, *The Chinese Written Character as a Medium for Poetry*. ed. Haun Saussy, Jonathan Stalling, and Lucas Klein (Bronx, NY: Fordham University Press, 2008), 41.

48. Ernest Fenollosa and Ezra Pound, *The Chinese Written Character as a Medium for Poetry*, 42.

49. Ernest Fenollosa and Ezra Pound, *The Chinese Written Character as a Medium for Poetry*, 42–43.

50. Ernest Fenollosa and Ezra Pound, *The Chinese Written Character as a Medium for Poetry*, 24.

51. In *Transpacific Displacement*, Yunte Huang notes that in the original manuscript a "pencil mark [that] was characteristically the editor Pound's" struck-through paragraphs "to champion the cause of China's independence" (20). The excised text is as follows: Especially for Great Britain and for the United States . . . They alone, of modern people, still bear the torch of freedom . . . They alone, perhaps, possess the tolerance and the sympathy required to understand the East, and to lift her into honorable sisterhood. The peoples of Continental Europe fear the possibilities of selfhood in the East; therefore they aim to crush her . . .

> . . . Strange as it may seem, the future of Anglo Saxon supremacy in the world is probably bound up with the future of the East. If the better elements in her be crushed, and the worse be chained in slavery to some Western form of Despotism, time may come to blow out our torch. Far beyond a sentimental sympathy, our loyalty to our own ideals should urge us to champion the cause of China's independence . . . (Qtd. in Huang 20, from Fenollosa's draft, *The Chinese Written Language as a Medium for Poetry*, 1–2 in the Yale Collection of American Literature, Beinecke Rare Book and Manuscript Library).

52. Ernest Fenollosa and Ezra Pound, *The Chinese Written Character as a Medium for Poetry*, 45.

53. Ernest Fenollosa and Ezra Pound, *The Chinese Written Character as a Medium for Poetry*, 46.

54. Ernest Fenollosa and Ezra Pound, *The Chinese Written Character as a Medium for Poetry*, 51.

55. Ernest Fenollosa and Ezra Pound, *The Chinese Written Character as a Medium for Poetry*, 59.

56. Recall that Pound describes the role of the artist as "the antennae of the race." (*ABC of Reading* [New York: New Directions, 1934], 73) and that, as we saw in Chapter 1, McLuhan takes this image of the poet as radio and runs with it; indeed, he makes it one of the main motivating metaphors of his own identity as poet-critic, literary-media scholar.

57. Christopher Bush, *Ideographic Modernism: China, Writing, and Media* (Oxford: Oxford University Press, 2010), 3.

58. Christopher Bush, *Ideographic Modernism*, xviii.

59. Christopher Bush, *Ideographic Modernism*, xxix–xxx.

60. Eric Hayot, *Chinese Dreams*, 33.

61. John Irwin, *American Hieroglyphics: The Symbol of the Egyptian Hieroglyphics in the American Renaissance* (New Haven, CT: Yale University Press, 1980), 29.

62. Ira Nadel, "Constructing the Orient," 17.

63. Yunte Huang, *Transpacific Displacement*, 12. Huang cites a seventeenth century text, An Historical Essay Endeavoring a Probability that the Language of the Empire of China is the Primitive Language (1669), by Englishman John Webb that "sought to prove that Chinese was perhaps the language from which all others sprang" (12).

64. Michael Heim, *Metaphysics of Virtual Reality* (Oxford: Oxford University Press, 1993), 93. In "Erotic Ontology of Cyberspace," Heim calls the seventeenth century philosopher Leibniz "one of the essential philosophical guides to the inners structure of cyberspace"

(in *Reading Digital Culture*, ed. David Trend [Malden: Blackwell, 2001], 76). In *Electric Language: A Philosophical Study of Word Processing* (New Haven, CT: Yale University Press, 1987), Heim explains that the binary number system used centuries later by John von Neumann in developing electronic computers was based on Leibniz's invention (83). See also Martin Davis "Chapter One: Leibniz's Dream" in *The Universal Computer: The Road from Leibniz to Turing* (New York: W.W. Norton & Co., 2000).

65. Michael Heim, *Metaphysics of Virtual Reality*, 36.

66. Michael Heim, *Metaphysics of Virtual Reality*, 92.

67. Ezra Pound, *Gaudier-Brzeska*, 103.

68. Jacques Derrida, *Of Grammatology*, trans. Gayatri Chakravorty Spivak (Baltimore: The Johns Hopkins University Press, 1998), 76.

69. Jacques Derrida, *Of Grammatology*, 76.

70. Jacques Derrida, *Of Grammatology*, 76.

71. Jacques Derrida, *Of Grammatology*, 80.

72. See William Gibson's *Neuromancer* (1984), although, he also described cyberspace as a "mass consensual hallucination" earlier, in his short story, "Burning Chrome" (1982).

73. David J. Gunkel, "Lingua ex Machina: Computer-Mediated Communication and the Tower of Babel," *Configurations*, vol. 7, no. 1 (1999): 64. The science and rhetoric of genetics is also intertwined in the discourse about universal language and translation. Indeed, biogenetics can be described as the effort to pursue machine translation of human codes.

74. See Rita Raley, "Machine Translation and Global English," *The Yale Journal of Criticism*, vol. 16, no. 2 (2003): 291–313.

75. Warren Weaver, "Translation," *Machine Translation of Languages*, eds. William N. Locke and A. Donald Booth (Cambridge, MA: MIT Press, 1955), 23.

76. Warren Weaver, "Foreword: The New Tower" in *Machine Translation of Languages*, eds. William N. Locke and A. Donald Booth (Cambridge, MA: MIT Press, 1955), vii.

77. Rita Raley, "Machine Translation and Global English," 300.

78. Ezra Pound, "Ogden and Debabelization" (1935) reprinted in *Machine Art and Other Writings: The Lost Thought of the Italian Years*, ed. Maria Luisa Ardizzone (Durham: Duke University Press, 1996): 126–128.

79. Ezra Pound, "Ogden and Debabelization," 126.

80. Ezra Pound, "Ogden and Debabelization," 127.

81. Ezra Pound, "Ogden and Debabelization," 128.

82. In *Empires of the Mind: I. A. Richards and Basic English in China, 1929–1979* (Palo Alto: Stanford University Press, 2004), Rodney Koeneke shows that Richards's "Basic English campaign in China would come to encapsulate some of Richards's most deeply held critical concerns of the Twenties" (41).

83. See I. A. Richards's *How to Read a Page: A Course in Efficient Reading with an Introduction to 100 Great Words* (Boston: Beacon Press, 1942).

84. I. A. Richards, *Basic English and its Uses* (New York: W. W. Norton and Co., 1943), 11.

85. Lydia H. Liu, "iSpace: Printed English after Joyce, Shannon, and Derrida," *Critical Inquiry*, vol. 32, no. 3 (2006), 10.

86. Claude Shannon, "Prediction and Entropy in Printed English," in *The Bell System Technical Journal* (January 1951), 50.

87. Lydia H. Liu, "iSpace," 16.

88. Lydia H. Liu, "iSpace," 16.

89. For more on the protocols enabling the Internet, TCP/IP, and the various layers of protological functions (link layer, Internet layer, transport layer, application layer) they support as well as how these protocols are standardized by Internet governing boards such as the Internet Engineering Task Force (IETF), see Alexander Galloway's *Protocol: How Control Exists After Decentralization* (Cambridge, MA: MIT Press, 2004) and Laura DeNardis's *Protocol Politics: The Globalization of Internet Governance* (Cambridge: MIT Press, 2009).

90. Laura DeNardis, *Protocol Politics*, 6. DeNardis traces the new protocol (IPv6) proposed by the Internet Engineering Task Force (IETF) in 2008 to expand Internet address space, and she explains that the selection of these particular protocols "involved complex technical choices, controversial decisions, competition among information technology companies, resistance from large American companies to the introduction to any new protocols, and an institutional choice between a protocol developed within the prevailing Internet governance institutions and one promoted by a more interactional institution" (4).

91. See Alexander Galloway, *Protocol*.

92. See Wendy Hui Kyong Chun, *Control and Freedom: Power and Paranoia in the Age of Fiber Optics* (Cambridge, MA: MIT Press, 2005).

93. See Lev Manovich, *The Language of New Media*, chapter 1 (45–48, in particular).

94. Lev Manovich, *The Language of New Media*, 46.

95. Kittler writes, "All code operations, despite such metaphoric faculties as call or return, come down to absolutely local string manipulations, that is, I am afraid, to signifiers of voltage differences" Friedrich Kittler, "There is No Such Thing as Software."

96. In the language of the Linguasphere Observatory, a transnational research organization focused on multilingualism, Chinese is the "official language of the most populous nation on earth, and English, [is] now the most widely used and studied language of the world, http://www.linguasphere.org/language.html.

97. Joe Lockard, "Resisting Cyber-English," *Bad Subjects* no. 24 (February 1996), accessed October 22, 2012, http://bad.eserver.org/issues/1996/24/lockard.html.

98. Jacques Derrida, *Of Grammatology*, 80.

99. Gayatri Chakravorty Spivak, "Guest Column," *PMLA*, vol. 120, no. 3 (May 2004), 719.

100. Gayatri Chakravorty Spivak, "Guest Column," 719. Digital poet and Chinese translator John Cayley expresses a similar sense of concern as Spivak that engagement with the Internet will have a constrictive effect on Chinese, although his focus is on creative poetics. In "Digital Wen: On the Digitization of Letter-and-Character-Based Systems of Inscription," Cayley writes, "contemporary Chinese poetic seems to be lacking in an engagement with the formal and rhetorical resources of its own language, at what is a crucial moment for the development of writing and culture given the predominance of digital transcription and remediation" (in *Reading East Asian Writing: The Limits of Literary Theory*, ed. Michel Hockx and Ivo Smits, New York: Routledge, 2002), 285.

101. The first code for networked computing technology was American Standard Code for Information Interchange (ASCII), adopted in 1968, which represented English characters as numbers by assigning each letter a number from 0 to 128. As ASCII was based on English, it fell short of being able to translate such languages as Arabic, with its multiple vowels and diacritical signs, and, of course, Chinese. Projects to rectify this situation include Unicode, which uses 16 bits for each character instead of ASCII's 7 bits and can

thus accommodate over 65,000 unique characters. Unicode is produced by The Unicode Consortium, a nonprofit organization founded in 1991, and its motto is "Unicode provides a unique number for every character, no matter what the platform, no matter what the program, no matter what the language," available online from http://www.unicode.org/standard/WhatIsUnicode.html [cited March 2007]. For more on Unicode, see Jukka K. Korpela's *Unicode Explained* (Sebastopol, CA: O'Reilly Media, 2006). For more on the problems Chinese poses to Unicode and the Unicode conventions pose to Chinese, see Chih-Hao Tsai's "On Unicode and the Chinese Writing System," accessed April 21, 2011, http://technology.chtsai.org/unicode/ (1995).

102. Sandy Baldwin, "The idiocy of the Digital Literary (and what does it have to do with digital humanities?)" *Digital Humanities Quarterly*, vol. 7. no. 1 (2013), para. 75, accessed July 29, 2013, http://67.207.129.15:8080/dhq/vol/7/1/000155/000155.html.

103. Young-hae Chang Heavy Industries's *Nippon* can be accessed at www.yhchang.com

104. Ming Xie, "Pound as Translator," in *The Cambridge Companion to Ezra Pound*, ed. Ira Nadel (Cambridge, MA: Cambridge University Press, 1999), 217–218.

105. As I noted in Chapter 3, when discussing YHCHI's *Dakota*, it is impossible to describe and transcribe *Nippon* into print. I continue here the formatting I employed in Chapter 3, wherein, for the sake of differentiating between consecutively flashing screens and line breaks contained on a single screen, I use the conventional backslash (/) to denote a line break and thick dashes (—) to designate the flashing replacement of text on screen. Also, YHCHI consistently use the Monaco font and substitute the zero sign for the capital "O"; I follow them on the latter.

106. In "Reveal Codes: Hypertext and Performance" (in *Postmodern Culture*, vol. 12, no. 1 [2001]), Rita Raley argues that electronic literature operates through "an-anamorphosis—the digitized version of anamorphosis—[which] paradoxically references the anamorphic but flattens out its volume" (para. 18). To illustrate her point, she compares the experience of reading electronic hypertext to Jasper Johns's painting *Flags* (1965), which produces an anamorphic optical illusion in which "one flag is marked only by losing the other" (ibid.). *Nippon* is not a hypertext and, in some ways, is the opposite of hypertext (because in a hypertext, one lexia replaces another in the production of its an-anamorphic effect while YHCHI's animation is a single Flash file that contains no buttons for reader-controlled navigation), but it does operate through an aesthetic of anamorphosis.

107. For a more extensive close reading of *Nippon* as a meta-reflexive examination of code, see Jessica Pressman, "Reading the Code between the Words: The Role of Translation in Young-hae Chang Heavy Industries's *Nippon*," *Dichtung-Digital* (2007), accessed October 22, 2012, http://dichtung-digital.mewi.unibas.ch/2007/pressman.htm.

108. Jacques Derrida, "Des Tours de Babel," *Difference in Translation*, ed. Joseph F. Graham (Ithaca: Cornell University Press, 1985), 165.

109. Jacques Derrida, "Des Tours de Babel," 171.

110. As some critics have posited in larger critiques of post-structuralism, Derrida seems to reject a logocentric paradigm by substituting cacophony for harmony, positioning a different center of origin rather than overturning the origin narrative altogether.

6. Coda

1. For a definition and explanation of "ergodic," see Aarseth, *Cybertext*.

2. See Bonnie Mak's *How the Page Matters* and Lisa Gitelman's *Scripts, Grooves, and Writing Machines: Representing Technology in the Edison Era* (Palo Alto: Stanford University Press, 1999).

3. *House of Leaves* (2000) is about a family living in a house that grows an internal labyrinth of hallways. The narrative revolves around a short film called *Five and a Half Minute Hallway*, which is also the title of a song in referenced in the book and contained on the actual musical album, *Haunted* (by the novelist's sister, Poe), which is, I argue, part of the novel's transmedial network. For more on the connection between novel and album, see my essay, "*House of Leaves*: Reading the Networked Novel," *Studies in American Fiction*, vol. 34, no. 1 (Spring 2006).

4. See Alison Gibbons, "Chapter 1: This is not for you" in *Mark Z. Danielewski*, ed. Joe Bray and Alison Gibbons (Manchester: Manchester University Press, 2011).

5. Since this book contains two narratives and two sets of page numbers on each page, I cite text by naming the narrator (H for Hailey, S for Sam) followed by the page number from that narrator's narrative. When the same text appears in both registers, both Sam and Hailey's narratives, on the same page number, the citation will read (S/H) followed by the page number.

6. Mark Z. Danielewski, qtd. in "Interview with LAist" (October 23, 2007), accessed October 22, 2012, http://www.laist.com/2007/10/23/laist_interview_55.php.

7. "Who are the Montagues and Capulets there?," Danielewski queries aloud in an interview, "It's The Law. They're the people who care—and they are pursuing them. But what about those two that are unpursued? There's no family, no society, no law that cares about them," qtd. in Anthony Miller's review, "Revolutionary Roads," *LA City Beat* (September 25, 2006), accessed October 22, 2012.

8. Mark Z. Danieleswki, qtd. in Anthony Miller, "Revolutionary Roads."

9. The narrative surrounding Sam and Hailey's efforts critiques the institutionalization of marriage in America. The characters are told by various officials that they cannot marry because they are too young and are of mixed race. "Searching for someone/to legitimize our union. Worries so plenty" (H/S 241). Now seeking the law, they go through the "rigarmorale, Social permission" (H 244) and "Civic permission" (S 244) to discover that in the United States, "Love's not enough" (S 264).

10. James Joyce, *Ulysses* (Vintage International, 1990 [Modern Library 1934]).

11. For more on how Danielewski indirectly references the *Wake*, see Dirk van Hulle, "Only Evolutions: Joyce's and Danielewski's Works in Progress," in *Mark Z. Danielewski*, ed. Joe Bray and Alison Gibbons (Manchester: Manchester University Press, 2011), 123–140.

12. Eric McLuhan relates that the origin of his research subject stemmed from a shared experience with his father. "It was, in fact, about 1966, a couple of years before the writing of *War and Peace in the Global Village*, when my father and I first tackled Joyce's ten thunders. We had been reading the Wake off and on together for a year or two, for sheer enjoyment and delight in playing with language, and as a way to whet our wits . . . now and then we would stumble across a thunder, and wonder what in blazes Joyce was doing there. Eventually, we grew sufficiently curious about these odd 'words' to compile a list of all ten. We spent several days reading the thunders and puzzling over them" (*The Role of Thunder in Finnegans Wake* [Toronto: University of Toronto Press, 1997], xiii).

13. Eric McLuhan, *The Role of Thunder in* <u>Finnegans Wake</u>, x. He writes, "Each thunder, far from being a random collage of sounds, articulates words and themes from its context that echo and dramatize particular characters and events occurring in the wake of technological man" (x). He writes, "The first thunder, for example, dramatized the effects of the first palaeolithic and neolithic technologies: fire, building of walls (and with them various forms of architecture)" (x).

14. Mark Z. Danielewski, qtd. in Kiki Benzon, "Revolution 2: An Interview with Mark Z. Danielewski," *Electronic Book Review* (March 20, 2007), accessed October 22, 2012, http://www.electronicbookreview.com/thread/wuc/regulated.

15. Mark Z. Danielewski, qtd. in an "Interview with LAist."

16. Mark Z. Danielewski, qtd. in an "Interview with LAist."

17. Mark Z. Danielewski, qtd. in an "Interview with LAist."

18. I discuss the *House of Leaves Bulletin Board* in my essay "*House of Leaves*: Reading the Networked Novel."

19. Danieleswki published another book in between *House of Leaves* and *Only Revolutions*, a short novella titled *The Fifty Year Sword* (2005) released by Dutch publishing house De Berzige Bij in an extraordinarily limited print run. It was republished by Pantheon, October 2012.

20. Mark Z. Danielewski, "THAT" (August 17, 2005) post to *House of Leaves* Bulletin Board, http://www.houseofleaves.com/forum/showthread.php?t=3967.

21. Mark Z. Danielewski, qtd. in Benzon

22. Mark Z. Danielewski, qtd. in Benzon.

23. Mark Z. Danielewski, qtd. in Benzon.

24. Mark Z. Danielewski, qtd. in Benzon, In "Print Interface to Time: *Only Revolutions* at the crossroads of Narrative and History," (in Bray and Gibbons, 178–197), Mark B. N. Hansen writes, "without being in any way thematically focused on digital technology, the book is thoroughly if indirectly permeated by it, both through the history of its composition and in the infrastructure underlying its appearance" (179).

25. Mark B. N. Hansen, "Print Interface to Time," 187.

26. Henry Jenkins, *Convergence Culture: Where Old and New Media Collide* (Cambridge, MA: MIT Press, 2006), 243.

27. On the historical deconstruction of authorship, see Mark Rose's *Authors and Owners: The Invention of the Copyright* (Cambridge, MA: Harvard University Press, 1993); on the DJ as artist exemplar of the digital age, see Lev Manovich, *The Language of New Media* (chapter 3).

28. Ezra Pound, "The Tradition," 92.

Index